Older Wards and Their Guardians

Older Wards and Their Guardians

PAT M. KEITH AND
ROBBYN R. WACKER

PRAEGER

Westport, Connecticut
London

Library of Congress Cataloging-in-Publication Data

Keith, Pat M.
Older wards and their guardians / Pat M. Keith and Robbyn R. Wacker.
p. cm.
Includes bibliographical references and index.
ISBN 0-275-94424-7 (alk. paper)
1. Guardian and ward—United States. 2. Capacity and disability—United States. 3. Guardian and ward—Social aspects. I. Wacker, Robbyn R. II. Title.
KF553.K45 1994
346.7301'8—dc20
[347.30618] 94-6375

British Library Cataloguing in Publication Data is available.

Library of Congress Catalog Card Number: 94-6375
ISBN: 0-275-94424-7

First published in 1994

Praeger Publishers, 88 Post Road West, Westport, CT 06881
An imprint of Greenwood Publishing Group, Inc.

Printed in the United States of America

The paper used in this book complies with the Permanent Paper Standard issued by the National Information Standards Organization (Z39.48-1984).

10 9 8 7 6 5 4 3 2 1

Copyright Acknowledgment

The author and publisher gratefully acknowledge permission to use the following:

Excerpts from "Implementation of Recommended Guardianship Practices and Outcomes of Hearings for Older Persons," by Pat M. Keith and Robbyn R. Wacker in *The Gerontologist*. Copyright 1993, Vol. 33. Used by permission of The Gerontological Society of America, Washington, D.C.

For Ressie Keith Maddux who has watched over many in her 99 years.

—Pat M. Keith

To my parents, Reinhart and Alta Wacker, who taught me at an early age, that learning was a joyous activity, and to Jani Malkiewicz, who helps me keep life's little annoyances in perspective and who challenges me to excel, both off and on the golf course.

—Robbyn R. Wacker

Contents

Tables and Figures

TABLES

FIGURES

Acknowledgments

This project was supported by the American Association of Retired Persons (AARP) Andrus Foundation. I have appreciated more than I can say the opportunities that have come about from my association with the organization. Iowa State University and the University of Northern Colorado also aided us in our inquiry.

We owe much to the staff members of the courts where we conducted our research. Without their tolerance, cheerfulness, and sometimes eagerness to assist, we would not have been able to complete our research. We often added an extra burden in already-crowded quarters where they worked. Their helpfulness and our thanks to them can never be overestimated.

Our work benefited immensely from the superb data management skills of Dr. K. A. S. Wickrama. We have come a long way since our first conversations in rural, southern Sri Lanka. Sheri Wilson assisted with the design and formatting of the guardian questionnaire. Her thoughtful questions contributed to our investigation.

There are other colleagues whose continuing friendship and expertise are much appreciated. Professor Cynthia Dobson has generously shared her materials and ideas on gerontology. I am ever grateful to A. C. III for his counsel on data management and his understanding of the time demands of research and writing. And my newest colleague, Andy Terry, an undergraduate student at Iowa State University, brought his keen mind, computer skills, careful editing, and willingness to work hard on mundane chores to our effort. Thanks also to Bridget M. Austiguy for her very capable assistance with the editing.

In our division of labor on the project, Robbyn R. Wacker undertook the considerable task of supervision of data collection from the court records. She trained and monitored the work of coders in the three states. She assumed responsibility for chapters 3, 4, and 9. I collected data from guardians, supervised data management and analyses, and was responsible for the remainder of the chapters.

Finally, I remain indebted to the guardians who provided often poignant accounts of their work not heretofore studied. Their comments made this a most compelling piece of scholarship for me.

Pat M. Keith
Iowa State University

Older Wards and Their Guardians

1
Introduction

This book is about older men and women who were thought to need help beyond what they could provide in caring for their person, their property, or both. And it is about the legal process the elders went through, the final outcome of the proceedings, and about those who ultimately cared for them in some capacity. The book goes beyond providing information on older persons deemed in need of assistance from others, most of whom eventually became wards. It also considers whether outcomes of hearings for elders were different prior to and following changes in guardianship legislation.

The research, which used court records and information obtained directly from guardians, was conducted in three states, Iowa, Missouri, and Colorado. As shown in later chapters (e.g., chapters 2, 9, and 10), these states have revised their statutes and have quite different legislation specifying how they decide whether to appoint a guardian, a conservator, both, or neither. Consequently, it was possible to consider the influence of different revised statutes on decisions of the court about the capacity of older persons.

Although specific aspects of statutes differ by state, there are many common features of the process of establishing guardianship as it is practiced throughout the United States. Individual states, however, are able to vary requirements associated with each step of the process. Within states there is further variation in decisions by jurisdiction (Zimny, Gilchrist, Grossberg, & Chung, 1991). As we began the research, our assumption was that different specific requirements for guardianship procedures, as well as changes in them, should be reflected in the kinds of decisions ultimately made about guardianship of older persons. Similarities and differences between the guardianship legislation in the three states chosen for more intensive study, along with other selected states, are presented and compared in chapter 9. First, however, we consider some of the primary concerns about the guardianship system that are currently expressed in an increasing body of literature.

SOURCES OF INFORMATION ABOUT GUARDIANSHIP

Timely information on guardianship is presented in a variety of formats and is found in numerous sources. There are at least five primary types of literature on guardianship: (1) articles in popular magazines and newspapers (Associated Press, 1987; Topolnicki, 1989); (2) reports of empirical research usually conducted by social scientists about characteristics of wards and guardians, roles of family and professionals in decision making, and outcomes of the legal process for wards (Bulcroft, Kielkopf, & Tripp, 1991; Iris, 1988; Iris, 1990a, 1990b; Wilber, 1991); (3) articles in law journals that explicate changes in guardianship statutes, describe needed legislation, and provide insight into potential difficulties with the legal process (Anderer, 1990; Frolik, 1981; Schmidt, 1990), some of which include empirical research as well (Friedman & Savage, 1988); (4) view of guardianship from the perspective of the health and medical professions (Kapp, 1987); and (5) writings by philosophers and ethicists raising ethical questions about the conduct of guardianship (Schafer, 1988). Thus, legal scholars, social scientists, philosophers, health professionals, and journalists all have shaped both the available information and our thinking about guardianship.

These five types of literature on guardianship overlap somewhat both in content and goals. Although much of the literature has themes in common, the methods by which data are acquired and the tone and premise of these sources of information on guardianship vary. The literature often includes a shared core of data and information about elderly wards, and there is a common interest in protecting the rights of the ward and in ensuring due process. Some articles in the popular media have as their point of departure the existence of graphic abuses in the guardianship system. This particular type of literature, as well as other kinds, strongly emphasizes the vulnerability of the aged ward. Striking anecdotes are sometimes used to document the need for reform and the need for increased protection of older proposed wards. In chapter 3, "Concerns about the Guardianship Process: A Review of the Literature," perspectives about guardianship and research findings are drawn from these five general kinds of literature. The social context of guardianship as we view it is described and framed by research and writing in the fields mentioned above. The framework and questions guiding the research questions discussed in chapters 5 through 11 have their origins in the thinking about guardianship presented in chapter 3. In this chapter dominant concerns about the guardianship system, some recent and some not so current, are delineated. By the conclusion of chapter 3, we learn that some of the issues motivating current reforms in state guardianship legislation have a long history and are experiencing a renaissance. Subsequent chapters in this book then address several of the past and current questions about the guardianship system.

THE TIMELINESS AND PERVASIVENESS OF CONCERNS ABOUT GUARDIANSHIP

Issues of civil rights and involuntary commitment, due process and judicial reform, evaluation of capacity, the psychological effect of guardianship, the role of guardians, and the need for guardians have fostered widespread professional concern (Hightower, Heckert, & Schmidt, 1990). An appraisal of current thinking about guardianship suggests investigation of it is timely, and cognizance of its importance is not limited to scholars, journalists, and members of the legal profession just in the United States.

First, beyond consideration of the possible unwarranted intrusion on individual rights in establishing guardianship, why is the study of guardianship salient now? Research on guardianship is opportune because of the increased longevity of the population. The most rapid growth is among the very old, who likely will have the greatest future needs for protective services. Citing the ominous predictions of increased numbers of frail and incapable older persons as one reason for the recent attention to guardianship, Iris (1991) pointed to the tasks facing more families as they seek to provide for their vulnerable elders. In addition to noting the falling birth rate and the aging of the population as reasons for examination of the practice of guardianship, Schulte (1989) commented on the increasing numbers of nonfamily households and accompanying social and cultural trends that have significance for mental health and for the care of the aged. Furthermore, increasingly, older individuals want to determine their own plans for care if they should become incapacitated.

Hughes (1989) described the link between guardianship and the health care system for the aged. A three-stage process represents the relationship between aging and the protective services: initially there is little need for supplemental care and protection, followed by increasing needs for community-based services, and finally institutionalization for some. An aging population accelerates claims on the health system, and a corollary of enhanced needs for health care is increased demand for guardianship (Hughes, 1989). Because those who care for and give medical attention to the aged may want legal protection prior to administering a particular treatment, requests for guardianship are likely increased for those who reside in community care facilities.

The connection between the guardianship system, aging populations, and statutory reform has been noted by scholars from Australia (Creyke,

1989), Canada (Hughes, 1989), England (Hogget, 1989), Germany, and Austria (Schulte, 1989; Zenz, 1989). Consequently, concerns similar to those voiced by scholars and professionals in the United States have prompted legislative reform in many countries.

Furthermore, these issues have implications for developing countries, where the largest numbers of aged persons already live. The most rapid growth rates of older persons will be in these areas, in which intricate systems of protective services are not yet in place. Some of the countries recently instituting reforms of their guardianship systems have a high percentage of the population who are now aged. Historically these countries have shared some views of the obligation of the state to protect individuals, perhaps from others and/or themselves, as well as a commitment to personal autonomy. Many countries, however, will have differing conceptions of the nature of the responsibility of the state for the welfare of its citizens juxtaposed to the preservation of individual liberty.

The assumption of the responsibility by society to care for those who are unable to attend to their own affairs is long-standing. And the notion that another may have to act for those who lack the capacity to take care of their own self-interest also is not new. Guardianship, as a concept, has its origins in Roman civil law and English common law (Rogers, 1984). Guardianship is derived from the doctrine of *parens patriae*, "father of his country," in which the state has the right and the responsibility to care for the person and property of those unable to protect themselves (Iris, 1988). Historically, as personal and property rights were defined, it was necessary to take into account the welfare of individuals unable to act on their behalf. The designation of guardians then permits the court, representing the state, to execute its duty to care for individuals who because of incapacity are not able to care for their person, assets, or property. As will be seen, the type and quality of the assessment leading to the conclusion that an individual is in need of care, and the procedural safeguards employed to ensure the most appropriate judgments are made, dominate the concerns shared by scholars in North America and in portions of Europe.

Writing about guardianship laws and reform in Western Europe, Schulte (1989), who is affiliated with the Max-Planck Institute, Munich, underscored the commonality of concerns across selected nations. He described some of the conditions leading to reform, the substance of the reforms, the outcomes of statutory revisions, and gave suggestions for further changes. Schulte noted several troubling issues such as the unnecessary limitations imposed or upheld by the court, lack of legal representation, treatment of incapacity as a lifelong condition, and inexperience and lack of knowledge of guardians about the problems of wards or about the facilities and services that are available. Revised legislation provides for less restrictive forms of guardianship or for alternatives used in lieu of guardianship. Newer legislation clarifies and reduces the powers of the guardian and prescribes more restrictive judicial control over the action of the guardian. Revised statutes also question the necessity to maintain the guardianship in light of improvement by the ward (Schulte, 1989).

Further illustrating concerns about guardianship practice beyond the United States, Hughes (1989:619–620), in writing about Canada, observed that in general,

> The laws have not recognized degrees of incapacity or that incapacity can change over time or depending on the situation or environment. Persons either are found to be mentally competent and hence not in need of a guardian for anything, or mentally incompetent and in need of a guardian for everything. Thus, once the court determines that a person is mentally incompetent, that adult may be considered to have a blanket disability that prevents exercise of any civil rights.

Hughes (1989:621) also noted the lack of a requirement for "time-limited orders" and of "mandatory periodic review or accountability of the guardian." Recommended reform of the guardianship system includes annual or periodic monitoring and court supervision of guardianships (Hurme, 1991). In response to this need, experimental guardianship monitoring programs have been implemented in the United States (Newsnotes, 1990).

Thus, scholars from other nations echo those in the United States in their attention to procedural safeguards. Some of these safeguards include specificity in petitions, adequate notice, adequate information for wards and guardians, adequate representation by an advocate, and an advocate who will take an adversarial role. Objective standards to assess individuals' abilities to handle daily personal or financial matters are called for with the encouragement of limited guardianships and consideration of alternative plans to guardianship.

Despite considerable effort devoted to reform of the guardianship system, little attention has been given to the extensiveness of implementation of revised legislation. Later we ask why more limited guardianships have not been awarded.

Schulte's (1989) assessment of the outcomes of some of the reforms is instructive. He observed the expectation was that statutory revisions would contribute to decreased use of guardianships; however, this did not occur. Schulte (1989) reasoned that the courts may be reluctant to use newer and more complicated procedures, especially when they involve differentiation of the extent of incapacity. He also suggested a positive experience with new guardianships may have led to the inclusion of a wider range of problems and more frequent use of this option. Furthermore, there may have been some inertia in the review of existing guardianships attributable to a lack of time and personnel. "The new legislation may, however, have been introduced by Parliament too fast and its substance may be based on too little consultation with the medical and legal professionals involved" (Schulte, 1989:598). This implies greater attention should be given to the context in which legislation is introduced and especially to the involvement of those who are responsible for implementation of innovative statutes. In chapter 10, we examine the extent to which outcomes of wards' hearings were associated with revised legislation.

Finally, as a corollary to the emphasis on protection of individual rights, it has been suggested that greater consideration be given to guardianship of the person. Hughes (1989) observed that Canadian guardianship law has focused primarily on the management and protection of property rather than on the guardianship of the person. As a part of the revised legislation to address some of the reforms mentioned earlier, greater efforts necessarily will be directed toward review of guardianship of the person. The chapters that follow describe wards and their guardians of the person.

Guardianship statutes and their accompanying terminology vary considerably from state to state (Hurme, 1991). To maintain consistent terminology throughout the book, we will use "guardian" to refer to the person designated to protect and care for an individual. Conservator will refer to a person who is appointed to protect and care for an estate. The focus of the research was on guardians of the person; however, some were also conservators. Therefore, some of the guardians studied were appointed by the court to care for both the person and the estate.

THE OUTLINE OF THE BOOK

This book, then, reviews current thinking on guardianship reform, describes characteristics of the process by which persons became wards, considers the impact of revised statutes on outcomes for older wards, and finally profiles the concerns of those who were appointed as guardians. A description of the data collection procedures and the samples comprise chapter 2, "Procedures." Chapter 3, "Concerns about the Guardianship Process: A Review of the Literature," contains a review of contemporary literature on guardianship from several perspectives. By drawing on literature from the five fields—law, social science, health and medicine, philosophy and ethics, and the popular media—the convergence and disparity in approaches to the practice of guardianship become evident.

The focal point for the establishment of guardianship is the determination of incapacity and identification of the need for assistance beyond what individuals can accomplish for themselves. Chapter 4, "Can You Spell 'World' Backward? Assessing Incapacity in Guardianship Hearings," is an essay on the concept of capacity and comprises a selective review of assessments of function. The chapter emphasizes the need to consider individual capacities. Whereas some persons will be best served by a full guardianship, others may require only modest assistance in daily life and then perhaps for a limited time (Hughes, 1989). Furthermore, capacity is viewed differently by practitioners and scholars from various disciplines.

Taking into account the interface between a determination of capacity and simultaneous protection of the rights of proposed wards, recommendations for future assessment tools are made.

Chapter 5, "Becoming a Ward: Characteristics of Wards and Their Guardians," begins with a demographic profile of wards studied in the three states. Selected activities that comprise the three stages of the guardianship process (Iris, 1990a) are included in chapter 5 and in chapter 11, "Use of Recommended Guardianship Practices and Outcomes for Older Prospective Wards." The three stages are: preadjudication (the stage during which need is established); adjudication (from filing the petition to the hearing); and postadjudication (activities following the disposition of the case and the selection of the guardian). Corresponding to the preadjudication stage, critical incidents leading to guardianship and guardians' assessments of the capacity of their ward are investigated in chapter 5. Views of guardianship by court visitors and wards, alternatives to guardianship, and characteristics of guardians and their activities on behalf of their wards are instructive about the features of the ward-guardian relationship.

Guardians are agents of the courts and have some clear tasks and specific responsibilities to carry out (Rogers, 1984). Yet, the roles of guardians also are encumbered by unclear expectations. Beyond certain expectations for all guardians as required by the courts, additional activities on behalf of their wards varies considerably. In chapter 5, some of the specific activities that guardians engaged in with their wards are described. Most of the assistance was not specifically required by statute; rather, they provided some indication of the kind of relationship guardians may have maintained with their wards.

In chapter 6, "Pathways to Guardianship," and chapter 7, "Themes of Meaning in the Guardianship Experience," the characteristics of guardians and candid reflections on their roles augment our view of the lives of both wards and guardians. In chapter 6, the decision to seek guardianship, involvement of family and nonrelatives in the process, reasons for the selection of the specific individual, services used by guardians, and activities made possible by guardianship contribute to an understanding of how guardians came to assume and perform their roles. Continuing the study of the lives of guardians, chapter 7 emphasizes themes of meaning in caregiving. Both the intrusiveness and the joys of guardianship become clear. Guardians graphically described their hardships, detailed the benefits in their roles, and gave advice to others. Finally, they recounted how guardianship had shaped their views of old age and their future.

Chapter 8, "Role Strain of Male and Female Guardians: Tests of Two Models," is comprised of two multivariate studies. Both studies build on the qualitative descriptions of guardians presented in the previous chapter. The first study explores correlates of role strain of male and female guardians. The second study investigates how family relationships and role strain differentiated among four patterns of guardianship: the tough, the sad, the challenged, and the sympathetic. In chapters 6, 7, and 8, some of the major stressors of guardians are identified. Suggestions by guardians for others who would undertake this role reveal some of their greatest difficulties.

Without a clear sense of the expectations of the role of a legalized caregiver, and perhaps with minimal support to carry out the tasks, guardians may experience unnecessary strain. To the untrained, the very complexity of the guardianship process is a major barrier to negotiating the system. The services and individuals who were most helpful to guardians are identified, and other assistance that would have been useful are noted. In the views of some guardians, guardianships were established to address difficulties that could have been resolved better in other ways. Some of their suggested alternatives, as well as recommendations to make the guardianship system more effective, are presented.

Despite the fact that guardians often are targeted as being among the villains in the guardianship system and are thought to occupy a central and quite powerful position, data are rarely obtained from them. Juxtaposed to stereotypes, guardians' reflections sometimes indicated uncertainty, insecurity in their role, and vulnerability. By attending to the strain of guardians, the information presented in chapters 6, 7, and 8 differs from that derived from court records alone.

Chapter 9, "The Context of Guardianship Legislation in Selected States," provides a framework within which to view the legislation of the three states chosen for more detailed study. Following a discussion of five areas of recommended guardianship reform, we examine revised legislation in nine states. By investigating closely the three states central to this research in which a range of legislation has been initiated, it was possible to view the contrasts among them and any potential differences in outcomes more clearly.

In chapter 10, "Guardianship Reform: Do Revised Statutes Make a Difference in Outcomes for Prospective Wards?," action taken by the court is investigated in relation to the period in which the case was heard, that is, before or after statutory changes. the types of guardianships requested, the extensiveness of powers granted, and the use of evidence prior to and following the adoption of new legislation are studied. To determine whether outcomes reflected the varying orientations of the state statutes, some of the decisions of the court are analyzed separately by state.

Chapter 11, "Use of Recommended Guardianship Practices and Outcomes for Older Prospective Wards," addresses whether use of suggested practices that are adopted has an effect on decisions about the care of older persons. In chapter 11, we investigate how implementation of recommended guardianship practices influenced outcomes for proposed wards regardless of whether the actions represented statutory change. The practices included attributes of the petition for guardianship, representation by counsel, involvement of the ward, and observations of proposed wards and court visitors about the circumstances of the ward. These selected practices were examined in relation to outcomes of hearings for the proposed wards. When possible, practices that were implemented and had been targeted for change by those interested in reform were considered irrespective of whether they were included in recent statutory revisions. A final chapter, "A Concluding Glimpse of Wards and Their Guardianships," summarizes the major findings and their implications for the practice of guardianship.

SUMMARY

The book has three major parts. The first portion describes the context in which questions about the guardianship system have been raised. It demonstrates the need for the research reported here and places it in the context of earlier literature (chapters 1–4).

The second part describes wards and their guardians (chapters 5–8). At the social-psychological level, it addresses strains of individuals as they go about their work as guardians. The third part (chapters 9–11) considers issues at the macro level by linking statutory change with decisions made at hearings for older proposed wards.

And now a word about what the book is not. It is not comprehensive in its coverage of legislation from all states, nor is it a test of outcomes for older persons in all jurisdictions. Comparative reviews of selected aspects of state statutes are available elsewhere (Hurme, 1991; Zimny, Gilchrist, & Diamond, 1991). Rather, wards and guardians in three states that have very different revised statutes were studied in some detail. The number of records reviewed was substantially larger than those usually investigated.

The primary strengths of the book lie in four areas. First, the research was an effort to correlate statutory revisions with decisions about outcomes for older wards. This usually has not been done. Often calls for reform have not been examined in relation to outcomes of implementation of revised legislation.

Second, we also investigated the association between practices that were not necessarily a part of revised statutes and outcomes for prospective wards. We asked, "When recommended practices were implemented, were they reflected in decisions about proposed wards?"

Third, we attempted to provide a view of how individuals conceptualized their lives as guardians. Our intent was to profile guardians' responsibilities, hardships, and joys rather than to malign or label them negatively. No general sociological theory about law and society is set forth. Rather, only modest tests of the role strain framework are made.

Finally, the book brings together literature on guardianship from a variety of perspectives. The literature review demonstrates the wide range of concerns. But before a discussion of the literature on guardianship, procedures used in data collection are described in chapter 2.

2
Procedures

In this chapter, we describe the procedures used to secure data from court records and from the questionnaire completed by guardians. The content of each instrument and some of the variation in data collection procedures across the three states are presented. The sampling procedure for obtaining information from court records is discussed first.

SAMPLES FROM COURT RECORDS

Two types of data were collected and analyzed for this book. The first type of data was obtained from court records in Iowa, Missouri, and Colorado. Samples in the three states were drawn that conformed to the following criteria. First, the means of obtaining a guardianship was involuntary. That is, a third party had requested protective intervention by the court. This condition for inclusion in the sample was necessary in order to examine whether outcomes (i.e., action taken by the court) for the proposed elderly wards differed prior to and following changes in guardianship legislation. Furthermore, legislative protections are written primarily for involuntary petitions. A second criterion was that the proposed ward must have been 60 years of age or older at the time the petition was filed. Third, because one of the objectives was to study the roles of guardians of the person and ward-guardian relationships, it was necessary to select cases in which the petition included a request for guardianship of the person. Therefore, an effort was made to include cases in which a guardianship or a combined guardianship/conservatorship was requested. With the following exception, petitions for conservatorships alone were excluded. In Colorado, earlier guardianships encompassing care of the person were described as conservatorships.

Fourth, to consider outcomes prior to and following statutory revisions, it was necessary to select cases filed before and after legislation was adopted. In this book, the records will sometimes be designated as "pre" and "post" statutory change data (i.e., those cases heard prior to and following the passage of revised legislation, respectively). As noted below, the dates for the pre and post records differed for the three states. Because the majority of petitions were heard within four to five years of one another within the pre and post designations, period effects would not be expected to be great. The records reviewed, for example, would have been compiled under statutes passed before the 1988 American Bar Association (ABA) Wingspread National Guardianship Symposium, held to make recommendations about guardianship reform, and prior to other recent widespread calls for change in the guardianship system.

Fifth, because the study of the role of the guardian involved contacting the guardians by mail, the most recent cases in both the pre– and post–statutory change periods were selected regardless of whether they were open or closed. That is, even though the date of legislative change used to differentiate between pre and post cases may have been 1984, as in the instance of Iowa, the most recent post records were selected (e.g., beginning with 1990). This was done so that cases would more likely still be open, and addresses of guardians would be more current. In the instance of pre cases, the same procedure of choosing the most recent records was followed with selection of the records compiled nearest to the close of the prechange period. As is described later, accessing the earlier records in all three states was somewhat more difficult than obtaining the more recent ones.

Finally, because the initial plan was for a guardian to have an opportunity to complete a mail questionnaire that would then be matched with the data from the court record of his or her ward, an effort was made to select guardians who were guardians for only one person selected in the sample. This decision was made for several reasons. First, guardians with a large number of wards were less likely to have a personal relationship with them and consequently might be less able to respond to questions about each in detail. For example, in one community, which was not selected as a primary site for the data collection, one of the guardians had well over 100 wards. Second, even if the guardians had been willing to complete a questionnaire regarding their relationship with several of the wards, who otherwise would have been included in the sample, a portion of the questions on attitudes and strain of being a guardian likely could not have been completed with each ward in mind. Therefore, use of multiple responses from guardians would have precluded treatment of the questionnaire data as independent observations. However, although guardians may have been a guardian for only one ward included in the sample, a few served as guardians for others who were not selected for study.

Using the above criteria, a total of 1,160 court records were sampled. The following numbers of records initiated prior to and after legislative changes were sampled in the three states; the number of records that were open and closed is in parentheses: Iowa, 152 pre and 208 post (175 open and 185 closed); Missouri, 199 pre and 207 post (162 open and 244 closed); and Colorado, 97 pre and 297 post (176 open and 218 closed). The number of cases examined before the change in legislation in Colorado is smaller than in the other two states because of the difficulty in accessing the oldest records. Most records were closed because of the death of the ward.

DATA COLLECTION PROCEDURES FROM COURT RECORDS

The probate court in Iowa is responsible for the administration of wills, guardianships, and conservatorships. Each case filed with the court is assigned a docket number and hand recorded in a bound ledger containing approximately 500 pages. Each page of the ledger contains a summary of the activity of a case, such as the type of case (e.g., estate, guardianship, conservatorship), the date the petition was filed, the date of the hearing, and when the fees were paid. The names of the petitioner, the proposed guardian, and respondent (the proposed ward) are noted as well. Ledgers are not separated by type of case and specific age is not included in the summary. Both minor guardianships and adult guardianships are listed in the same ledger. Because primarily guardianships were to be included in the research, each page of the ledger had to be reviewed for cases that were

Figure 2.1
Code Sheet for Information from Court Records

Location ____________ Volume ____________

Docket Number	Date	Type Petition	Name	Age	Open/ Closed

designated as guardianships or guardianship/conservatorships. Once the docket number and the name of each guardianship/conservatorship case were noted, individual files had to be obtained and inspected for the age of the proposed ward and the type of guardianship (i.e., involuntary or voluntary). The project required a proposed ward to be 60 years of age or over to be included in the sample. Involuntary cases and those not dismissed prior to a hearing were selected. Figure 2.1 shows the type of initial information recorded for each state. Approximately 25 ledgers of 500 cases each were reviewed in order to obtain the sample in Iowa. Data were collected primarily in Des Moines, Iowa.

In Des Moines, open cases are located in the probate clerk's office, and the closed cases are maintained in the basement of the courthouse. Earlier records are stored on microfilm. The most recent post–statutory change cases (those after May 24, 1984) and the most recent pre–statutory change cases (prior to May 24, 1984) were selected regardless of whether the case was open or closed.

The probate court in Missouri also administers wills, guardianships, and conservatorships. Data were collected primarily in Independence, Missouri, although some records were reviewed in Kansas City and one smaller community.

The Missouri records studied, however, are maintained and referenced differently from those in Iowa. Computer printouts contain the docket numbers, names of the respondents and petitioners, the type of case, and an indication of the outcome (i.e., appointment of the guardian or dismissal). Unlike in Iowa, code numbers are assigned to each case indicating whether the case was a guardianship, conservatorship, or both and whether the case involved a minor. Non-minor guardianship and guardianship/conservatorship cases were selected for the research, but it was necessary to obtain individual files in order to determine the age of the proposed ward. Current, open cases are kept in the courthouse. Closed, but more recent, cases are maintained in warehouses, and older records are on microfilm. The most recent post–statutory change cases (after October 1, 1983) and pre–statutory change cases (before October 1, 1983) were selected. The information indicated in Figure 2.1 was recorded for these cases as well.

Colorado records are organized similarly to those in Missouri. The most recent cases are recorded on a computer printout that gives the name of both the ward and the guardian. The type of guardianship and whether the ward is an adult or a minor are indicated on the printout. To determine the age of the adult ward, however, the records had to be accessed. As in the other states, the data in Figure 2.1 were compiled from the computer printout, and the sample was drawn from this listing. Data were collected in Colorado Springs, Denver, Fort Collins, and Greeley, Colorado.

Records in Colorado were selected for study primarily because of the required court appointment of a visitor in guardianship proceedings unless the individual has his or her own counsel. This requirement was mandated in 1979. The duties and responsibilities of the visitor are carefully specified. Data from the visitors' reports are included as a part of the record and were available for use in this project. Employment of a visitor provides more extensive information about the proposed ward than likely would be available to the courts in the other two states. At the time of our study, court visitors conducted initial intensive screening of wards, but annual reports were not required in Colorado although they had been proposed (Dice, 1987). Annual reports, however, are mandated in Iowa and Missouri.

Data collection procedures in the three states varied depending on the particular office. The extent to which researchers were permitted to have ready access for files varied considerably. In some offices, researchers were able to use the electrical retrieval systems to secure records by themselves. In other offices, it was necessary to fill out a separate card requesting each record and wait until a staff member could retrieve the documents. When this process was followed, work was impeded somewhat. Furthermore, in all three states it was necessary to look at many records to meet the criteria of an involuntary guardianship or joint guardianship/conservatorship in which the ward was 60 years of age or older.

Access to older court records in all three states was somewhat difficult and time-consuming. These earlier records were important in determining the outcomes of changes in legislation. Older records tended to be on microfilm, and there was usually only one microfilm reader. These machines were heavily used by county staff whose work had first priority. Thus, depending somewhat on the organization of the offices, methods of retrieving both current documents and those stored on microfilm usually took much longer than anticipated.

To a great extent the ease of the researchers' efforts was contingent on the good will and the interest of employees of the court. The spaces in which county employees worked were often quite crowded. The nature of the research meant research assistants spent many hours in close proximity with county staff. Explanation of the project and the development of rapport with office personnel were critical, as well as careful orientation, training, and monitoring of coding by researchers who obtained data from the court records. Office staff were extraordinarily helpful, interested, and patient. Our work would have been impossible without them.

Researchers who coded information from the records were hired at the sites. They were trained and carefully monitored. Training and checking the work of coders was important. Repeated checks of information coded on the court record questionnaire were made by referring to the records. This step was critical because records varied widely in the information they contained and in the organization of the material.

The Questionnaire for Court Records

Information from court records was hand recorded on questionnaires that were then coded, and the data were entered for use on the computer. The available information varied somewhat for the three states. Some of the difference was due to variation in guardianship statutes. Therefore, a few specific questions applied only to single states. Where appropriate, these differences will be noted. An obvious example would be data from court visitors available only in the Colorado records.

Information from the Petition and Records. The first group of questions in the court record questionnaire covered information on the petition: the type of petition, characteristics of the ward (age at filing, current age, sex, marital status, living arrangement, financial status [value of real estate, value of personal property, amount of income]), identification of the proposed guardian, relationship of the ward and the guardian, presence of co-guardians, and evidence presented to establish incapacity. Whether a specific physical or mental condition was stated in the petition (other than statutory language) was noted. The presence or absence of a request for specific powers by the guardian in the petition was coded. Information about the hearing including representation of the ward (own attorney or court-appointed), attendance by the ward at the hearing, and the action taken by the court were recorded on the questionnaire. A sample of a petition is in the Appendix.

Information about additional petitions filed following the appointment of the guardian, and the court action on them, were also recorded. For example, petitions for medical procedures, for the sale of real estate/personal property, and other petitions (e.g., petition to prepay funeral expenses, petition to make investments, petition to appoint a conservator following the appointment of a guardian, and a petition to transfer the ward from hospital to nursing home) were coded.

Some information was available about the activities of the guardian on behalf of the ward. Information on guardian activities is reported in chapter 6. Data from reports of guardians to the courts included: presence of initial reports for each action; presence of annual reports (in states in which it was applicable); and submission of plans for the care of the ward and the guardian's agreement with the plan (Missouri only). From Iowa records, the presence of information on the physical and mental condition of the ward and the health rating observed in the most recent annual report were coded. For Missouri, the presence/absence of any major changes in the ward's physical or mental condition during the preceding year were noted as well as the nature of the changes. Only selected portions of these data are presented in this book.

When they were available, a series of personal activities the guardian might undertake on the ward's behalf were coded. These activities were: visiting the ward, taking the ward shopping, providing personal items, taking the ward to visit family, doing laundry, selecting and preparing meals, assisting with needs in daily living and personal care, providing emotional support, taking the ward to a physician, and managing paperwork (filing forms, taxes, etc.). The following activities of the guardians who also were granted conservatorships were available: establishing a checking account, establishing a savings account, changing assets to the conservator's name, paying bills, collecting income, and filing lawsuits on behalf of the ward. For both guardians and conservators, activities in addition to those specified were coded in an "other" category.

Information from the Court Visitors' Reports. Data included on the visitor questionnaire were coded from the Colorado court records. Following the date of statutory change in Colorado (1979), a report from a court visitor became a required part of the record if the ward did not have an attorney. The visitor questionnaire included information on the characteristics of the proposed ward. Characteristics of the ward that were coded were: orientation to time and place; understanding of the petition; preference for an attorney; type of assistance needed in caring for self; preference for those who might provide help; identification of closest family members; acquaintance with the proposed guardian; relationship of proposed guardian to the ward; extent of the powers viewed as necessary or desirable by the visitor; belief by the ward that powers should be limited and in what ways; attitude of the ward toward the scope and duration of the guardianship; attitude toward the proposed guardian; the visitor's assessment of why the ward needs assistance; identification of who, if anyone, has been caring for the ward during the past three months; planned changes in residence; physical diagnosis of the ward's condition by a physician; and functional capacity of the ward as noted by a physician.

The following conclusions by the visitor about the situation of the ward were coded: the nature and degree of the physical and functional incapacity of the ward; evaluation of appropriateness of the guardianship; recommendation that powers should or should not be limited; recommendation that an attorney, a guardian ad litem, and/or a physician should or should not be appointed. Systematic data from court visitors were available only in the Colorado records, and they were a primary factor in the selection of this state for study and distinguished it from the other two. These data from the court records were used to describe the sample of wards and guardians (chapter 5).

Other information from the records was analyzed to answer some of the primary questions of the study. For example, the data from court records were employed to study potential differences in the decisions of the courts on behalf of wards prior to and following the changes in guardian legislation (chapter 10). Other guardianship practices included in the court records (e.g., statement of ward's condition in the petition, presence of the ward at the hearing, the type of counsel representing the ward) were considered in relation to decisions of the court (chapter 11).

The wording of questions, individual items, response categories, and coding from the court records are described in the text where they are used. Statistical tests are clearly indicated in the tables or in the text if no table is presented.

The Sample of Guardians

The second type of data presented in this book was obtained from a questionnaire sent to guardians of some of the wards about whom information from court records was collected. The questionnaire data from guardians were matched with those from the court records.

The questionnaire included information from guardians that was not available in the court records. Generally, data about guardians contained in the court records were restricted to the family/nonfamily relationship of the guardian and the ward, the sex of the guardian, whether the proposed guardian was also the petitioner, living arrangement of the ward (residence with the guardian or with others), and the presence of co-guardianship.

The guardian questionnaire comprised several aspects of the relationship between the ward and the guardian. Two versions were constructed for each state and worded in present and past tense to reflect open and closed guardianships, respectively. The concern that guardians with closed and open cases might respond differently to questions was addressed. Correlations among all variables that were used in later multivariate analyses were calculated separately for guardians with open and closed cases. This made it possible to examine any differences in patterns of interrelationships among the responses of guardians with open and closed guardianships. Variables from both the court records and the guardian questionnaire were included. In another set of calculations, open and closed cases were coded as a dichotomous variable and correlated with other indicators of interest from both the court records and the guardian questionnaire. Following inspection of these data, we concluded that data from guardians with open and closed cases could be combined.

Mail questionnaires were sent to guardians at the addresses listed in the court records. A little more than half of the cases were closed. Therefore, some questionnaires were sent to addresses no longer kept updated through annual reports as they should have been for open cases in two of the states. For closed cases, as well as open cases in states not requiring an annual report, there is potentially greater opportunity for incorrect addresses. In Colorado, unless courts order guardians to submit annual reports, they are not required. Examination of court records indicated guardians were rarely required to submit an annual report. Therefore, this mechanism for obtaining more current addresses was not available.

Not all guardians were sent questionnaires. Because the pre–statutory change records in Colorado were filed before 1979, and current addresses would have been especially difficult to obtain, these guardians were not sent the guardian questionnaire. Resources were not available to trace and update addresses.

A letter describing the study and including the elements of informed consent, a questionnaire booklet, and a postpaid envelope were sent in the first mailing. About two weeks later a reminder postcard was sent. This included a phone number to call collect in the event guardians had not received or had misplaced the questionnaire.

Completed questionnaires were received from 387 guardians by the deadline, and three were returned late. This represents a return rate of 49 percent when the following were excluded: those who were not reached in the initial mailing or with the reminder card due to outdated addresses; those who returned the questionnaire indicating their ward had died shortly after their appointment as guardian; those whose petitions were denied; and the pre–statutory change sample from Colorado. Those who were not reached tended to have been guardians prior to the change in legislation and to have cases that were closed.

For the majority of cases, data from guardianship questionnaires were linked with information from the court records of their ward. Questionnaire data from 15 guardians were not matched with information for their wards because these questionnaires were from co-guardians and represented instances in which both guardians responded. The responses of only one guardian were linked to the data for wards, although responses from all guardians to the mail questionnaires were used in analyses that did not require use of data from court records.

Content of the Guardian Questionnaire. The guardian questionnaire included questions in the following areas: (1) proximity to, amount of contact with, and amount of time spent on duties of guardianship; (2) the process of becoming a guardian, including relationships with family members and family involvement in guardian selection; (3) resources needed to perform the role of guardian; (4) reflections on the role of guardian, advice for others, and thoughts about aging; (5) functional capacity of the ward; (6) role strain and difficulties of guardianship; and (7) demographic characteristics. Specific questions are stated and response categories are listed when they are used either in tables or in the text of the book. When scales or indices are analyzed, scale items and procedures are discussed in the chapters as they occur. By and large, information from the mail questionnaire was used to illuminate characteristics of the role of the guardian. Therefore, data from the guardian questionnaire comprised primarily chapter 6, "Pathways to Guardianship," and chapter 7, "Themes of Meaning in the Guardianship Experience."

Data from the court records are presented primarily in three chapters. These are chapter 5 ("Becoming a Ward: Characteristics of Wards and Their

Guardians"), chapter 10 ("Guardianship Reform: Do Revised Statutes Make a Difference in Outcomes for Prospective Wards?"), and chapter 11 ("Use of Recommended Guardianship Practices and Outcomes for Older Prospective Wards"). Finally, in chapter 12, "A Concluding Glimpse of Wards and Their Guardianships," some of the major findings from both the records and the guardian questionnaire are summarized and recommendations for practice are presented.

Next we provide a review of the literature about the guardianship process and the characteristics of wards and guardians who were participants in the system. Chapter 3 reflects the views and research of scholars from a variety of disciplines. The chapter establishes the context from which questions are raised about wards, guardians, and the guardianship process that are explored later.

3

Concerns about the Guardianship Process: A Review of the Literature

GUARDIANSHIP LAW WITHIN THE CONTEXT OF THE LEGAL SYSTEM

Within our society there exists a body of law, created in part through legislation, that regulates a variety of social and economic relationships. Laws are created because there is a belief about how the law ought to be regarding a particular social relationship and because there is an assumption that the social context, as it currently exists, has deficiencies (Grace & Wilkinson, 1978; Jenkins, 1980). Therefore, in the larger societal context, laws have a number of functions. First, laws describe an ideal order of events—human conduct and behavior that *should* occur in society. Second, laws act as a *passage* from the current social order to a described ideal order (Jenkins, 1980). Guardianship law is but a small part of a larger body of law whose function is to provide for an orderly transference and regulation of decision-making activities, and for the continuation of social relationships for individuals who can no longer conduct routine social and financial matters on their own. In this light, guardianship law has a functional purpose for certain members of society and for legal, financial, and medical institutions. There is agreement among those in the legal, medical, and social science fields about the basic function or purpose of guardianship law: to provide a formal substitute decision maker for individuals who are unable to care adequately for themselves. Most scholars do not dispute the purpose of guardianship law per se, but rather, their concern is about how guardianship laws are written. Indeed, a great number of articles have been written about the need for guardianship reform, about how much individual choice or protection should be granted to the proposed ward, about how to define and determine incapacity, and about defending of the civil rights of individuals who are the subject of a guardianship. The purpose of this chapter, then, is to present what scholars from various fields have written about guardianship law reform.

THE HISTORICAL CONTEXT OF GUARDIANSHIPS

The roots of guardianship law extend back to the sixteenth century, when the power of the state to look after its citizens was based on the ideology of *parens patriae* (Sherman, 1980). Under this ideology, the king had a legal and moral obligation, authority, and duty to take care of personal and financial matters of those found by a jury to be lunatics or idiots. Only those who had estates of any size, however, were subjected to an appointment of a guardian (Mitchell, 1978). Thus, the primary purpose was to preserve the prosperity of the incompetent.

Because guardianship law has deep historic roots in benevolence, it has been only recently that scholars in a wide variety of disciplines have questioned its basic underlying assumptions and procedures (Alexander, 1977, 1979; Frolik, 1981; Hommel, Wang, & Bergman, 1990; Iris, 1988; Mitchell, 1978; Stevenson & Capezuti, 1991). As a result, a genre of literature about the guardianship process has emerged, coming from legal scholars, social scientists, reports in the lay press, health law advocates, and ethicists. In each area of scholarship, writers have raised questions about using guardianships to intervene in the lives of those deemed to be marginally incompetent, and perhaps more important, about the process and methods used by the courts to determine incapacity.

The reason for great concern about the guardianship process is due to the ramifications of being found incompetent. Guardianships are obtained through a judicial process that may be traumatic and frightening to the respondent, and the procedure represents a dramatic intrusion on basic individual liberties (ABA, 1986). Once found incapacitated, the aged person's relationship with the guardian becomes similar to a parent-child relationship, whereby decisions regarding daily living activities and management of finances are made by another individual. In addition, this action may strip the aged person of basic freedoms, such as the right to marry, vote, continue in their professions, or to enter into contractual arrangements (Mitchell, 1978). One legal scholar, Elias Cohen, has remarked that "outside of execution, guardianship is the most radical remedy we have" (Topolnicki, 1989).

Many professionals concerned about the guardianship process agree that guardianships do provide a valuable service to those who are in need of such intervention. But observers of the guardianship process have voiced a number of criticisms about guardianship procedure and the outcome for proposed wards. We will present a brief explanation of the guardianship procedure, followed by a review of the guardianship literature drawing from the legal profession, social sciences, popular press, health professions, and ethicists.

GUARDIANSHIP PROCEDURES

When others suspect that an individual is no longer able to make responsible decisions regarding his or her welfare or assets, a concerned individual, or in some instances, a corporation or government agency, can file a petition with the court for guardianship or conservatorship powers. Although state statutes vary somewhat in terminology, a guardianship typically refers to the authority that allows another to make decisions on behalf of the alleged incompetent (often referred to as the ward) in matters such as place of residence, health care, daily care and comfort; conservatorships grant the authority to make decisions regarding the assets of the incapacitated person. In most jurisdictions, the process of obtaining a conservatorship is the same as for a guardianship. In addition, some states use the terms guardianship and conservatorship interchangeably to encompass the functions attributed to both. We will use the term guardianship to denote both guardianship and conservatorship, as the processes of obtaining these legal authorities are virtually the same.

In every jurisdiction, in order to obtain a guardianship, a petition must be filed with the court, evidence of the need for a guardian must be presented at a hearing, and the court must make a determination regarding the need for a guardian. We will discuss, in some detail, each of the specific steps in the guardianship process in subsequent sections.

THE LEGAL LITERATURE

Because the process of obtaining a guardianship involves the legal system, it is not surprising that the legal literature contains the vast majority of the debate and discussion about guardianships. Criticisms about the guardianship process first appeared in the 1960s, due in part to the concerns being voiced about involuntary civil commitments of persons with mental illnesses. In some instances, case law concerning commitment procedures of allegedly incompetent individuals to mental institutions were cited as a basis for guardianship reform. For example, the doctrine of providing less restrictive alternatives has its legal beginnings in the civil commitment case of *Lake v. Cameron* (364 F. 2d 662; see Horstman, 1975). Lake was a 60-year-old woman whom police found wandering on the streets of Washington, D.C. Against her wishes, police took her to a local hospital and subsequently transferred her to a psychiatric hospital. At the incompetency hearing, the psychiatrists testified that she had frequent difficulty with her memory and occasionally could not tell the date or her present location. The court determined, however, that she was not a danger to herself or others. On appeal, the court ruled that there should be a full exploration of less restrictive alternatives to the more restrictive commitment to a psychiatric hospital, thereby reversing the lower court's decision.

A second notable case, *Lessard v. Schmidt* (349 F.Supp. 1078) was instrumental in securing procedural safeguards in commitment hearings. Two police officers picked up Alberta Lessard in front of her home and took her to a mental health facility. The court authorized the mental health facility to hold Lessard a period of approximately two weeks, during which time she was never notified of the hearings authorizing her to be detained. One day before the full hearing on her commitment to the mental health facility, she was able to obtain an attorney and to secure one additional week to prepare for the commitment hearing. After the lower court found Lessard mentally ill, a class action suit was filed challenging the due process procedures used in her case. The higher court found that the procedures used for civil commitment of Lessard were unconstitutional. The court found that Lessard failed to receive effective and timely notice, that there was no adequate notice of all rights, including a trial by jury, that she was not represented by counsel, that hearsay was permitted as evidence, and that the court failed to require a less restrictive alternative be considered.

These are just two involuntary civil commitment cases that have served as legal precedents for individuals advocating guardianship reform. It is clear that the protection of legal rights for individuals who are subjected to involuntary civil commitment are similar to those for individuals who are subjected to a guardianship proceeding. Consequently, the guardianship reform movement has benefited from the procedural changes sought in civil commitment hearings. Since the early 1960s legal scholars have conducted a few empirical studies and written numerous articles about the need for guardianship reform.

EMPIRICAL STUDIES

One of the first empirical studies to examine issues of competency and guardianship was initiated in 1962, and funded by the National Institute of Mental Health. Three attorneys, Allen, Ferster, and Weihofen, conducted the Mental Competency Study, which examined court records of incompetency hearings in ten states: California, Colorado, Maryland, Massachusetts, New Jersey, New York, North Carolina, Ohio, Texas, and the District of Columbia. To identify possible problem areas and obtain suggestions for reform in addition to the examination of court records, personal interviews were conducted with 213 individuals involved in civil competency procedures, including psychiatrists, psychologists, judges, and attorneys.

Another early study, by Alexander and Lewin (1972) examined 513 New York court records of individuals who were appointed conservators. As a part of this research, the authors conducted a review of guardianship statutes in 50 states. In other early empirical research, the National Senior Citizens Law Center examined 1,010 guardianship and conservatorship cases filed in Los Angeles from 1973–1974 in order to ascertain the type of evidence submitted, the degree to which wards were present at hearings and represented by counsel, and the outcome of the hearings (Horstman, 1975).

These studies are important in that they represent initial attempts to gather empirical data and to question guardianship practices. The findings and criticisms expressed in these three studies—the Mental Competency Study, Alexander and Lewin's research, and the National Senior Citizens Law Center—now approximately 20 years old, serve as benchmarks against which we can measure the progress of guardianship reform. The results of these studies are discussed later in this chapter.

LEGAL COMMENTARY

While there have been relatively few empirical studies of guardianships, there have been many more commentaries offering critical insights about guardianships. Several law review journals have published articles examining the entire guardianship process and suggesting various solutions (Barnes, 1992; Horstman, 1975; Regan, 1972; Sherman, 1980). Although most of these articles discuss individual state statutes, the suggestions made by the authors are applicable to other states since most jurisdictions have similar guardianship processes. These include the filing of the petition, serving the notice of the hearing, the conduct of the hearing, the appointment or dismissal of the proposed guardian, the appeal of the decision, and the frequency and content of the guardian's report. The rest of this chapter will examine the guardianship process and suggestions made by legal scholars concerning the petition, notice of hearing, standards used to assess competency, legal representation of the proposed ward, the scope of the powers granted to the guardian, court supervision of the guardian and termination of guardianships.

PETITIONING FOR GUARDIANSHIP

In most states, individuals seeking a guardianship use one of two procedures to initiate a guardianship. These two procedures are typically referred to as voluntary and involuntary guardianships. For voluntary guardianship procedures, a person who is still competent but feels that his or her capacities may be declining, can file a petition requesting a guardian. The voluntary guardianship option was created with the intent of diminishing the stigma attached to involuntary guardianships (Allen, Ferster, & Weihofen, 1968). In Iowa, for example, a voluntary petition does not require a notice or a hearing, unless, of course, the court determines a hearing is necessary. The powers given to the guardian, however, can be just as extensive as those obtained through an involuntary guardianship procedure. In the voluntary process there is usually no statutory-mandated inquiry into the ward's competency because the court assumes that the ward is competent enough to consent to a guardianship. In summary, a voluntary guardianship can grant powers that are quite extensive without conducting a hearing about the extent of the need for protection, or without an inquiry into the intentions of the guardian.

One variation of a voluntary guardianship is the standby guardianship. Standby guardianships allow the proposed ward to file a petition before any incapacity emerges, to indicate the preferred guardian and to specify the type of incapacity required to be present before a guardianship can be granted. A verified statement indicating that the specified incapacity has occurred activates the petition.

Even though in some states the court can appoint a guardian through the use of a voluntary petition, the outcome of reduced personal liberties and autonomy is the same as it is in involuntary guardianships. The procedures to establish voluntary guardianships, however, stand in marked contrast to those followed for involuntary guardianships.

Interested third parties can file petitions for involuntary guardianships with the court. Since the consent of the proposed ward is not obtained, involuntary guardianships are considered to be adversarial proceedings. Any interested person, corporation, and in some instances, a governmental agency acting as a "public guardian," can file with the court of appropriate jurisdiction a petition that initiates the guardianship action.

Interested individuals can also obtain involuntary guardianships on a temporary or emergency basis. The court can grant full or limited powers to a temporary guardian. The majority of states provide for a temporary guardianship, whose duration is for a time either specified by statutory language or by the court. For example, in Iowa, there is no time limit specified in the statute and the court determines the duration of the temporary guardianship. Therefore, it is quite possible for an individual to obtain a temporary guardianship without having had a hearing before the guardianship expires after a few months. In other instances, the temporary guardianship continues until the court holds a hearing for a permanent guardianship. Researchers have not investigated the circumstances under which individuals seek temporary guardianships, or the duration and scope of powers granted under a temporary guardianship. The following comments about the guardianship process refer to involuntary guardianships, unless otherwise noted.

PETITION

In most states, the guardianship petition contains basic information about the proposed ward's address, age, assets, and sometimes, physical condition. Most petitions merely recite the statutory language requirements (e.g., the ward is unable to manage his person or estate) and do not explain in any depth the circumstances or reasons for the necessity of the guardianship (Sherman, 1980). In most instances the petition is a form that simply requires the petitioner to fill in the blanks, without providing any details (see a representative example in the Appendix). Colorado is an exception in this regard. The guardianship petition requires that the petitioner declare the nature and degree of incapacity; the extent of authority that the court should give the guardian to arrange for medical or professional care; and the nature and extent of the care, assistance, and protection necessary. Legal scholars and advocates have called for petitions to contain explanations of the serious nature of the guardianship and to set forth the facts that support the need for a guardianship (Horstman, 1975; Mitchell, 1978).

ADEQUATE NOTICE

The service of the two legal documents, notice of the hearing and the petition, to the proposed ward is a basic legal requirement in all states. In most states, a sheriff or process server personally serves the notice of the hearing and the petition to the proposed ward. Its purpose is to notify the alleged incapacitated person about the nature of the proceeding and the date, time, and location of the hearing. The notice also serves to provide adequate time to prepare a defense (Allen, Ferster, & Weihofen, 1968). In their investigation of guardianship cases, Allen, Ferster, and Weihofen (1968) found that of 103 cases, only 9 wards did not receive a notice of the hearing. Because the service of the notice is such a basic step in all types of legal cases, criticisms about notification generally concern the content of the notice. Many legal scholars have argued that notices provided to the alleged incompetent announcing the start of a guardianship proceeding are not adequate (Horstman, 1975; Mitchell, 1978; Sherman, 1980). Specifically, the notices often do not include information regarding the nature of the proceeding, the reasons for the need of a guardian, the consequences of the adjudication of incompetency, and the legal rights available to the alleged incompetent, such as the right to a jury trial, the right to attend the hearing, and the right to cross-examine witnesses and be represented by counsel (Mitchell, 1978). New York and Rhode Island have recently passed statutory changes that require the notice to be in large type and to include a clear statement about the proposed ward's rights (Wood, Stiegel, Sabatino, & Edelstein, 1993). In addition, because of the confusing language often used in the notices, scholars have called for them to be written in plain language, or in another language if needed (Sherman, 1980). For example, illustrating complicated language, the notice used in Texas reads, in part, as follows:

At or before 10 A.M. of the Monday next after the expiration of 10 days after the date of service of this citation by filing a written answer to the application of (petitioner) filed in said court on the (date) alleging said ward has no guardian and praying for the appointment of the person and estate of said ward. At said above mentioned time and place, said ward and all other persons may contest said application if they so desire. (Associated Press, 1987)

Many authors believe that a trained individual who can explain the guardianship process, its ramifications, and the rights of the proposed ward should personally serve the notice and petition to the proposed ward (Atkinson, 1980; Mitchell, 1978).

GUARDIANSHIP HEARING

The character of the guardianship hearing has been the topic of numerous discussions about guardianship reform. This is not surprising, as the hearing is of vital importance to the proposed ward. It is at the hearing where the petitioner presents evidence supporting the proposed ward's incapacity; it is where the ward has an opportunity to be present and rebut any allegations made; it is where the judge determines if the proposed ward is in need of a guardian and either appoints a guardian or dismisses the petition; and it is where the judge determines the scope of the guardian's power over the ward. Clearly, the hearing is the most critical stage of the process.

Nonadversarial Hearings

Legal scholars have characterized guardianship hearings as informal or nonadversarial, because in most instances, only the petitioner and his or her attorney are present, and as a result, no one is able to challenge any of the evidence submitted (Mitchell, 1978). The authors of the Mental Competency Study reported that hearings were often so perfunctory that it was not a hearing in any meaningful sense. The alleged incompetent person was seldom present at the hearing, and in some cases was discouraged from attending the hearing or was not fully advised of the right to attend the hearing (Allen, Ferster, & Weihofen, 1968). The nonadversarial nature of the hearing results in evidence going unchallenged, often making the medical evidence the only grounds the court uses to grant a guardianship (Mitchell, 1978). Almost ten years after the Mental Competency Study, the National Senior Citizens Law Center study (1974) revealed that the only persons present at 84 percent of the hearings were the judge, the petitioner, and the petitioner's attorney. Allen, Ferster, and Weihofen (1968) reported that in California, a state that required affidavits attesting to the ward's physical or mental inability to attend the hearing in the event that the ward was unable to attend, only 32 of the 46 cases contained affidavits. No inquiry was made why the proposed wards were not present because the courts were relying on the information contained in the affidavits that are usually filed by the petitioner's attorney. Further, the informality of the hearing resulted in very few cases being heard by a jury. Trial by jury is a fundamental legal right, recognized either by statutory language or case law, but it is an option seldom provided to the proposed ward. Allen, Ferster, and Weihofen (1968) reported that 40 percent of the sample of professionals involved in guardianships believed that trial by juries should be dispensed with entirely.

Determination of Incompetency

The appointment of guardian rests solely on whether the court is persuaded that there is enough evidence to support the allegation of incapacity as defined by statute. How statutes define incapacity is critical in determining whether the proposed ward is in need of a guardian.

Definitions. One of the first empirical studies to investigate definitions of incompetency was the Mental Competency Study (Allen, Ferster, & Weihofen, 1968). Researchers identified 55 different terms used to define incompetency in the guardianship statutes of the 50 states and the District of Columbia, and found that the various terms used to define incompetency were ambiguous and archaic. Some terms such as "unsound mind" varied widely in their interpretation. In their assessment of incompetency determinations, Alexander and Lewin noted that by 1972, most of the older terminology associated with guardianships had been altered. No longer, for example, did statutes refer to prospective wards as being "imbeciles," "idiots," "insane," or "lunatics," but rather as being incompetent or incapacitated.

Along with criticisms of the terminology used in guardianship statutes, concerns about the actual definitions of incapacity are still being articulated by legal scholars. Anderer, Coleman, Lichtenstein, and Parry (1990) have identified three different categories of incapacity in various state statutes—the traditional-causal, the Uniform Probate Code (UPC), and the functional therapeutic. The traditional-causal type defines incapacity as resulting from a physical or mental deficiency. This type of definition generally takes a "two-part test" (Ratcliffe, 1982). First, in order to prove incapacity, there has to be an evident cause, such as mental illness, mental deficiency, or old age. Second, as a result of one of these causes, persons must be unable to manage their financial or personal affairs. For example, the Iowa law states that a person is considered to be incapacitated if the proposed ward "by reason of mental, physical or other incapacity lacks sufficient capacity to make or carry out important decisions concerning the proposed ward's person or affairs" (Iowa Code §633.552[2] [a]). Critics suggest that courts do not fully examine the link between this cause and effect. Often, it is the medical evidence by the examining physician that takes precedence without establishing the effect of the medical condition (Atkinson, 1980).

A second type of definition is similar to the UPC, which emphasizes an individual's impaired decision-making and communicative abilities. The Colorado statute is representative of this type of definition of incapacity:

> Any person who is impaired by reason of mental illness, mental deficiency, physical illness or disability, advanced age, chronic use of drugs, chronic intoxication, or other cause (except minority) to the extent that he lacks sufficient understanding or capacity to make or communicate responsible decisions concerning his person. (Colorado Revised Statutes §15-14-101 [1])

The Colorado definition differs slightly from the UPC in that it includes old age as one of the causes of incapacity, and as a result, may encourage the stereotypical link between old age and incapacity (Alexander, 1979).

The third type of incapacity definition is the functional therapeutic, which is based on impairment of functional abilities or ability to care for oneself. Missouri is one example of this type of definition of incapacity:

> An "incapacitated person" is one who is unable by reason of any physical or mental condition to receive and evaluate information or to communicate decisions to such an extent that he lacks capacity to meet essential requirements for food, clothing, shelter, safety or other care such that serious physical injury, illness, or disease is likely to occur. (Missouri Revised Statutes §475.010 [8])

Unlike the other statutes, which broadly mention functional incapacity as "responsible decisions concerning his or her person," the Missouri statute has a more narrow test of what must be the outcome of a physical or mental impairment, based on the functional ability of the proposed ward. Therefore, simply having a physical or mental condition is not sufficient to warrant the appointment of a guardian unless the person is unable to take care of essential daily needs.

As demonstrated by the three statutes, definitions of incapacity can vary considerably. Frank (1993) suggests that all three types of definition are imprecise because they do not define incapacity in specific, observable behaviors. The nature of the statutory definition of incapacity has a direct effect on the type of evidence presented to support incapacity, and also acts as a barrier that keeps individuals from entering the guardianship process if they can be served by other, less restrictive alternatives.

Amount and Type of Evidence. Another criticism of the determination of incapacity at the hearing concerns the evidence presented to support incapacity. It is often unclear what kind of evidence would support the contention that the alleged incompetent is unable to manage his or her financial affairs. Eccentric behavior? Poor decision making? Unproductive investments? Incorrect entries into a check register? One article has suggested that the abstract inability to manage personal and financial affairs should not be the criterion to determine incompetency, but rather the criterion should be the effect of that inability (Comment, 1976). Critics of the guardianship system argue that the appointment of a guardian is warranted only if the court does indeed determine that the proposed ward would incur an actual hardship if no guardian is appointed (Comment, 1976).

Alexander and Lewin (1972) examined the nature of the allegations concerning the extent to which wards were incapacitated and the kind of medical proof necessary to warrant an appointment of a guardian. Based on their research, they noted a number of criticisms about the determination of incompetency. For example, the courts did not use objective standards as a measure of capacity. Even though statutes have changed from declaring a person to be "insane" to being "mentally incompetent," the testimony appeared to be the same. The test of mental competency was still a question of how bizarre the person's behavior was, and the testimony of medical professionals overshadowed the facts of the case. The authors concluded that the movement for guardianship reform should be away from mental competency to a more precise investigation of functional capacity. Some scholars have suggested that courts should use tests of functional capacity that measure the ability to perform activities of daily living (Hafemeister & Sales, 1984; Nolan, 1984; Scogin & Perry, 1986). The issue of how incapacity is determined will be discussed in greater detail in chapter 4.

Legal Standards Used in Judging Evidence. While the burden of proof of incapacity rests with the petitioner, the breadth and scope of the evidence required to prove incapacity varies from state to state. In some instances, the statute is silent on the standard required, and any amount of evidence can be deemed sufficient. Law can, however, specify different legal tests of the evidence. "Preponderance of the evidence" is the lesser of the tests; the more strict test of evidence is referred to as "proof beyond a reasonable doubt" or "clear and convincing." Horstman (1975) argued that the legal standard used to determine incompetency should be "proof beyond a reasonable doubt" as opposed to the less strict standard of "preponderance of the evidence." Given the serious consequences of an involuntary guardianship, statutes should instruct courts to use the more stringent standard of proof on the evidence submitted to support incapacity.

Adequate Legal Representation

Legal scholars and advocates have noted that in many instances, proposed wards are not at the hearings, and perhaps more important, are not represented by counsel. The National Senior Citizens Law Center (1974) reported that attorneys represented proposed wards in only 2.9 percent of

1,010 cases, and the court appointed a guardian ad litem (GAL), who might act in the best interests of a person lacking capacity, in only one case.

In all jurisdictions, proposed wards are entitled to legal counsel, but states handle the appointment of legal representation differently. In some states, such as Iowa, the decision to appoint legal counsel for proposed wards is at the judge's discretion. In contrast, Missouri courts appoint an attorney to represent the proposed ward once the petition is filed, provided that the ward does not already have an attorney. In practice, however, wards are generally not represented by an attorney and they are often unaware of their right to request representation.

In some states courts appoint GALs as legal counsel for the proposed ward. Typically, the role of the GAL is to act in the best interests of the ward, which does not ensure that the attorney will act as an advocate charged to represent the wishes of the ward. Therefore, even though courts might appoint a GAL, there is no guarantee that the GAL will rigorously defend the wishes of the ward. Allen, Ferster, and Weihofen (1968) reported that in three jurisdictions where the courts appointed attorneys as guardians ad litem, the GALs did not function as partisan representatives of the proposed ward, but rather as "paper checkers." It was the authors' recommendation that courts inform proposed wards of their right to counsel and have the discretion to appoint counsel to represent the proposed ward.

More recently, one legal scholar has called for mandatory appointment of legal counsel for every proposed ward (das Neves, 1991). In many instances, the proposed ward is unable to challenge adequately the petitioner and the petitioner's attorney, due to inexperience with the legal system or physical or mental limitations. Das Neves argues that the appointment of an attorney, who will be a "zealous advocate" on behalf of the proposed ward, will protect the rights of the client at every stage in the guardianship process. An attorney would be able to prepare a defense sooner in the process, to ensure the presence of the proposed ward at the hearing, and to challenge the petitioner's allegations.

APPOINTMENT OF THE GUARDIAN

Critics of the guardianship process contend that the appointment of a guardian should be based on perceived benefits for wards, as opposed to benefits any potential heir will receive (Alexander, 1977). Moreover, the appropriateness of the proposed guardian is often not a consideration. Allen, Ferster, and Weihofen (1968) concluded from their interviews that courts gave little or no thought to whether a particular guardian was acceptable to the ward. The interviewees did recommend that courts explore the proposed guardian's integrity, financial standing, time available for estate management, history of his or her relationship with the proposed ward, and any prior mental or criminal record. They reported one judge as saying that "since about 95 percent of the cases are uncontested, there is no need for the court to make any inquiry at all. The court merely passes on what the petitioners have proposed as a matter of form" (Allen, Ferster, & Weihofen, 1968:91). Some statutes simply direct courts to appoint a guardian who is "suitable" or identify an order of preference for appointment. In some states, statutes specifically direct courts to ascertain the ward's preference for a guardian. For example, Colorado law requires the visitor to comment on the appropriateness of the proposed guardian and to ascertain the proposed ward's views about the proposed guardian and the scope of his or her duties. In Oregon, proposed guardians must disclose if they have ever been convicted of a felony, and anyone suspended from practicing law is disqualified from being a guardian or conservator. Very few state statutes, however, specifically require the court to examine the interests and intentions of the guardian.

POWERS GRANTED TO THE GUARDIAN

Once the court establishes the need for a guardianship, it gives the guardian the legal authority to make personal decisions on behalf of the ward. According to Colorado law, "a guardian has the same powers, rights and duties respecting his ward that a parent has respecting his unemancipated minor child" (CRS §15-14-312 [I] [e], Supp. 1990). Guardianships grant guardians the authority to determine the ward's residence, to consent to medical care and treatment, and to take reasonable care of the ward's personal effects, unless restricted by the court. For example, Iowa law requires court approval if the guardian wants to move the ward to a more restrictive setting or if the guardian believes the ward needs elective surgery (IC §633.635 [2] [a] [b], Supp. 1987).

Perhaps because no one in the process makes a distinction between wards with varying degrees of capacity; courts seldom limit the guardian's power over the ward. The authors of the Mental Competency Study noted that as soon as the court determined the proposed ward to be in need of a conservator, "the system is superimposed on him regardless of his actual specific needs," a phenomenon they called "overkill" (Allen, Ferster, & Weihofen, 1968). Others argue that the powers granted to guardians should match the specific functional limitations of their wards (ABA 1989; Barnes, 1988; Nolan, 1984). In addition, other legal scholars have called for statutes to require courts to consider "least restrictive alternatives" to guardianships. This would require that courts consider alternative community resources that could protect the individual without having to appoint a guardian (ABA 1989; Horstman, 1975). In New York, the court must find, when appointing a limited guardianship, that the powers given to the guardian are the least restrictive form of intervention consistent with the ward's functional limitations (Wood, Stiegel, Sabatino, & Edelstein, 1993).

ADEQUATE REPORTING OF GUARDIAN ACTIVITIES

In most states, statutes require guardians to file an annual report describing any activities conducted on behalf of the ward. The frequency and detail of the guardian report vary from state to state. Oregon requires the guardian to file a written report each year. The report provides information regarding the current location and description of the ward's placement; the ward's physical and mental condition; contacts made with the ward; major decisions made on behalf of the ward; source of income and expenditures for the ward; and reasons why the guardianship should continue (Oregon Revised Statutes §126.137 [6], Supp. 1989). In contrast, Colorado law does not require guardians to file any reports, unless the court orders otherwise (CRS §15-14-312 [1] [e], Supp. 1990).

Even if guardians file annual reports, it does not necessarily ensure that courts will scrutinize their activities closely or determine if such actions are in the best interests of the ward. Legal commentators argue that courts do not provide adequate supervision of guardians' activities (Alexander, 1977; Sherman, 1980). This lack of oversight may be due in part to the overburdened and understaffed judicial system.

The ABA has developed recommendations for court monitoring of guardianship activities based on an 18-month study of court monitoring activities (Hurme, 1991). The recommendations were as follows:

1. The guardian should be required to report on the ward's personal and financial status no less than once per year;
2. The guardian's written report should be designed to include narrative responses that will provide concise explanation of the ward's circumstances, the care provided, and continued need for guardianship;
3. The guardian should file with the court a written statement within 60 days after appointment including future plans to provide for the ward's care and the allocation of resources;
4. The guardian should explain in the annual report any deviations from and amendments to the plan;
5. The court should state the guardian's responsibility to report to the court in the initial order; and
6. The court should provide the guardian with reporting and accounting forms and samples it considers satisfactorily prepared.

The author of the study made some additional recommendations designed to improve the court's handling of guardianship reports.

Finally, if guardians are to act in the best interests of the ward and comply with reporting requirements, they must receive adequate guidance from the court. Frolik (1990) has suggested that courts should have written and videotaped training materials and qualified staff available to answer questions about the guardian's responsibilities to the court and the ward. He aptly noted that if guardians are to perform their tasks better, they must receive support and guidance from the court.

TERMINATION OF GUARDIANSHIP

Once the court appoints a guardian, termination of the guardianship only occurs upon the death of the ward or after a hearing finds the ward has regained competency. In some instances, it is up to the ward to file with the court a petition to end the guardianship and to present evidence that shows she or he is no longer incapacitated. Studies have shown that most guardianships remain in effect until the death of the ward. Alexander and Lewin (1972) reported that the court restored to capacity 7 percent of the wards they studied. Allen, Ferster, and Weihofen (1968) observed that restorations rarely occurred in the jurisdictions they investigated.

SUMMARY

In the past 20 years, concerns about the guardianship process remain relatively unchanged. Our review of the legal literature reveals continued misgivings about the current guardianship practices in most states. Scholars agree that the courts must begin to conduct guardianship hearings as though they were adversarial proceedings; proposed wards must be represented by attorneys who will zealously protect their rights; every effort must be made to ensure that wards are present at the hearings; and judges must weigh the evidence against the strictest legal standards. Moreover, the court should limit the powers of the guardian to those activities the ward is not capable of managing.

Finally, the appointment of a guardian must be in the best interests of the wards and not those who seek the guardianship. Alexander and Lewin (1972:136) concluded the following at the completion of their study:

> One startling conclusion about the whole process of incompetency was drawn from the realization that in almost every case examined the aged incompetent was in a worse position after he was adjudicated incompetent than before. The study could identify no particular benefit which flowed to the incompetent that he could not have received without a finding of incompetency.

Indeed, looking back over the last 20 years of guardianship reform, it may be that statutory wording has changed, but the process and outcome have not.

GUARDIANSHIP LITERATURE IN THE SOCIAL SCIENCES

In contrast to the legal literature, articles about guardianship have only sporadically appeared in the social science literature in the last 20 years.

Articles regarding guardianships first appeared in the social work literature. Older adults in need of "protective services" were often subjected to a guardianship as part of an intervention strategy used by social service departments. As a result, many authors debated the ethical consequences and possible benefits of this intervention (Lehmann, 1961; Regan, 1978; Schoenfeld & Tuzil, 1979).

Elias Cohen remarked in a 1978 editorial in *The Gerontologist*:"Research in the substantive issues in law and aging has been limited. . . . Empirical studies . . . are critically needed in the face of what some of us regard as an inappropriate and premature embrace of public guardianship" (p. 229). Despite this call for more empirical research, only a few empirical studies have been conducted in the last 15 years. A review of articles published in two gerontology journals—*The Gerontologist* and the *Journal of Gerontological Social Work*—from 1978–1988 revealed only 3 empirical articles examining guardianships or conservatorships. Since that time, however, 12 articles on guardianship have appeared in these journals. In spite of this growing interest in guardianship, empirically based information about guardianships is somewhat limited.

The studies that have been conducted, however, play an important role in our understanding of various aspects of the guardianship process. In one of the first studies on guardianship, Bell, Schmidt, and Miller (1981) reviewed public guardianship programs in 34 states and conducted on-site visits of guardianship programs in 6 states. On-site visits included a review of administrative records and interviews with public guardian officials, wards, and guardians. The Dade County (Florida) Grand Jury (1982) was responsible for the review of 200 guardianship cases filed in the county between 1979 and 1981. In another investigation of guardianships in Florida, Peters, Schmidt, and Miller (1985) examined 42 incompetency/guardianship cases filed in Leon County, Florida, during 1977–1982. Their investigation included a review of court records as well as observation of court hearings.

Iris (1988) completed an ethnographic study that described the decision-making process among family members, attorneys, guardians ad litem, and judges in Illinois. She collected data from 14 courtroom observations and 11 interviews with attorneys and program administrators.

Grossberg, Zimny, and Scallet (1989) conducted an empirical investigation of guardianship cases in which the Division of Geriatric Psychiatry at the St. Louis University Medical Clinic provided specialized diagnostic and treatment services. Data were collected from information provided by the Division of Geriatric Psychiatry regarding the diagnoses of the clients as well as a review of court records of those clients who were eventually granted guardians ($n = 13$).

More recently, Bulcroft, Kielkopf, and Tripp (1991) investigated 63 guardianship cases in Ohio and Washington, and Vittoria (1992) conducted a qualitative examination of guardianship hearings. Lisi and Hommel (1992) recently completed a national study on guardianship systems by gathering data from 563 guardianship hearings, 726 guardianship files, and 228 guardianship petitioners. The results of these studies are presented below.

Characteristics of Wards

Findings about the characteristics of wards were consistent across the various studies. Elderly individuals with guardians or conservators appointed on their behalf had characteristics similar to the elderly population as a whole. The majority were women, over age 70, and without a spouse (Bell, Schmidt, & Miller, 1981; Bulcroft, Kielkopf, & Tripp, 1991; Dade County Grand Jury, 1982; Grossberg, Zimny, & Scallet, 1989; Lisi & Hommel, 1992; Peters, Schmidt, & Miller, 1985). There was little information available regarding ethnicity of the wards, although Lisi and Hommel reported that 83 percent of the wards in their study were white.

The residences of proposed wards (when the petition was filed) varied somewhat. Peters, Schmidt, and Miller (1985) reported that the majority of proposed wards were living in a private residence, whereas Bulcroft, Kielkopf, and Tripp (1991) found that 44 percent of the proposed wards were living in a nursing home and 34 percent were living in their own home. In contrast, 34 percent of wards in Lisi and Hommel's study (1992) were living in a nursing home, and 47 percent were either living alone or living with others. Grossberg, Zimny, and Scallet (1989) reported that 9 of 12 respondents were living in residential care facilities.

The socioeconomic status of proposed wards is somewhat more problematic to assess. In some jurisdictions (for example, Colorado) the courts do not require guardians to report on the financial status of the proposed ward if a conservatorship is not also granted. In addition, studies of public guardianship programs may include wards whose economic status is different from that of wards with private guardians. Often wards in the public guardianship system may have limited incomes, perhaps indicating that those with fewer assets may be less likely to have a private guardian (Bell, Schmidt, & Miller, 1981).

Available information, however, suggests that the economic status of wards varies greatly from having no assets to having assets worth hundreds of thousands of dollars (Bulcroft, Kielkopf, & Tripp, 1991; Grossberg, Zimny, & Scallet, 1989; Peters, Schmidt, & Miller, 1985). The Dade County Grand Jury (1982) investigation reported that 46 percent of the wards had assets more than $50,000, whereas 15 percent had no assets. In two other studies, 43 and 47 percent of wards had estates valued less than $50,000 (Bulcroft, Kielkopf, & Tripp, 1991; Peters, Schmidt, & Miller, 1985). Grossberg, Zimny, and Scallet (1989) cited mean values of $16,426 for real property and $65,667 for personal property. Lisi and Hommel (1992) obtained information about the ward's income status from petitioners. Using information collected from petitioners willing to reveal the income status of their ward, they reported that 54 percent had incomes less than $50,000, with 33 percent having incomes less than $10,000.

Characteristics of Guardians

Court records contain very little information about guardians. At the very least, the petition lists the name and address of the proposed guardian. The extent of any additional information about guardians in the record depends on whether the statute directs courts to collect such information. Petitions may require a statement of the relationship of the guardian to the proposed ward and reasons why the court should appoint the petitioner (usually the statute gives priority to the spouse and in succession to children and other relatives).

It is clear from research that in the majority of cases, petitioners and consequently guardians were relatives of the proposed ward (Dade County, Grand Jury, 1982; Lisi & Hommel, 1992; Peters, Schmidt, & Miller, 1985). Most often, the petitioners were adult children of the proposed ward, even though many of the wards may have had a spouse (Bulcroft, Kielkopf, & Tripp, 1991). An almost equal percentage of daughters and sons acted as guardians (Bulcroft, Kielkopf, & Tripp, 1991; Grossberg, Zimny, & Scallet, 1989; Lisi & Hommel, 1992). Bulcroft, Kielkopf, and Tripp (1991) reported that most of the guardians resided in the same city and that 25 percent were also providing caregiving assistance to the wards.

Guardianship Process

Empirical findings regarding the judicial process are consistent with much of the criticism cited in the legal literature. Evidence submitted to support the need for a guardianship often consists of nothing more than a general statement about the ward's physical status. For example, Peters, Schmidt, and Miller (1985) found that in 38 percent of the cases reviewed, the rationale for guardianship was simply that the wards had mental or physical incapacities. Other studies reported that physical status or diagnosis, such as dementia, senility, or simply "confusion/disorientation," was the sole determination of incompetency (Bulcroft, Kielkopf, & Tripp, 1991; Peters, Schmidt, & Miller, 1985). Thus it is not surprising that the physician's diagnosis of the ward is often the key piece of evidence presented to support the proposed ward's incapacity (Bell, Schmidt, & Miller, 1981). Evidence that links the ward's physical status with functional incapacity is often absent from court records, and in some instances, the records do not contain any evidence that the alleged incapacity exists (Bulcroft,

Kielkopf, & Tripp, 1991). Iris (1988) observed that many of the hearings were more concerned with who should be appointed as guardian rather than whether the guardianship was needed. She concluded from her observations that the court often based its determination of incompetency on eccentric behavior, noting that such an interpretation carries with it ageist assumptions about appropriate age-related behavior.

The conduct of the hearing itself continues to come under a great deal of criticism. Proposed wards are seldom present (Bulcroft, Kielkopf, & Tripp, 1991; Grossberg, Zimny, & Scallet, 1989; Lisi & Hommel, 1992) and hearings tend to be nonadversarial, lasting only a few minutes (Bell, Schmidt, & Miller, 1981). Lisi and Hommel (1992) measured the length of the hearing in 515 cases and found that 50 percent of the hearings lasted 15 minutes or less.

Even though proposed wards have the right to be represented by counsel, not all have attorneys to represent them. Peters, Schmidt, and Miller (1985) found 43 percent of the proposed wards did not have attorneys appointed to represent them, whereas Grossberg, Zimny, and Scallet (1989) reported that 11 out of the 13 proposed wards had attorneys. Attorneys represented wards in 23 percent of the cases in Lisi and Hommel's study (1992). The number of wards having legal representation will vary depending on the jurisdiction. States such as Missouri require courts to appoint attorneys for proposed wards (if they do not have their own counsel) once the petition is filed. In other states, such as Iowa, the appointment of counsel for the ward is at the discretion of the judge. Perhaps the greater question is whether the appointment of an attorney to represent the ward influences the outcome of the hearing in any way. In chapter 11, we investigate the relationship between recommended practices and outcomes for proposed wards.

The outcome of guardianships appears to be consistent across all studies. That is, once a guardianship petition is filed, it is seldom denied or dismissed or the powers of the guardian limited. In their review of public guardianship cases, Bell, Schmidt, and Miller (1981) found that once cases reached the adjudication stage, courts "almost invariably" granted guardianships, rarely granted partial or limited guardianships, and seldom considered least restrictive alternatives. Peters, Schmidt, and Miller (1985), in an examination of 42 guardianship and incompetency cases filed in Leon County, Florida, reported that the court appointed guardians for all 42 proposed wards. Only one proposed ward was appointed a limited guardian. In a more recent study, Bulcroft, Kielkopf, and Tripp (1991) reported that all petitions resulted in the appointment of a guardian; however, 7 percent of those petitions resulted in limited guardianships. Lisi and Hommel (1992) found a similar outcome in their research, as 94 percent of guardianship petitions filed were granted and only 13 percent of those were limited in some way.

Another area of concern is the lack of oversight of the guardian's activities by the court. The Dade County Grand Jury (1982) found many of the court records did not have all the required annual reports of the ward's financial or physical status. Bell, Schmidt, and Miller (1981) concluded that court review of guardians' activities was "perfunctory at best."

In conclusion, results from these investigations reveal wards are likely to be unmarried, older women, who have children as their guardians. These studies, conducted at various times over the last decade, continue to find the same inadequacies in the guardianship process. These empirical studies confirm the notion that benevolent attitudes concerning guardianship result in nonadversarial hearings with proposed wards not present, not represented by lawyers who serve as advocates, with guardianships seldom denied or limited, and conclude with inadequate supervision of guardians' activities.

POPULAR PRESS

Just as scholars in the academic community were beginning to conduct empirical investigations of guardianships, the Associated Press (AP) exposed the problems associated with guardianships to the lay audience. In 1987 the AP, using reporters and editors, randomly selected 2,200 guardianship cases in 50 states and the District of Columbia for review. The results of this large national study were somewhat comparable to those discussed above. The average age of the wards was 79 years; the majority were female and almost three-quarters of the guardians were relatives, most of whom were children of the wards. The average size of the estates was $97,551, although 55 percent of them were below $50,000. Evidence supporting incapacity was conspicuously absent. Thirty-four percent of the cases had no statement from a physician and for 16 percent the only evidence of incapacity was a statement contained in the petition. Guardians ad litem represented wards in 31 percent of the cases, 17 percent had court appointed attorneys, and 44 percent had no legal representation. In keeping with other empirical research, the AP investigation found that the court approved 97 percent of the petitions filed.

As part of the investigation, the AP also reviewed state guardianship statutes. Their research revealed that only 14 states specifically required that the proposed wards be informed of their rights in the guardianship process and of the potential loss of liberties due to being adjudicated incompetent.

In March of 1989, *Money* magazine also brought the guardianship problem to readers of the popular press (Topolnicki, 1989). This investigation found that only 14 states required the presence of the proposed ward at the hearing and that in 26 states courts did not require the petitioner to submit medical documentation of the ward's incapacity. Furthermore, about one-half of the states did not require that guardians report on the status of their wards.

In conclusion, the findings of these two investigations mirror much of the empirical research conducted by social scientists. These reports have also provided the lay audience as well as policy makers with an inside view of the guardianship process.

HEALTH AND MEDICAL LITERATURE ABOUT GUARDIANSHIP

The guardianship process is also an important issue for those involved in health care professions. The concern is not with the legal process per se, but rather with the method of determining incapacity and the circumstances that necessitate the appointment of a guardian.

For those in the health care field, the individual's competency is crucial in a number of different areas. Competency is important in determining the mental capacity to consent to or refuse medical care, consent to the withdrawal of life-sustaining procedures, consent to drug experiments, or consent to care received in a long-term care facility.

Individuals have a constitutional right to autonomy, which is the right to make decisions that primarily affect themselves (Hall & Ellman, 1990). Individuals must be competent, however, to make those decisions. Problems can occur when an individual's competency is questionable and medical care and treatment decisions need to be made. When this occurs, families typically make medical care decisions on a de facto basis, that is, informally, without court intervention (Kapp, 1987). Recently, courts have ruled against families having the authority to make de facto medical decisions on behalf of their incapacitated member. A Missouri court refused to allow the parents to remove life-sustaining technologies from their daughter, Nancy Cruzan, who had been in a coma for a number of years. The court reasoned that the parents did not have the authority to take this action without a written directive authorizing such a decision (Furrow, Johnson, Jost, & Schwartz, 1987). Scholars have argued against the move away from granting family members the authority to be substitute decision makers (High, 1988; Jecker, 1990). Jecker believes that intimate others, including families, have the "subjective experience" necessary to make surrogate decisions for incompetent family members. If family members are not allowed to assist informally in decision making for an incapacitated family member, then they have to consider seeking a guardianship.

In a text written for individuals working in long-term care, Kapp (1987) identifies guidelines that are designed to assist in determining if residents are in need of a guardian. He suggests several circumstances that may need court determination of incompetency and the appointment of a guardian. They include: (1) when the decision to be made is of great consequence and the capacity of the individual is questionable; (2) when family members disagree; (3) when the decision made by the substitute decision maker is inconsistent with the previously known wishes of the individual with questionable competency; and (4) when the incapacity is great and likely to be prolonged.

In addition to their concern about the situations that may warrant the appointment of a guardian, health care professionals are also interested in the determination of incapacity. There are different aspects of competency that health care professionals should consider when determining an individual's capacity for making health care decisions. According to Kapp (1987), there are three main approaches to determining the capacity to make health care decisions. The *outcome approach* measures the decision made by the individual with questionable competence on the basis of whether it is consistent with the values of the caregiver. In the *status approach*, competence is judged by the physical or mental status or diagnosis without any further inquiry into how the status actually affects the person. Finally, the *functional approach* focuses on the individual's ability to function in decision-making situations. The functional approach centers on the thought processes used in arriving at a decision. Under this approach, competency is determined on a decision-specific basis, which acknowledges that an individual may be competent in some areas and not in others, may vacillate during the day, and may be influenced by medications and transient medical conditions.

Finally, health care professionals have suggested that a distinction be made between the capacity to make legal decisions and medical decisions (Hastings Center, 1987). The Hastings Center *Guidelines on the Termination of Life-Sustaining Treatment* suggest that being incompetent to make legal decisions does not necessarily translate to incapacity to make health care decisions. Other health care scholars have made the distinction between legal and health care competence, arguing that persons may not be able to manage their financial assets, yet be able to make health care decisions (President's Commission, 1981). Distinguishing between legal and medical competence is an important point that the courts should consider when determining the scope of a guardian's power over the ward.

SUMMARY

The treatment of competency from the perspective of health professionals can serve to inform the discussion of guardianship reform presented in the legal and social science arenas. Specifically, the delineation between legal and medical capacity, as well as the application of different criteria used in the assessment of capacity, are of particular benefit. Whether discussions about guardianship are from a legal, social, or health perspective, they all share a common concern about the ethical implications of guardianship.

ETHICAL CONSIDERATIONS OF GUARDIANSHIP

> The only freedom which deserves the name is that of pursuing our own good in our own way, so long as we do not attempt to deprive others of theirs, or impede their efforts to obtain it. Each is the proper guardian of his own health, whether bodily, mental or spiritual. (J. S. Mill, *On Liberty*, cited in Horstman, 1975)

Ethicists have also discussed guardianships, and have raised concerns about the determination of competency and the possible unwarranted intrusion of a guardianship into the lives of individuals who may not need protective oversight. Indeed, the basic dilemma in guardianships rests with balancing protection with the right to individual autonomy and self-determination. This issue is especially important as research has indicated that very often the justification for the appointment of a guardian is based on the odd or bizarre behavior of the proposed ward (Iris, 1988). This leads one to ask at what age and under what circumstances do we no longer tolerate "odd" or "unwise" behavior?

Two cases can serve as illustrations. *In re Estate of Segal* (82 A.2d 309) Segal believed that killers with atomic rays were pursuing her and responded by covering her windows with lead sheets. *In re Guardianship and Conservatorship of Sim* (403 NW 2d 721) the petitioners gave testimony that Sim, while watching a television evangelist, announced that the evangelist was going to kill her and put her up as a sacrifice. Does the behavior of these two women, without further evidence of inability to manage financial and personal activities, warrant the appointment of a guardian? When is it permissible to infringe on individual autonomy? When there is a clash between paternalistic intervention and individual liberty, which principle should individuals follow (Schafer, 1988)?

Upon closer examination, these cases raise questions regarding what society considers "appropriate" behavior for older adults, and moreover, suggests that society should have different standards for intervening into the lives of children and the aged. Schafer (1988:212) suggests that we should ask several questions before paternalistic intervention occurs:

> How likely is it that he will come to harm? How likely must it be that he will come to harm in order to justify infringing upon his liberty? How serious must be the predicted harm? How oppressive to the patient is the restriction of his liberty likely to be? . . . Is there any alternative means available to achieve the desired goal without depriving him of his liberty or without infringing to such an extent upon his autonomy?

Schafer believes that even though the assessment of all these questions is a complex task, we have an ethical and legal obligation to ask them.

To determine whether a person is in need of a guardian, is to determine the mental competency of the individual. Such a determination is undoubtedly linked to a subjective interpretation of cultural and age-based normative behavior. Schafer (1988:210) states:

> Undeniably, the life plans adopted by some people will appear imprudent or foolish to others. Nevertheless, even those who favor a range of paternalistic legislation to protect individuals from self-inflicted harm or foolish decisions concede that a competent adult is entitled to take some risks with his or her life, and even to follow a course of action which may produce serious injury to self. . . . We respect their right to make mistakes, even serious mistakes.

Indeed, the appointment of a guardian turns on a deeper and complex issue—the paternalistic rationale used (Alexander, 1985). Instead of selecting a rationale that seeks to protect the interest of the proposed ward, and satisfying the needs of others, the ethical direction should be that of minimizing the deprivation of personal autonomy (Alexander, 1985, 1990).

Ethical considerations raise more questions than answers about the use of guardianships to "protect" older adults. Perhaps these questions can serve as markers to caution us about the assumptions and the application of the reform measures directed toward guardianships.

CONCLUSION

The various areas of scholarship have contributed to bringing the need for guardianship reform to the attention of legal, social, and health professionals, as well as to the general public. Examining the guardianship process from a multidisciplinary approach provides practical as well as philosophical suggestions for change in the process. As discussed in chapter 9, many states have responded to the call for statutory changes in guardianship law. But as the number of empirical studies increase, old concerns about the guardianship process remain, and new ones will undoubtedly emerge. Are the legal rights of the proposed ward being rigorously protected at each stage in the process? Are guardians appointed only for those who need assistance? Does the scope of the guardians' powers match the decision-making deficits of the wards? What can be done to assist judges, attorneys, and guardians in securing community resources that provide the least restrictive alternative for wards? Are guardians providing the appropriate amount of aid to wards when it is needed? What benefits do wards receive by having a guardian appointed? Researchers must now direct their investigations toward answering these questions and studying the impact of the statutory reforms on the outcomes of guardianships.

In summary, the purpose of guardianship law is to provide a substitute decision maker for individuals who do not have the capacity to make personal, financial, and health care decisions on their own. The law itself, however, is still evolving from its current inadequacies into what scholars hope is the ideal guardianship law.

4

Can You Spell "World" Backward? Assessing Incapacity in Guardianship Hearings

In our day-to-day interactions with others, we rely on the assumption that persons in our social milieu will predictably and sufficiently carry out expected roles and responsibilities. We assume certain types of behaviors will accompany the different roles others occupy, and we orient ourselves to those patterned expectations (Merton, 1949). Furthermore, we expect that individuals will behave according to the specific expectations of a particular role given a particular social context (Moreno, 1934, cited in Turner, 1986). Older adults are no exception in this regard. In later life individuals occupy various roles—spouse or partner, grandparent, parent, sibling, neighbor, patient, and within the larger society, aged adult. We presume their behaviors will be in accordance with the expectations associated with each role. Problems occur when older adults begin to deviate from those role expectations—decisions made in the role of a patient no longer appear "rational" to the physician; family members report that mother "isn't acting herself lately." Depending how far older adults stray from the expected normative behavior and how many social roles are thought to be affected, they may find their competency questioned and that they are the subject of a guardianship hearing.

Determining an individual's competency is a difficult task. What is the meaning of incompetence? How should it be assessed? When is it permissible to exhibit "incompetent" behavior? Finally, who should make the assessment of competency and what interventions do a lack of capacity require? Consider Mrs. Smith, who does not know where she is or the name of her doctor. Upon further examination she cannot subtract serial 7s from 100 and is unable to spell "world" backward. Another test reveals she is unable to interpret the saying "a rolling stone gathers no moss." On the basis of these findings, the psychiatrist reports to the court that Mrs. Smith has senile dementia, is incompetent, and in need of a guardian. But what is it exactly that we know about the social, legal, or medical competency of Mrs. Smith? Can she enter knowingly into a contract? Consent to medical treatment? Decide where she should live? Can she care for herself? Are there any decisions the court should allow Mrs. Smith to make?

In the past, legal scholars have criticized the courts for basing the determination of incapacity on subjective or even stereotypical assumptions about the proposed wards' age and medical or psychiatric diagnosis. According to Mitchell (1978), courts err on the safe side and appoint a guardian because "merely filing a petition . . . raises a strong a priori presumption in a judge's mind that the person *is* incompetent." Furthermore, if the capacity of proposed wards is questionable, courts may believe proposed wards will eventually need a guardian at some point, because of the "inevitable" decline that accompanies old age, and appoint a guardian.

What can be done to ensure proposed wards' capacity is accurately assessed before guardians are appointed? In this chapter we address this issue by examining the various definitions of incompetency, the criticisms of these, and the methods used to assess incompetency in the guardianship process. We will use the terms incompetency and incapacity interchangeably in this discussion.

DEFINITIONS OF INCAPACITY

The terminology describing an individual's inability to make and communicate personal decisions has changed over the years. For example, the term "incompetency" has given way to the term "incapacity" in many state guardianship statutes in recent years (Hommel, Wang, & Bergman, 1990). This may be due in part to the fact that incompetency meant one had a mental illness or disability, and advocates have encouraged using the less stigmatizing term of "incapacity" (Allen, Ferster, & Weihofen, 1968). Though the terminology has changed, the problems associated with defining incompetency or incapacity remain.

The meaning of competency or capacity differs depending on which discipline is conducting the assessment. Social scientists conceptualize competency as "social competency," in which an individual can "manage an effective lifestyle" (Kraus & Popkin, 1989). The definition of social competency can cover many different areas of functioning. For example, Kraus and Popkin (1989:277) define competency as the following:

> In its broadest sense, it may refer to the ability to carry out the requirements of productive existence [or] in a narrow reading it may refer to the ability to perform quite specific tasks, such as managing a checkbook or bathing, thought to be necessary to maintain legal control over the conditions of his or her living situation.

In the health care field, patients must be competent in order to give informed consent for medical procedures (Kapp, 1987). In order to be able to give informed consent to accept or refuse medical treatment, the individual must understand and appreciate the diagnosis, possible treatments, and any risks involved (Kapp, 1987). Finally, legal competency is an important consideration in a number of areas. Besides the determination of competency for guardianship cases, courts are concerned with determining competency in order to ascertain whether individuals have the ability to participate in legal proceedings and to stand trial, to enter a contract, and to make a will (Petrila, 1985).

These definitions are not mutually exclusive and may overlap. It is plausible that persons who are unable to give informed consent are also unable to maintain any level of social or legal competence. Conversely, individuals could provide informed consent, yet lack social competence. When courts determine the capacities of the proposed ward, it is not clear which area of capacity is being assessed, as most statutory definitions of incapacity are nonspecific and vague.

Defining Incapacity for Guardianships

The definition of competency is pivotal in the guardianship process. Courts appoint a guardian only if there is evidence to support the contention that proposed wards are incompetent as defined by statute. Over the years, the statutory definitions and language of incapacity have been changed (Allen, Ferster, & Weihofen, 1968; Alexander & Lewin, 1972). Along with the statutory changes designed to protect the due process rights of the proposed ward, statutes no longer refer to incapacitated persons as "imbeciles" or "idiots." Mitchell (1978) argues, however, that procedural safeguards will mean little if the substantive legal standard of incapacity is so open-ended as to encompass potentially anyone. Therefore, a primary criticism of statutory definitions of incapacity is the absence of specific guidelines to serve as standards that assist the court in its determination (Mitchell, 1978).

The following are examples of definitions of incapacity in three different state statutes—Oregon, Colorado, and Missouri, respectively. Each definition gives courts in that state a different test to use to determine whether proposed wards are incapacitated.

(1) "Incapacitated person" means a person, other than a minor, who is unable, without assistance, to properly manage or take care of self or personal affairs of the person. (Oregon Revised Statutes §126.003[4], Supp. 1987)

(2) "Incapacitated person" means any person who is impaired by reason of mental illness, mental deficiency, physical illness or disability, advanced age, chronic use of drugs, chronic intoxication, or other cause (except minority) to the extent that he lacks sufficient understanding or capacity to make or communicate responsible decisions concerning his person. (Colorado Revised Statutes §15-14-101[1], 1973, Supp. 1988)

(3) An "Incapacitated person" is one who is unable by reason of any physical or mental condition to receive and evaluate information or to communicate decisions to such an extent that he lacks the capacity to meet essential requirements for food, clothing, shelter, safety or other care such that serious physical injury, illness, or disease is likely to occur. (Missouri Revised Statutes §475.010[8], 1956, Supp. 1989)

The Missouri and Colorado definitions take the two-step approach (Frolik, 1981). In both definitions, incapacity is caused by a physical or mental condition, and as a result, the individual lacks the capacity to manage personal or business affairs. Therefore, it should not be surprising that the evidence used to prove incapacity in jurisdictions with this type of definition relies primarily on the disability or diagnosis presented by a physician or psychiatrist (Peters, Schmidt, & Miller, 1985). Stevenson and Capezuti (1991) in their study of guardianships found physicians' statements contained only a brief outline of disabilities, references to medical conditions, and vague definitions, including "old age." Often these diagnoses go unchallenged, and as a result the medical diagnoses are the only criteria used as evidence (Creyke, 1989). Hommel, Wang, and Bergman (1990) suggest the problem with sole reliance on a medical diagnosis is its lack of usefulness in evaluating overall day-to-day functional capacity. They recommend the emphasis of statutory definitions or labels be replaced with an objective standard using functional assessments. Further, statutes not requiring a demonstration of lack of functional capacity may in some ways perpetuate the assumption that a diagnosis is automatically associated with or results in a lack of capacity.

The Missouri definition differs from the Colorado definition in requiring that the lack of essential personal needs must result in serious harm to the proposed ward before the courts appoint a guardian, thus using a higher threshold for incompetent behavior. Although the Missouri statute retains the specification of physical and mental incapacity, the test is whether the individual has the capacity to meet daily needs (Borron, 1983). Carney and Tait (1991) have written that definitions should include both the functional and social consequences of impairment, just as in the Missouri statute. But they go on to say that only those social handicaps with a high degree of severity, which pose an imminent crisis, and are solvable by law, should be included in the definition of incapacity.

Oregon's statutory definition eliminates the label or diagnosis and removes the link of a physical or mental status with incapacity. In addition, if the proposed wards can properly manage with assistance, courts are to find that the proposed ward does not need a guardian. Theoretically, by using this type of definition, evidence to support incapacity should rely primarily on functional capacity rather than simply presenting a diagnosis with its implied assumptions of lack of functional ability.

A second problem inherent in statutory definitions of incompetency is the application of normative standards of appropriate behavior against which the proposed ward is measured (Wang, Burns, & Hommel, 1990). These would include definitions of incapacity that determine proposed wards are not able to make responsible decisions concerning their property or person. Normative standards may relate to how individuals should spend their money or maintain the cleanliness of their home. Responsible or normative standards for behavior leave individuals with little room for atypical actions. As Iris noted, "eccentric" behavior of the ward is the sole focus of many guardianship hearings. Moreover, such standards are not likely to allow for ethnic, cultural, and social class differences (Iris, 1990b). Two guardianship cases illustrate the judgment of normative behavior. In its decision to appoint a guardian, *In re Tyrell* (28 O.O.2d 337), the court observed that the proposed ward's "smile at times is not normal; his eyes do not focus properly at all times; and he is not laying his cane aside, but is dropping it." Similarly, *In re the Estate of Galvin* (445 NE 2d 1223) petitioners provided testimony that the proposed ward believed he had invented the snowmobile, had a pet black widow, could produce fire by pointing his finger, and that he had been the co-worker of the Shah of Iran. Yet, in this case, the appellant court agreed with the lower court's decision that there was sufficient testimony the proposed ward was adequately able to manage his affairs. Definitions of incapacity directing the court to focus on eccentric behavior fail to give adequate consideration to the proposed ward's functional capacity. As one observer noted, "A person may be a blithering, drunken idiot who doesn't know a dollar bill from a kleenex; but if his economic needs are being adequately satisfied, he should be permitted to blither in unmolested bliss" (Comment, 1976).

A third criticism of statutory definitions of incapacity is that they instruct courts to determine the global incapacity of the proposed ward. A definition stating that the incapacitated ward is one who is "unable to manage his person or affairs" tells the court nothing about which affairs or personal activities are important to assess, and implies that the proposed ward is either competent or incompetent. Such an approach ignores the fact that individuals possess varying degrees of competency. Moreover, competency varies depending on the task at hand. For example, the level of capacity needed to enter into a long-term commercial contract differs from the capacity needed to contract to purchase food (Dickens, 1989). Similarly, Anderer (1990) suggests that individuals are neither completely proficient in performing tasks nor completely unable to perform them, but have varying degrees of skill along a continuum. Furthermore, the social context in which individuals function can hinder or facilitate their individual proficiency. For example, two individuals may have similar ability levels but the living arrangements for one may require more self-reliance, or one person's finances may be more difficult to handle (Anderer, 1990). When determining least restrictive alternatives to a guardianship, courts should consider social support interventions that may eliminate the need for a guardian.

Whereas courts generally view competency as the ability to do a given task, competent behavior should also include the proposed ward's ability to secure assistance from others to complete a task. The tendency may be to use the lack of capacity as evidence for the need of a guardian, rather than viewing the ability to seek help as evidence of being able to function within the given social context. For example, one's ability to perform activities of daily living might be impaired; however, the management of one's social network to provide for those areas of diminished capacity should be considered competent behavior (Nolan, 1984, 1990). Oregon's definition addresses the notion of "assisted capacity" (Kapp, 1990) by excluding from guardianship those who can function with the assistance of others.

One final criticism of incapacity definitions concerns the lack of consideration given to the variant nature of competency. The time of day, type of medication taken, nutritional status, and stressful events can all influence an individual's competency (Anderer, 1990). Thus, the statutory definitions treating incapacity as a static dimension, and as such only requiring a one-time assessment, have the potential to result in an inaccurate measure of capacity.

In conclusion, competency has many different dimensions, and courts must cease from viewing it as a single or global state. Courts should make incapacity determinations about the proposed ward's social, medical, and legal functioning, and assess only those areas that are critical to enhancing the proposed ward's well-being. Any determination must be sensitive to the socioenvironmental influences on the proposed ward's capacity. The courts currently assess incapacity by associating medical diagnosis with incapacity and by not making distinctions in the proposed ward's abilities, and as a result, end up appointing a plenary guardianship for the proposed ward.

Recommendations for Definitions of Incapacity

There has been a great deal of discussion in the literature about the meaning of competency and its statutory definition (ABA, 1989; Anderer, 1990; Coleman & Dooley, 1990; Dickens, 1989; Frolik, 1981; Horstman, 1975; Kraus & Popkin, 1989; Lo, 1990; Mitchell, 1978). The more recent recommendations are presented below.

Coleman and Dooley (1990) report the recommendations from the American Bar Association's Wingspread Conference, convened to discuss the guardianship process and to suggest reforms. The definition of incapacity was one of many areas cited as being in need of reform. The conference recommended that an acceptable definition of incapacity should have the following elements:

1. Recognize that incapacity may be partial or incomplete;
2. Incapacity is a legal not medical term and it should not be linked to a diagnosis alone;
3. Because incapacities change, a finding of incapacity should be supported by evidence of functional impairment over time;
4. Determination of incapacity should include the notion that the respondents are likely to suffer substantial harm;
5. Labels identifying the person by his/her age, eccentricities, poverty or medical diagnoses alone do not justify a finding of incapacity.

Other recommendations have also appeared in the literature. Anderer (1990) suggests the standard for incapacity includes: (1) functional inability, wholly or partially to care for self or property; (2) the inability to make or communicate decisions concerning person or property; and (3) the functional impairment endangers physical health or safety or leads to dissipation of property.

In conclusion, the statutory definition of incapacity should specify to the court the areas of competency it is required to assess. By treating competency as an "all or nothing" determination, the courts are unable to match the proposed ward's specific incapacities with guardian powers. If the proposed ward's functional, medical, and legal incapacity is examined in detail, the court can make orders that correspond to the individual's incapacities and appoint more limited guardianships.

Changing the definition of incapacity is the crucial first step in ensuring that the court appoints guardianships for individuals who truly need them. Even though many states have reformed their guardianship statutes, they still fail to give the court full guidance on the subject of incapacity (Frank, 1993). Any change in the definition of incapacity must also be accompanied by a mechanism by which court personnel can evaluate incapacity.

THE ASSESSMENT OF INCAPACITY

What Should Be Assessed?

The assessment of incapacity is usually completed by the proposed ward's attending physician, who provides the court with a list of ailments or diagnoses of physical illnesses. As previously mentioned, courts all too often assume that functional incapacity is an automatic result of physical incapacity. This assumption may be unfounded in many instances. For example, many older adults suffer from an array of chronic physical problems, and when compared to younger individuals, their list of chronic conditions looks quite debilitating. Many, however, are able to carry on basic activities of daily living. Almost 40 percent of those who report having at least one chronic condition observed they were not limited in their activities (Wildner, 1971). The majority of older adults continue to function well despite having a number of chronic conditions. Therefore, when assessing functional capacity, courts should keep in mind that it is not uncommon for older adults in the general population to have a myriad of chronic conditions. As a point of illustration, a physician might report to the court that an older patient has arthritis, hypertension, unsteady gait, gastrointestinitis, and is hard of hearing. The court should not focus on the number of physical impairments of proposed wards, but rather on their functional capacity.

Anderer (1990) proposes that the assessment of incapacity should be based on a detailed inquiry in three main areas. First, courts should inquire into the proposed ward's disorders or disability. This inquiry should include the nature of the condition, how it was diagnosed, and the level of contact between the professional and the proposed ward. The second area to be considered is the proposed ward's functional capacity. This includes the ability to care for self (in such areas as nutrition, clothing, personal hygiene, health care, residential safety); and the ability to care for property (the acquisition, administration, and disposition of finances). The third area to be included in the assessment of incapacity is the decision-making and communication ability of the proposed ward. This includes (1) *personal decision making* regarding nutrition, clothing, hygiene, and living arrangements (in such areas as awareness of needs and alternatives, expressing a preference, understanding and reasoning); (2) *property decision making* regarding the acquisition or disposal of property, awareness of their deficiencies and the danger they might pose, awareness of the various alternatives to resolve the problem, and an inquiry about the experience the respondent has had in such matters; and (3) *decision making on other legal actions* such as decisions to marry, engage in lawsuits, testify, be a juror, vote, and drive. Anderer suggests that courts ascertain whether individuals are performing these activities, if they are capable of performing the activities, and consider the likelihood of harm in the absence of intervention.

How Should Capacity Be Assessed?

Typically, when courts determine the capacity of the proposed ward, they rely on one and sometimes two different types of evidence. First, as previously mentioned, physicians provide the court with a list of the ward's diagnoses, such as Alzheimer's disease, senile dementia, or Parkinson's disease. Second, when the proposed ward's mental status is evaluated, clinicians usually conduct psychological assessments. Clinicians use mental status tests such as those that measure orientation to time, place, and person; ask the names of current and past presidents; require the proposed ward to count backward by serial 7s or greater, to spell "world" backward, or to recall objects previously mentioned by the interviewer (Kraus & Popkin, 1989). These tests are usually administered through instruments such as the Philadelphia Geriatric Center Mental Status Questionnaire, the Mental Status Questionnaire, the Mini-Mental State Examination, the Short Portable Mental Status Questionnaire, or the Wechsler Adult Intelligence Test-Revised (see Kraus & Popkin, 1989).

Although a detailed review of these tests is outside the scope of this discussion (see Groth-Marnat, 1990, for a review), there is some debate about the appropriate use of these tools. Kraus and Popkin (1989:283) state that tests such as those mentioned above "have considerable value as initial measures to determine which successive instruments should be used to assess cognitive competence. We do not concur [that] these measures [are] useful in determining the presence of and distinguishing among . . . dementia, depression . . . or in different diagnosis among dementias." Lo (1990) observes that one problem with mental status assessments is the absence of naturally defined "passing scores" and that such tests might not be related to ability to make medical decisions. Although these types of assessments can provide the court with important information, they do not provide an assessment of the ward's functional abilities, and when used alone, have limited value.

Functional assessments measure what social scientists commonly refer to as activities of daily living (ADL) or instrumental activities of daily living (IADL). ADLs include such things as dressing, bathing, toileting, mobility, continence, and feeding. IADLs refer to activities such as using the telephone, traveling, shopping, preparing meals, managing money, doing housework, and taking medication properly (Fillenbaum, 1985). Many scholars have advocated the use of functional assessments in guardianship cases (Hafemeister & Sales, 1984; Hommel, Wang, & Bergman, 1990; Nolan, 1984), but they have not been implemented on a wide scale by the courts.

Nolan (1984:211) provides the following justification for the use of functional assessments in guardianship hearings:

> The functional assessment differs from other sorts of evaluations and diagnostic methods primarily in its focus on resulting behavior. The functional evaluator records the extent to which a subject carries out activities of daily living effectively. Thus, for example, when the defendant is disoriented as to date and time, but uses newspapers and television announcements as cues to compensate for his deficits, functional evaluation would credit the adaptation as an effective use of resources. In contrast, a formal mental status evaluation would note the disorientation negatively. The functional evaluator is less interested, therefore, in the cause of the disability, the prognosis or the potential for treatment.

The functional evaluation should be made over time in order to account for fluctuations in behaviors and should be conducted in the environment in which the person feels most comfortable (ABA symposium recommendations, 1989, cited in Wood, Dooley, & Karp, 1991). By using an assessment of functional status, the determination of incapacity turns on a different question, away from mere physical and mental diagnoses. The key question is the proposed ward's ability to function within his or her environment. Physical, mental, and functional assessments can provide the court with a broad view of individual capacity, recognizing the variation that may occur in each area. For example, Gurland (1980) suggests it is possible to have low cognitive awareness, but have adequate self-care skills (cited in Kraus & Popkin, 1989). In addition, the use of functional assessments in conjunction with other measures can provide the court with enough detail to grant powers to guardians in only the areas in which functional capacity is diminished.

Many types of functional assessment instruments have been developed and used in a variety of medical and social settings. The Katz Index of Activities of Daily Living (Katz, Ford, & Moskowitz, 1963), the Barthel Index (Mohoney & Barthel, 1965), the Multidimensional Functional Assessment Questionnaire (Duke University, 1978), and the Five-Item Instrumental Activities of Daily Living Screening Questionnaire (Fillenbaum, 1985) are just a few of the tools available for functional assessments (see Gallo, Reichel, & Andersen, 1988, for a review of these and other geriatric assessment instruments). A functional assessment tool could be developed that measured the proposed ward's social, medical, and legal functioning and used in guardianship hearings. Multidimensional assessments would provide the court with a detailed review of the proposed ward's physical, cognitive, and functional capacity.

Rather than simply relying on an assessment scale, Nolan (1990) advocates the use of a narrative report that would describe in greater detail the ward's functional abilities. Specific areas of functioning that professionals would assess include cleanliness of self, environment, accessing transportation, health care management, financial management, environmental safety, use of social resources, and use of recreational resources. In each area Nolan suggests assessing capacity by determining the following: Does the person have the resources needed to function acceptably? How is the person using the resources? Can the person get help to supplement these resources? Does the individual agree resources are needed? Is the person able to use resources, and if not, is the person satisfied with his or her life situation?

Comprehensive information provided by these assessments could provide the court with valuable information to help the court make a decision about the need for a guardianship, as well as tailor a guardianship to the specific needs of the ward. But again, during the assessment, one must be cautious of personal biases, which might lead to a subjective evaluation of the proposed ward's answers and situation. As mentioned at the outset, older adults may be unfairly scrutinized because their behaviors stray from normative expectations. Wood, Dooley, and Karp (1991) caution against interjecting societal and individual values into the assessment of incapacity. They state (1991:126):

> It may be easy for the courts and community workers to inject societal values or their own values into capacity assessments. A patient who refuses surgery, a frail elderly person who refuses to have home or nutrition services, a testator who gives money to an obscure or unpopular group, an aged man whose will favors a young girlfriend rather than family, or an individual whose personal lifestyle is simply eccentric may be seen as "crazy" or "out of his/her mind."

Many have argued that society and the courts should allow older adults to live with risk and make risky decisions, just as it allows the rest of the population to do so (ABA, 1986; Wood, Dooley, & Karp, 1991).

Who Should Conduct the Assessments?

In general, petitioners provide the assessments of incapacity as evidence to prove the need for a guardian. Of course, the proposed ward also may obtain an assessment to use as evidence against the need for a guardian. Typically, the petitioner or proposed ward (respondent) will have a physician, psychologist, or psychiatrist complete an evaluation and submit the report to the court. Besides the petitioner's or respondent's evaluation, the court may request a health professional to conduct an independent report. In some jurisdictions, the court may appoint a guardian ad litem or court visitor to interview the proposed ward. Simply requiring an assessment is a necessary, but not sufficient criterion in ensuring an informed report to the court. Those conducting the assessments, especially the guardians ad litem and court visitors, may not have the necessary training in the various disciplines needed to work with the elderly. Furthermore, most assessments are made during a single visit, lasting only a short time. Such an assessment cannot accurately evaluate an individual's competence, which can fluctuate from hour to hour or day to day. Finally, there are no standards to guide what specific element of capacity the evaluator should assess.

Many writers have suggested that interdisciplinary teams conduct evaluations of proposed wards (Hafemeister & Sales, 1984). Others have suggested using individuals with training in gerontology to conduct standardized functional assessments (Scogin & Perry, 1986) or other professionals such as social workers, nurses, or physical therapists (ABA, 1989; Kraus & Popkin, 1989; Nolan, 1990). Professionals should conduct assessments in an environment familiar to the proposed ward (ABA, 1989), with follow-up assessments incorporated into the determination of capacity (Kraus & Popkin, 1989). Court visitors can supplement the multidimensional assessment provided by the evaluation team with information regarding the proposed guardian, attitudes of the proposed ward, and proposed living arrangements for the ward (Hommel, Wang, & Bergman, 1990).

Finally, the role of the court should be to ensure that assessments of medical condition, functional abilities, and psychological condition are made. These assessments should include what the proposed ward understands, feels, thinks, believes and values; the environment and its demands on the individual; the social support network and its impact on individual functioning; and the financial situation of the proposed ward (Anderer, 1990).

CONCLUSIONS

The determination of incapacity is critical in the guardianship hearing. Perhaps as a result of the benevolent motives behind the appointment of a guardian, statutory definitions and assessments of incapacity have been less than rigorous. In most jurisdictions, standards used to judge incapacity do not exist and as a result the courts are left to make inconsistent or haphazard determinations.

Definitions of incapacity must shift the focus away from use of the physician's medical diagnoses and psychiatric testing as sole measures of incapacity. Medical diagnoses and psychiatric testing shed little light on the ability of the proposed ward to perform the tasks of living (Barnes, 1992). The evaluation of incapacity must be extended to include functional ability as well as cognitive functioning. A standardized assessment tool, based on those already in existence, should be created specifically for the purpose of determining capacity in guardianship hearings. Such assessments should be used in all guardianship cases and conducted by professionals trained in geriatric evaluation. Multidisciplinary teams of lawyers, physicians, and social scientists must find a common language that would contribute to greater precision in a competency determination (Barnes, 1992).

How the statutes define incapacity and what the courts use as evidence of incapacity are critical to the entire guardianship process. The statutory changes designed to increase due process rights for proposed wards may not have the desired effect if the means by which incapacity is measured are ineffective, or worse, inaccurate indices of individuals' functional abilities.

5

Becoming a Ward: Characteristics of Wards and Their Guardians

In this chapter and the next we consider the characteristics of wards and their guardians whom we studied and the processes resulting in their guardianships. Much of this information about wards and guardians was drawn from court records from Iowa, Missouri, and Colorado. The major sections of this chapter examine the demographic characteristics of those who became wards; critical incidents leading to the request for guardianship; alternatives to guardianship; assessments of the proposed ward and the guardianship by guardians, court visitors, and wards; characteristics of guardians; and some of their activities on behalf of their wards as reported in the court records. The process of becoming a guardian is discussed in chapter 6, and qualitative descriptions of the guardianship experience and responses to it are presented in chapter 7. Chapters 6 and 7 are derived from data contained in a mail questionnaire completed by guardians.

Most of the information about wards in this chapter was obtained from court records. Observations of proposed wards about their condition and their preferences for the guardianship, and reflections of court visitors about the circumstances of proposed wards, are described. These data were available only from the Colorado visitor reports which are part of the court records. The thoughts and feelings of those who eventually became wards are rarely studied. Insofar as proposed wards were questioned about their attitudes toward a potential guardianship, data from the visitor questionnaire may represent a large portion of the information in the court records provided directly by the ward. Consequently, in states not requiring a report from a court visitor or a similar procedure, the desires of wards are less likely to be known. For an action (i.e., awarding guardianship) with potentially such pervasive outcomes, surprisingly little is known about the response of those for whom the transition may be the greatest. As described in chapter 1, a recommended change in the guardianship system is that the preferences of proposed wards be taken into account to a greater extent than previously. Information gathered by a visitor is one medium to learn about the preferences of wards. This chapter brings together information about wards and their preferences, views of court visitors, and activities of guardians drawn primarily from 1,160 court records obtained in Iowa, Missouri, and Colorado.

CHARACTERISTICS OF WARDS

Sex, Age, and Marital Status

Similar to attaining a very old age, becoming a ward is predominantly a female experience. Most of the wards, more than two-thirds, were women, and they were quite old. At the time the petitions were filed, proposed wards ranged in age from 60 to 106 years, with an average age of 81 years. In general, the characteristics of the wards from the three states were similar, and comparable to those described in other research (Stevenson & Capezuti, 1991). Stevenson and Capezuti, for example, found wards ranged in age from 60 to 101 years with a mean age of 81 years, and 71 percent were women.

In the population as a whole, older males in their mid-70s tend to be married (75 percent) whereas two-thirds of their female peers are widowed (Atchley, 1991). Of those who became wards, 21 percent were married, 50 percent were widowed, 24 percent were never married, and 5 percent were divorced. Male wards were more likely to be married (35 percent) than female wards (14 percent, $X^2 = 61.23$, 1 df, $p < .001$). Having a spouse in very old age, especially for men, is a resource that may diminish the threat of institutionalization. Yet, marriage did not protect over one-third of these men from being adjudicated as incapacitated and having a guardian appointed. Spouses served as guardians in 9 percent of these cases.

Income and Assets

Three different types of assets held by wards were considered. Annual income, value of real estate, and value of personal property were coded into nine categories, which are shown in Table 5.1. The data in Table 5.1 include information for wards from the three states both prior to and following legislative changes and, thus, could span varying lengths of time. The data should be interpreted cautiously, and the lengthy period of time should be taken into account. In later statistical analyses, codes from 0 to 9 were used to represent values of income, real estate, and personal property.

It should be noted that data were missing in 24 percent of the cases for values of real estate, in 23 percent of the cases for the amount of the personal estate, and in 31 percent of the cases for personal income. The intentional

Table 5.1
Amount and Types of Assets of Wards

	Annual Income	Real Estate	Personal Property and Other Assets
	Percent	Percent	Percent[a]
None	3	45	12
$ 9,999 or less	71	8	29
10,000-19,999	18	10	12
20,000-29,999	5	8	9
30,000-49,999	2	12	7
50,000-74,999	0.7	8	8
75,000-99,999	0.1	3	4
100,000-149,999	---	3	6
150,000 or more	.2	3	14

[a]Percentages do not total 100 percent.

overrepresentation in the sample of guardians of the person may have figured in the incomplete reports for these three indicators of finances. Indeed, only 7 percent of guardianships that were joint guardianships of the person and conservator of property had incomplete information on financial status, compared to about one-third of those established to oversee the welfare of the person alone. Other research has noted more incomplete reports for guardians of the person than for conservatorships of property (Zimny, Gilchrist, & Diamond, 1991).

The financial status of these wards varied considerably. As noted in chapter 3, dramatic variation in the size of wards' estates has been documented (Bulcroft, Kielkopf, & Tripp, 1991). About three-quarters of the wards had incomes of less than $10,000, and nearly half had no real estate. Indeed, only one-fifth of the wards had real estate valued at $50,000 or more. For over half of the sample, personal property and other assets were valued at less than $20,000. For some wards, of course, assets available earlier may have been depleted by the costs of care or disbursed to others, perhaps in an effort to qualify for Medicaid.

Unlike in the larger population of older persons, for the most part, there were few differences in the financial status of wards by sex or marital status. An analysis of the three indices of finances shown in Table 5.1 indicated women had somewhat larger personal estates ($\bar{X} = 3.35$) than did men

($\bar{X} = 2.95$, $t = 2.95$, $p < .05$). Amount of income and value of real estate did not differ for men or women. The married owned real estate of greater value ($\bar{X} = 2.61$) than did the unmarried ($\bar{X} = 1.91$, $t = 3.29$, $p < .001$). But other indices of financial status did not differ by marital status. In summary, sex and marital status differences in finances often observed in later life were not present among these wards (Keith, 1989).

The level of assets available to wards may in part reflect our intentional selection of primarily guardianships of the person or joint guardianships of the person and conservatorships of property, rather than conservatorships of property alone. A sample of exclusively conservatorships of property likely would include more wards with greater personal income and larger estates. A partial test of this theory was possible by examining levels of assets by type of guardianship received. Finances were compared between wards who had only guardians of the person and those with a joint guardianship/conservatorship. The value of personal property and real estate did not differ for wards who had a conservator and those who did not. But wards with conservators had somewhat higher incomes than those with a guardian alone ($\bar{X} = 1.40, 1.24$, respectively, $t = 2.38$, $p < .05$). This difference may reflect that liquid assets are more readily available, require management, and can be controlled with more ease than real estate. Peters, Schmidt, and Miller (1985) observed a relationship between the size of the estate and the assumption of guardianship by relatives. If the estate was larger than $50,000, relatives more often assumed guardianship.

Living Arrangements

It is instructive to recall the dominant living arrangements of older persons who are not wards. We find the majority of men 75 years of age or older head households with a spouse present (66 percent), and less frequently live alone (22 percent), while the majority of women live alone (52 percent), and less frequently live with a spouse (21 percent; Hess, 1991). The remainder of both sexes live with other relatives, nonrelatives, or in group quarters.

Because of the presumed need for care signaled by guardianship, we were especially interested in the characteristics of persons who lived alone after the guardianship was awarded. As they age, men and women increasingly live alone, although women are much more likely to do so than men (Keith, 1989). Several factors affect living arrangements of the aged, but perhaps marital status has the most influence. Among older people, Fillenbaum and Wallman (1984:348) concluded that "married couples almost invariably lived together." When they do not live together, health difficulties and needs for functional assistance by either or both spouses may figure in their living arrangements. For most, those who must have needs met and

Table 5.2
Current Living Arrangements of Wards

Living Arrangements	N	Percent
Alone	132	12
With spouse	47	4
With children	45	4
With other relative or unrelated adult	23	2
Hospital	271	24
Nursing or boarding home	592	52
With proposed guardian	20	2

require assistance from others are more likely to live with other persons, whereas the less dependent may choose to live alone.

The living arrangements of wards following the establishment of the guardianship are shown in Table 5.2. Slightly more than three-quarters of the wards lived in congregate facilities; of these, a little over one-half resided in nursing homes, and approximately another quarter were hospitalized. Not surprisingly, significantly higher proportions of wards were institutionalized than is found in the population of older persons as a whole. Among the proposed wards contacted by court visitors in Colorado prior to the hearing, 45 percent had lived in nursing homes in the preceding three months, and another 10 percent had resided in board and care facilities during that time. Although no change in residence was planned for about 70 percent of the wards who were visited, visitors observed it was expected that one-fifth would move into a nursing home.

The remaining one-quarter of the sample from the three states studied lived in the community either alone (12 percent) or with family members or nonrelatives (12 percent). Only 4 percent resided with a spouse, although 21 percent were married. Among the majority of the married wards in the sample, the need for a guardian apparently had intervened to shape the living arrangements of the couple. For many wards, a change of residence accompanied guardianship; the majority moved after the petition was filed and the guardianship was established.

To understand more about the distinguishing characteristics of wards who lived alone, the living arrangements described in Table 5.2 were divided into three groups: (1) living alone (n = 132, 12 percent); (2) living with others but outside a nursing home or medical facility (n = 135, 12 percent); and (3) living in a nursing home or hospital (n = 863, 76 percent).

Sex of wards and guardians, age of ward, assessments of dependency, and financial situation were considered in relation to living arrangements.

Female wards lived alone a little more often (14 percent) than male wards (8 percent, $X^2 = 8.85$, 2 df, $p < .01$). Of course, as widowhood increases, women who are not wards more often live alone than do men. Wards who lived alone were older ($\bar{X} = 83$ years) than those in hospitals or nursing homes ($\bar{X} = 81$ years) or than those who resided with others in the community ($\bar{X} = 80$ years, $F = 5.37, p < .01$). Finally, the gender of the guardian was not associated with the residential choice of these wards ($\bar{X} = .60$, ns). This indicates that female guardians were not any more likely than men to have responsibility for 24-hour care of their wards. In some types of caregiving women have greater involvement with the more dependent aged (Montgomery, 1992).

As noted above, dependency may figure in the living arrangements of the elderly who are not in the guardianship system. As well as being a determinant of whether they became wards, it also would be expected that impairment or incapacity would be a significant correlate of living arrangements of most wards. Data were not available to describe specifically the physical, mental, functional and social capacities of all proposed wards. In lieu of somewhat sketchy and inconsistent information in the records, two types of assessments were used to discover characteristics of wards who lived alone. Two partial indicators of wards' well-being were considered: the assessment of the ward's capacity by the guardian, and judgments by Colorado court visitors about the need for a limited guardianship. These two indicators were investigated in relation to the wards' living arrangements.

In the mail questionnaire, guardians were asked to estimate the capacity of their wards by how often they were able to carry out five activities: write checks and pay bills, dress and undress, prepare food, understand and communicate, and manage medication (if used). Responses ranged from "all of the time" (1), "some of the time" (2), to "not at all" (3). For use in statistical analyses, an index of the ward's condition was formed by summing responses across the five activities. A higher score indicated greater incapacity of the ward. Scores ranged from 5 to 15 ($\bar{X} = 12.7$, sd = 2.20).

Because not all guardians completed a questionnaire, assessments of wards' capacity were available for only 43 wards who lived alone, 35 who lived with others in the community, and 259 who resided in congregate facilities. A one-way analysis of variance indicated guardians' estimates of their wards' capabilities were significantly associated with living arrangements ($F = 7.59, p < .001$). As might be expected, wards in hospitals and nursing homes were described as most impaired. Guardians did not differentiate between wards who lived alone and those who lived with others in the community in their capacity to manage activities of daily living.

Court visitors observed whether they believed the powers of the guardian should be limited. We assumed a recommendation for a limited guardianship was an indicator that the ward possessed greater capacity than one for whom a full guardianship was requested. The relationship between a recommendation for a limited guardianship and living arrangements of the ward was not significant. However, somewhat more wards who lived alone (17 percent) compared with those in institutions (10 percent) received recommendations for limited guardianships by court visitors. In conclusion, of the indicators of capacity that we used, guardians' estimates of the capabilities of their wards were more closely associated with the living arrangements of the latter than were observations of visitors. Guardians' assessments included functional capacities that would likely predict the ability to live independently, or conversely, the need for supervised living arrangements.

Assets may have been important in the decision for some wards to continue to live alone. With the awarding of guardianship, others may have been divested of personal property and real estate. Wards living alone had larger personal estates than those in other living arrangements ($F = 11.07$, $p < .001$). They also owned real estate of greater value than wards who were in hospitals or in nursing homes ($F = 8.74$, $p < .001$). But wards in the three types of living arrangements had similar levels of income ($F = .24$, ns). Decisions about property (both personal and real estate), along with altered living arrangements, may have reflected some of the considerable change that occurred with the awarding of the guardianship.

CRITICAL INCIDENTS LEADING TO GUARDIANSHIP

In his work on family decision making, Cicirelli (1992:60) reminds us that "the degree of dependency of the elderly parent (i.e., the type and amount of help needed during caregiving) is related to paternalistic caregiving." The caregiver/care receiver dyad exists because of the presumed dependency needs of the older person. Presumably, the very existence and degree of dependency are among the reasons care is sought in the first place. The balance between paternalistic decision making and autonomy of the elder is contingent on the dependency of the latter. Following this thinking, indices of dependency should predict paternalism, perhaps culminating in a petition for substitute decision making. Although he does not specifically discuss critical incidents as factors in the shifting relationship between autonomy and paternalism, Cicirelli implies the occurrence of such events. These critical events indicating dependency may foreshadow a decline in the autonomy of the older person: "the caregiver's allowance or promotion of the exercise of the elder's autonomy continues until the elder reaches a point of decline or deterioration such that some degree of paternalistic decision making becomes necessary to care for the elderly person's needs and autonomy begins to decline" (Cicirelli, 1992:60). Cicirelli observes that the threshold will vary and will be dependent on the type of dependency—physical, mental, emotional, or a combination.

Thus, a critical incident may prompt a shift in the continuum of autonomous to paternalistic decision making between the caregiver and the recipient of the assistance. As observed in chapter 1, for most persons the path to becoming a ward is likely one of gradual decline and movement through the health care system (Hughes, 1989). But Frolik (1981) notes that particular events may prompt the decision to petition for a guardianship.

Families may vary in their response to the dependency of their elder, which in turn is reflected in the types of formal services they select. Sometimes caregivers do not identify themselves as in need of assistance. Critical concerns are the type of dependency and the perceptions of families about their capacity to manage it on their own or whether they should seek assistance. There may be multiple and overlapping types of dependencies.

To assess whether guardianship was requested in response to a specific event, guardians were asked: "Was there a particular incident that prompted the request for a guardian?" For a majority of the wards (77 percent), a critical incident had occurred that led to filing a petition for guardianship. Thus, although in several instances the progression to guardianship likely was somewhat gradual, there was an identifiable event or series of events occurring close together defined by guardians as having significance in the decision to petition for protective services. In most cases, then, there were markers on the continuum from autonomous to paternalistic decision making that were clearly identifiable. Much as dependencies

Table 5.3
Critical Incidents Leading to Guardianship

Incidents	N	Percent[a]
Physical emergency	127	45
Incapacity and dependency	72	25
Altered personal relationships	19	7
Assistance with financial management	19	7
Legal changes	19	7
Institutionalization	12	4
Contact with police and social services personnel	11	4
Other	5	2

[a]Percentages do not total 100 percent.

may be overlapping, investigation of critical incidents showed that sometimes they too were not entirely unique but had shared elements. In the sections that follow we present examples of incidents that guardians said prompted requests for guardianship (Table 5.3).

Physical Emergency

Although in instances the incidents overlapped, the largest group of events involved a physical emergency (45 percent). There was usually a pivotal incident that exacerbated previously existing difficulties. These incidents ranged from illness to having been physically assaulted in robberies or by neighbors or family. For example: "My ward had a stroke and was beaten and robbed by a neighbor." Thus, sometimes physical emergencies of wards were heightened by deviant behavior of others.

Other physical emergencies were independent of the misbehavior of others and represented changes in physical health: "She (the ward) had a mild heart attack, and I found her on the floor. The hospital needed someone to sign the paperwork." "The ward had sores filled with maggots and was living in filth and pain."

Incapacity and Dependency

One-quarter of the guardians indicated their wards were no longer able to care for themselves; these persons said their wards had gotten lost, did not eat, and in general were not able to care for themselves. In some instances, there was a combination of difficulties. One guardian said his ward "was leaving the gas stove on, wandering out at night, and getting lost."

For others, physical health emergencies were sometimes prompted by the inability or failure of wards to care for themselves: "He almost died in 100 degree heat from drinking, malnutrition, and dehydration." "She left the door open in the middle of winter and was wandering around in a four-lane street." "She had wandered from her house on New Year's Eve and someone found her in the street." "He left the nursing home on a freezing night in house shoes and no coat; he ran away." This category of incidents included mental incapacity that if left unattended might have resulted in a greater physical emergency.

Altered Personal Relationships

Less often than the occurrence of physical emergencies, there were changes in personal relationships so that more formal caregiving was thought necessary. Frequently the change in personal relationships involved stressful life events. The death of a spouse, the death of another relative who provided care, or divorce prompted the petition for guardianship for some (7 percent). For example: "After my aunt died, my uncle could not take care of himself—he lost it totally." These types of incidents first may have impacted a significant other of a ward, resulting in altered plans for care and a petition for guardianship.

Assistance with Finances

The need for assistance with finances, a need sometimes prompted by material abuse, was mentioned as the reason for the request for guardianship by 7 percent of the guardians. Compared with physical and emotional abuse, material abuse has received little attention (Wilber, 1990). Although the prevalence is not known, research suggests material abuse may be a significant problem. The misuse of an older person's assets may be referred to as "financial exploitation, exploitation of resources, material exploitation, fiduciary abuse, financial mistreatment, financial maltreatment, financial victimization, economic victimization, extortion, theft, and fraud" (Wilber, 1990:90).

Suggesting a need for assistance and prompting the request for guardianship, several of these incidents involved financial exploitation of the finances of the ward by others. For example: "The ward was fleeced by a young man with a criminal record." "The ward's youngest daughter financially exploited him to the tune of over $70,000." "An ex-trustee abused funds of the ward; my mother took him to court to obtain guardianship instead of his being appointed guardian." "My sister and her husband were living on my mother's income." "Other family members were borrowing money from the ward in large amounts without giving a note or mortgage, etc." "A grandson was living with her (the ward) and mentally abused her, plus he was in the process of getting her to sign her money over to him." "Approximately $20,000 had disappeared. She did not know what she did with it." In contrast to a common image of guardians as villains, these individuals commented on abuse of their wards by other. In chapter 6, in a discussion of what guardianship enabled guardians to do for their wards, we describe the protection they believed they afforded their wards.

Legal and Medical Aspects of Caregiving

Another 7 percent noted incidents involving legal arrangements for caregiving previously in place that had in some way changed (e.g., power of attorney had lapsed, another relative filed for conservatorship). In 4 percent of the cases the ward was institutionalized, and the institution requested that a petition for guardianship be filed. When institutionalization prompted the request for a guardianship, a change in the ward's condition may have been a factor as well. In these instances the intent of the guardianship was to facilitate medical and health care decisions.

Contact with Police and Social Services

Police and social services personnel were involved to some extent and were instrumental in encouraging the request for guardianship in 4 percent of the families. Sometimes the behavior of wards resulted in their contact with the police and was identified as the critical incident prompting the petition for guardianship. One guardian, for example, reported: "The ward discharged a gun into the wall of an adjoining apartment." Others noted more than one instance of aberrant behavior; for example, "There were several incidents of public disturbances resulting in multiple arrests." "She slipped out at night (when the nurse staying with her was asleep), went to the 7-Eleven store, called the police, and said she was being held against her will." As described by guardians, activities that warranted oversight by the police often indicated multiple difficulties of the ward.

These, then, were the types of incident identified by guardians as prompting the requests for guardianship. Some of the incidents, such as financial or physical abuse and changes in previously established legal arrangements for care, were events prompted by others. But the majority of critical incidents reflected changes in the well-being of the proposed ward, and they often were consequences of multiple incapacities of the ward.

ALTERNATIVES TO GUARDIANSHIP

Coleman and Dooley (1990:50) observe: "For many, guardianships are sought to resolve problems that could be addressed in other, less intrusive ways. Often the problem lies in identifying the alternative means of problem resolution through good screening and diversion techniques." Indeed, in legislative reform to strengthen procedural safeguards, the rigorous standard of proof includes the expectation that the court has reviewed and considered alternative plans suitable to care for the ward and has examined least restrictive alternatives (Wang, Burns, & Hommel, 1990).

Stiegel (1992:12) defines alternatives to guardianship as "various legal tools, social services, and government programs that *may* delay or prevent the appointment of a guardian for a person who is not capable of making decisions on his or her own behalf." Stiegel divides guardianship alternatives into two types. One type includes those that allow individuals to plan for their own incapacity or that of another, including health care power of attorney, durable power of attorney, living will, voluntary guardianship, and trusts. The second type can be implemented to respond to current incapacity. These include, among others, money management, representative payeeship, protective services, health care consent laws, and limited guardianship.

Coleman and Dooley (1990) comment that the increasing alternatives to guardianship are heartening, and note approaches such as money management programs, homemaker and health services, and case management. Some of the services used by the guardians in the study both before and after awarding of the guardianship are described in chapter 6. In addition to services provided by communities that may sustain independent living, other practices had been suggested to some of the guardians as alternatives to guardianship.

Individuals have been admonished to seek guardianship when they believe other alternatives have been exhausted (Wilber, 1991). Therefore, we might expect that guardians in the study would be able to document alternatives suggested to them. In fact, alternatives were called to the attention of only one-third of the guardians.

A little over one-fifth of those who responded to the questionnaire said that power of attorney was noted as an alternative prior to the establishment of their guardianship. One view is that durable power of attorney may be superior to securing a guardianship, but another perspective suggests the holder of a durable power of attorney is not obligated to maintain records or inform the family about the ward's condition (Friedman & Savage, 1988).

Sixteen percent of the guardians reported that 24-hour nursing care was recommended as an alternative to guardianship. Joint bank accounts were suggested in lieu of guardianship to 10 percent of the persons who later became guardians.

Seven percent observed that a limited guardianship rather than a plenary guardianship was presented as an alternative. As noted in chapter 9, the three states studied have the option of circumscribing the guardian's authority by use of a limited guardianship. Yet, less than 10 percent of guardians were reminded of this choice. There was some variation among the states. In Missouri, 4 percent of the guardians had been apprised of the option of limited guardianship, compared to 9 percent in Iowa and Colorado. It is perhaps significant that no alternatives were suggested to about two-thirds of the guardians. As guardians remembered the process, most were awarded guardianship with no alternative, less restrictive measures called to their attention. Insofar as the use of least restrictive alternatives is among the tenets of the guardianship reform movement, the procedures these guardians participated in were largely untouched by a major component of the drive to increase protection of wards.

ASSESSMENTS OF WARDS AND GUARDIANSHIPS

Guardians' Assessments of the Functional Capacity of Wards

It was thought that guardians who contacted their wards regularly would be able to assess the frequency with which the latter were able to perform various activities. As we noted earlier in this chapter, guardians

Table 5.4
Guardians' Estimates of Functional Capacity of Wards at the Awarding of the Guardianship

Capacity	All of the Time		Some of the Time		Not at All	
	N	Percent	N	Percent	N	Percent
Able to write checks and pay bills	5	1	48	13	325	86
Able to dress/undress	103	27	138	37	136	36
Able to prepare food	12	3	83	22	279	75
Able to understand and communicate	44	12	223	59	109	29
Able to manage medication (if used)	6	2	77	21	287	78

who responded to the questionnaire indicated how often their ward was able to perform selected tasks of daily living at the time the guardianship began. Other than the often scant material in the court records on functional capacity, these data from guardians provide insight into some of the functions that individuals were able to carry out at the time they became wards. More detailed potential assessments of functional capacity were discussed in chapter 4. Because of space limitations in the questionnaire, we asked guardians whom we contacted to indicate the frequency with which their wards were able to undertake the five types of activities described in this chapter.

The majority of wards (three-fourths or more) were unable to perform three of the tasks: write checks and pay bills, prepare food, or manage medication (Table 5.4). Dressing and undressing was the activity performed all of the time by the largest percentage of wards (27 percent). But the majority of the wards, as described by their guardians, were unable to complete the five selected activities on a regular basis. Perhaps a more complete list of activities of daily living would have revealed aspects of personal care that a greater proportion of the wards could have undertaken. Performance of the tasks considered, however, would suggest possible placement of persons on the continuum between autonomy and dependence as described by Cicirelli. It might be expected that more alternatives to guardianship would be suggested for prospective wards with greater capacity to behave autonomously. However, the capacity of the ward as estimated by the guardian was not associated with the presentation of alternatives ($t = 1.37$, ns). Thus, proposed wards with greater capabilities became a part of the guardianship system with no more consideration given to alternatives than was given for their presumably less able peers.

Court Visitors' Assessments

In Colorado, assessments of wards and their circumstances by court visitors are a part of the court record. In Iowa and Missouri, court visitors are not mandated by statute. Court visitors' reports are a part of the records only in Colorado. Their visits are important because they take place before a decision about guardianship is made. Court visitors see the wards in the circumstances in which they are located at the time the request for guardianship is filed. Because their mission is an objective appraisal of the capacity of the ward and an assessment of the ward's need for guardianship, visitor reports provide a unique perspective on circumstances of the ward. Visitors describe resources available to the prospective ward, including both personal capacity and other types of support.

Appropriateness of the Guardian and Limitations on the Guardianship. Visitors in Colorado evaluated the appropriateness of the individual who petitioned to become a guardian as "positive," "neutral," and "negative." The majority of the court visitors believed the specific individual who petitioned for guardianship was appropriate (89 percent) while 4 percent disagreed, and 6 percent were neutral. Even though the proposed guardians were viewed by most visitors as needed, following contact with proposed wards almost one-fifth believed there should be limitations placed on the powers of the guardian. This view suggests visitors may have observed capacities of some wards that they thought would make it possible for them to function with fewer restrictions on their decisions about personal care and/or management of their assets or property.

Proposed Wards' Perceptions of the Guardianship

Questioning prospective wards about their well-being and their perceptions of the proposed guardianship was among the tasks of the court visitors. A visit with someone from the court gave prospective wards an opportunity to describe their personal circumstances and to articulate perceptions of their needs for intervention. Because guardianship as a judicial process transfers decision-making responsibilities from a person who is thought to be incapacitated to someone else, we might expect that considerable information from the individual who will lose decision-making power would be available. But guardianship records are quite silent about actual preferences and assessments from proposed wards. That is, in most records there is no systematic effort to note the specific desires and concerns of future wards. Even if proposed wards attend their hearings, their involvement is minimal. And the process is structured to diminish the contribution of those who may soon lose their decision-making power (Vittoria, 1992). Therefore, insights about the responses to guardianship such as those supplied by prospective wards to court visitors are all the more uncommon and warrant attention.

Wards' Specific Assessments of Their Needs. Of those who were about to become wards, a substantial minority (46 percent) felt they did not need help to care for themselves, while 54 percent agreed they needed assistance with certain tasks. Prospective wards who wanted assistance generally observed they required help with personal care (42 percent), and often concluded they could use aid with multiple needs (39 percent). Needs for assistance with finances were less frequently identified (7 percent). Of course, some wards likely were already recipients of assistance in several areas. Furthermore, acknowledging a need for help did not mean the desired assistance was a guardianship. In the end, most received guardianships, even those who did not disclose any needs for help.

Wards were asked two further questions to elicit their response to the proposed guardianship. They were first asked their view of the scope and duration of the guardianship. The responses were coded as "positive," "negative," "don't know," "neutral," or "do not care." The designated scope and duration of the proposed guardianship were viewed negatively by 34 percent of the wards, although a similar percentage, 36 percent, were satisfied with the specific proposal indicated in the petition. Seven percent of the wards visited specifically indicated they did not want a guardianship.

In a similar, but more general, question wards were asked how they felt about the proposed guardianship. Slightly less than half (48 percent) of the wards felt positively about the guardianship whereas one-third tended to be negative toward the proposed guardianship as a whole. About one-fifth were neutral or did not care about the outcome of the proposed proceedings. The majority of wards, then, were either positive or neutral about the guardianship. In chapter 11, assessments of visitors and wards are considered in relation to the extensiveness of powers granted by the court.

CHARACTERISTICS OF GUARDIANS

In most instances an outcome of the hearing was the appointment of a guardian. In general, the characteristics of guardians revealed in the court records studied were comparable to those observed in other research (see chapter 3). Like their wards, guardians were more often women (57 percent) than men (39 percent), although 4 percent of the wards had co-guardians who were both male and female. As in other types of caregiving, family members assume the greatest responsibility for guardianship. Even within the family there is a hierarchy of members who are most likely to be appointed as guardians. In other forms of caring for older persons, the selection of a caregiver tends to conform to a

Table 5.5
Relationship of Guardians and Petitioners to Wards

	Relationship of Guardians to Wards		Relationship to Wards of Petitioners Who Were Not Appointed Guardians	
	N	Percent	N	Percent[a]
Spouse	87	9	9	5
Adult daughter	234	23	15	8
Adult son	159	16	11	6
Two or more adult children	33	3	3	2
Other relative	287	28	23	12
Nonrelative	163	16	5	3
Dept. of human services	27	3	58	30
Financial institution			1	.5
Health care institution	1	.1	16	8
County attorney/ public administrator	18	2	45	23

[a]The remaining responses (2.5 percent) were categorized as "other."

hierarchical pattern of informal support in which the principle of substitution is followed (Shanas, Townsend, Wedderburn, Friis, Milhoj, & Stehouwer, 1968). Substitution means the activation of informal resources in order from those closest and most intimate to those most distant. If available and physically able, the spouse generally is looked to first as a caregiver, followed by children, usually an adult daughter, siblings, more distant relatives, friends, and neighbors. The pattern of hierarchical support may be modified somewhat in the selection of guardians. Because guardianship usually involves older, quite vulnerable persons, spouses even if they are present may not be viewed as capable of performing the needed tasks to care for the proposed ward's person or property. Indeed, as noted earlier, relatives other than the spouse are most often designated to care for the person and finances of wards.

If they were available and capable of doing so, children become the first in line to serve as guardians. In the records studied, children of wards were appointed as guardians more frequently than were spouses (Table 5.5). Fewer than 10 percent of the guardians were spouses while about 42 percent were children, with daughters (23 percent) more often being guardians than were sons (16 percent). The remaining 3 percent of the children who were guardians were mixed-sex co-guardians. Relatives other than children were less likely to be guardians (28 percent). Twenty-two percent of the guardians were nonrelatives, including friends, representatives of state agencies, attorneys, public administrators, or health care institutions, in addition to other individuals who were not related to the ward. The proportion of guardians studied who were nonrelatives was fairly comparable to that found in other research. One-quarter of the guardians in a national sample, for example, were not family members, compared to 21 percent in the present research (AP, 1987). Because of our sampling criteria to minimize inclusion of multiple wards with the same guardians and to select guardians of the person, we had thought family members might be somewhat overrepresented.

Co-guardianships were awarded in 12 percent of the cases. As noted, co-guardians were sometimes adult children of the ward. In several instances one child lived in close proximity and the other was located farther away.

The petitioner for the guardianship may or may not also be appointed as guardian. In 82 percent of the cases reviewed, the petitioner also was appointed guardian. To the degree that the majority of petitioners hope to become the guardian, some of the instances in which they are not appointed may indicate that a careful review demonstrated selection of another person would best meet the ward's needs. Table 5.5 shows the relationship of the petitioner to the ward among the petitioners who were not appointed as guardians. Petitioners who were not appointed as guardians, were most often representatives of human services agencies, county attorneys, or public administrators. The critical incidents cited earlier sometimes involved interaction with agencies whose personnel eventually became petitioners. Others who were petitioners but were not selected as guardians included daughters, relatives other than children, and representatives of health care institutions (Table 5.5). In the next section, the nature of some of the contact between guardians and their wards during the first year of the guardianship is considered.

ACTIVITIES OF GUARDIANS

What do guardians do? What are they expected to do on behalf of their wards? The capabilities of a "good" guardian as described by the ABA Wingspread conferees are indeed formidable (Hurme, 1991). A good guardian should be "knowledgeable about housing and long-term care options, community resources, protection and preservation of the estate, accounting, medical and psychological treatment, public benefits and communication with elderly and disabled individuals." In addition, a guardian should "develop advocacy skills; assume 'case management' functions; monitor the ward's living situation; make decisions that are, to the greatest extent possible, in accord with the ward's values; avoid any conflict of interest; and regularly report to the court" (Hurme, 1991:25). The majority of these skills and attendant activities could not be developed and performed without something more than casual effort.

In a review of seven southern states, Johnson (1990) observed that powers and duties of guardians ranged from guidelines for specific conduct to no provision for conduct. In the seven southern states, some of the duties focused on activities with the goal of potential improvement of the ward's condition, for example, "training, education, and rehabilitation." Others related to enhancement of the ward's autonomy and treatment of the ward. These included "treating ward humanely, with dignity," "encouraging ward's participation in decisions," "helping ward develop, maximize, or regain self-determination," and "considering ward's preference." Other duties related to instrumental actions to comply with more specific legal requirements, such as "following court ordered prescription," and "consent for care." "Care of personal effects" and "regular physical/mental examinations" also were specified by some. Finally, one state mandated a range of potential personal interaction with the ward, described as "reasonable accessibility to the ward" and "regular contact with the ward."

The statutes of primary concern to this study are similar to those discussed above. The statutes of the three states studied vary in the scope and specificity of the duties of guardians. The Colorado, Iowa, and Missouri statutes instruct guardians to provide for the ward's comfort and medical and professional needs. Guardians in Iowa are to maximize the ward's potential and assist in developing their maximum self-reliance and independence. Missouri expects the guardians to assure that the ward is receiving treatment, rehabilitation, support, and maintenance, and that they are providing for the ward's safety and welfare. Missouri differs from the others, however, in that guardians are to assure that the ward resides in the least restrictive setting available. Colorado and Iowa specifically mention that the guardian must care for the ward's clothing, furniture, and vehicle.

Clearly, some of these objectives for guardian conduct are more easily attainable and certainly more open to measurement than others. For example, obtaining regular physical/mental health care can be assessed more readily than "treating the ward humanely, with dignity."

Once a guardianship has been awarded, what kinds of information are available about the relationships maintained by wards and guardians? Although certain obligations of guardians to their wards are designated and monitored by the court in varying degrees, guardians may engage in activities and provide assistance beyond that specified in state statutes. In Iowa and Missouri, guardians file annual reports that may detail some of their activities on behalf of the ward.

Table 5.6
Activities and Assistance Provided to Wards by Their Guardians

Assistance to Ward	Yes		No	
	N	Percent	N	Percent
Visit with ward	319	76	99	24
Provide emotional support	196	47	218	53
Purchase personal items	142	34	277	66
File forms and complete paperwork	129	31	286	69
ADLS	65	16	348	84
Prepare meals/food	48	12	366	88
Take ward to physician	46	11	366	89
Do laundry	40	10	379	90
Shop with ward	38	9	379	91
Take ward to visit family	26	6	388	94

The form for the annual report in Iowa contains several general questions or items that guardians report on and from which we coded ten categories of tasks performed by guardians. These give some insight into the nature of the contact between guardians and their wards. The information requested on the annual report form includes: (1) "The following is a summary of the medical, educational, vocational and other professional services provided for the ward"; (2) "The following is a description of the guardian's visits with and activities on behalf of the ward"; and (3) "Other information believed useful to the court." The items were open response.

In the Missouri annual report the guardian is asked to recall how many times he or she has seen the ward during the previous year and to describe the nature of the visits. The activities and assistance provided by guardians to wards in both states were coded into the following ten categories: visit with the ward, provide emotional support, purchase personal items, file forms and complete paperwork, assist with ADLs, prepare meals/food, take the ward to a physician, do laundry, shop with the ward, and take the ward to visit family (Table 5.6).

First annual reports in Iowa and Missouri were filed by 58 percent of the guardians. Reports of financial transactions and management of the assets of wards were filed by about 71 percent of the conservators, and these reports were more often complete. Reports about the activities of guardians other than on financial matters provided some insight into additional assistance these guardians provided their wards. Participation in these activities, drawn from guardians' first annual reports, is shown in Table 5.6.

Visiting with the ward was a dominant activity engaged in by guardians as indicated in their first annual reports (Table 5.6). As is observed in chapter 6, the majority of guardians who replied to the guardianship questionnaire reported quite frequent personal contact with their wards.

Perhaps as an outgrowth of their personal contact with their wards, one-half of the guardians believed that they provided emotional support to those for whom they cared (Table 5.6). There was somewhat less frequent instrumental assistance. For example, about one-third of the guardians purchased personal items for the ward or completed forms and paperwork. Presumably, some of the personal services included in managing the activities of daily living would have occurred most often when the ward and guardian lived in the same household. A high proportion of the guardians who undertook food preparation activities and laundry, for example, likely also shared a household with their wards. Obviously, the type of relationship that wards and guardians might maintain and the assistance the latter might provide were, in part, shaped by the living arrangements of the wards and their needs for direct care.

Using these ten types of aid, an index of helping was formed by counting the number of types of assistance that the guardian had provided over the year. This measure of helping does not assess the number of times each kind of aid was provided but rather how many, if any, of the types of assistance were extended to their wards. Because this assessment of helping does not address the entire amount of aid or the quality of assistance, it is a gross and unrefined measure. But other than financial reports, these are among the only indicators in court records about the nature of interaction between wards and guardians. The number of types of assistance provided ranged from none (16 percent of guardians) to ten (less than 1 percent of those responding). The average number of types of assistance mentioned by guardians was 2.48 (sd = 2.14).

One interest was in the relationship between the various types of helping and demographic characteristics of guardians and their wards. The personal characteristics were limited to those available in court records. Demographic factors considered in relation to the types of help were age and sex of ward, sex of guardian, length of guardianship, relationship of the ward and guardian (relative/nonrelative), living arrangements, and finances of the ward (value of personal property, value of real estate, and income).

Perhaps most significant was the lack of a relationship between several of the personal characteristics and the range of types of help provided. That is, receiving assistance from a guardian was largely independent of personal characteristics of either the ward or the guardian. For example, the socioeconomic status of the ward as reflected in assets in real estate ($r = .03$), amount of personal property ($r = .06$), and annual income ($r = 00$) was not associated with the range of help given by guardians. The number of types of help provided by guardians was independent of the length of the guardianship ($r = -.06$), the age ($r = -.03$) and sex of the ward ($r = 00$), and whether or not the ward and guardian were related ($r = -.05$).

Living arrangements figured in the range of help given by guardians. Wards who lived alone were a little more likely to receive a wider range of assistance from guardians than those who lived with others ($r = -.16$, $p < .01$). This greater assistance may have made it possible for wards to remain alone. Not surprisingly, wards who resided with their guardians who were relatives (spouse, child, more distant kin) were provided a greater range of types of assistance by the latter than wards who lived with and were cared for by nonrelatives ($r = -.31, p < .01$). In the group of wards cared for by nonrelatives, the guardian was less often the primary caregiver.

Finally, there was a tendency for male guardians to provide a smaller range of assistance than female guardians ($r = -.13$, $p < .05$). From the literature, it might be suggested that a gender difference in the amount of assistance could be accounted for by the different living arrangements of male and female wards. That is, it might be expected that wards would reside more often in households of female guardians and be in a position to receive a greater range of care from them. But as noted earlier, the wards studied were as likely to reside with male as with female guardians. In this way, some of the gender differences in guardianship did not correspond to patterns found among some other types of caregivers.

SUMMARY

In this chapter we considered the characteristics of persons who were adjudicated incapacitated and of those who cared for them. The majority of the findings presented here were somewhat limited by information available in the court records.

Clearly, the characteristics of the majority of wards differentiated them sharply from their peers who were not thought to need the protection of guardianship. Not surprisingly, substantially fewer wards lived alone than their counterparts outside the guardianship system. However, we especially were interested in personal or other resources that assisted individuals who functioned alone despite being found incapacitated.

Although the guardians' assessments of capacity were rudimentary, they did not differentiate between wards living alone or residing with others in the community but outside a nursing home or hospital. Their greater net worth may have made it possible for wards who lived alone to make arrangements for assistance. Wards who were alone were on average three years older than those who resided with others. Their greater age also may have reflected hardiness or a capacity to survive. Although they had characteristics of triple jeopardy—being older, female, and alone—they had greater resources of functional capacity and were better off on some economic indices.

Critical incidents that led to guardianship also were reflections of dependency. Such incidents were markers in the guardianship process for over three-quarters of the wards. In this way, critical incidents fostered a shift in the continuum from autonomous to paternalistic decision making (Cicirelli, 1992). And we know that even with minimal powers awarded to them, guardians often assume critical decision-making authority (Hurme, 1991). In chapter 6, the characteristics of those who assumed decision-making responsibility and their view of the guardianship process are described.

6

Pathways to Guardianship

This chapter provides a more in-depth examination of paths to guardianship than was available from information in the court records. Through use of a mail questionnaire, guardians were queried about becoming a guardian and the context in which they assumed the role of guardian. Some of the stages of the procedure that guardians were asked to address were decisions to seek guardianship, family involvement and response to the guardianship, and reasons for selection of the individual as guardian. Selected characteristics of the ward-guardian relationship (e.g., proximity, amount of contact, and change in the relationship) following establishment of the guardianship were studied. In this chapter, then, we consider how persons came to be guardians, changes in their relationships with family members and wards following their appointment as guardian, and their background characteristics. The data analyzed here were drawn from responses of 387 guardians to the mail questionnaire. We begin with a description of personal characteristics of guardians who participated in the research.

PERSONAL CHARACTERISTICS OF GUARDIANS

Reflecting the total sample from the court records, more of the guardians who completed the questionnaire were women (62 percent) than men (38 percent). Seventy-two percent were married, 15 percent were widowed, and the remainder were divorced/separated or never married (9 and 5 percent, respectively). Guardians ranged in age from 23 to 87 years. Their mean age was 58 years.

Several characteristics of guardians' households were considered, including the number of persons in the household and the number of persons age 60 years or over in the residence. A substantial minority (22 percent) of the guardians were living alone. Forty-eight percent resided in a two-person household, 13 percent lived in a three-person household, and the remainder lived in households with four or more persons. Few guardians and their wards lived in the same residence (8 percent). Forty-two percent of the households had no members age 60 or over; 28 percent had one individual age 60 or over; and 30 percent had two or more persons who were 60 years of age or over.

The majority of guardians had children; 12 percent had one child, and 74 percent had two or more living children. Fourteen percent had no children.

Forty-two percent of the guardians were employed full-time, 14 percent worked part-time, and 35 percent were retired. The remaining guardians were unemployed (2 percent) or were lifelong homemakers (7 percent).

Family income—yearly income from all sources—was classified in five categories: less than $5,000 (1 percent); $5,000-14,999 (15 percent); $15,000-24,999 (22 percent); $25,000-34,999 (18 percent); and $35,000 or over (44 percent). Educational levels ranging from less than high school to completion of work beyond a four-year college degree were grouped in six categories. Six percent of the guardians had received less than 12 years of schooling, while 40 percent had completed high school. About one-fifth (22 percent) had completed some college or held a technical or vocational degree. Almost one-third (32 percent) had completed a four-year college degree and/or had undertaken graduate studies. Guardians also rated their health as excellent (34 percent), good (49 percent), fair (15 percent), or poor (2 percent).

In short, the guardians who responded had higher average levels of education than their age peers found in the population as a whole, and the majority enjoyed good or excellent health. Gender differences in selected personal characteristics of guardians are described in chapter 8.

ESTABLISHING GUARDIANSHIP

The centrality of the family to the care of the aged is indisputable. Dwyer and Coward (1992) articulate the trend for the transfer of care for frail older persons from the purview of government, as the economy has declined, to the private sphere, especially that of women. Some of the motivations for caring for elders include love and affection for the person, repayment for previous assistance, and norms of spousal and filial responsibility (Doty, 1986). These motives were among those that emerged as guardians, both men and women, recounted the benefits and hardships from their efforts in caring for an older person (see chapter 7). Consequently, there was every reason to expect involvement of the family in the decision to embark on a procedure as dramatic as guardianship. It also was assumed that concern of family members would extend to the selection of the person who would serve as guardian. Even though the procedures involved in the decision to establish guardianship and to select a caregiver are more formal than those often used in more informal caregiving, we anticipated considerable family participation. Because not all wards have available family members, there might be differences in the selection of relatives and nonrelatives as guardians. Of course, many features of the process likely would be the same (e.g., critical incidents that prompt guardianship, selection of the best individual to serve). In some of the analyses that follow, we investigated whether there were differences in the establishment of guardianship and the ward-guardian relationship when guardians were relatives and when they were not related to the ward.

There has been considerable research on the strains and burdens of caring for the aged, and some of those related to guardianship are discussed in chapters 7 and 8. In general, many of the outcomes for those who care are negative, including emotional stress, diminished physical health, changes in life-style, and financial problems (Dwyer & Coward, 1992; Walker, Martin, & Jones, 1992). With some exceptions the efforts of men, often the sons of care recipients, have been neglected, with much research focusing only on women (e.g., Franks & Stephens, 1992; Walker, Martin, & Jones, 1992). This omission may be because daughters are more likely to be primary caregivers, or because the less frequent involvement of men is thought to make their experiences less critical to policy development (Montgomery & Kamo, 1989). Perhaps because the management of estates may be viewed as more congruent with the male gender role, men may be appointed guardians or guardian/conservators more often than they serve as other types of caregivers. One study found that sons usually became primary caregivers only when no female siblings were present, and even in this circumstance there was only a 24.8 percent rate of participation among men (Coward & Dwyer, 1990).

There is less information about the reasons for selection into caregiving than there is about responses of individuals to the tasks of caring (e.g., burden, strain, and benefit). Hence, there is more evidence about differences in male and female performance and response to caring roles than about reasons for their selection to assist an elder. How does involvement of males and females in caregiving differ? Men provide less direct personal care, perform fewer routine tasks, and in general seem to experience caring as less burdensome (Horowitz, 1985; Matthews & Rosner, 1988). One study found, for example, that men spent fewer hours providing care and were involved in less intensive tasks for shorter time periods (Montgomery and Kamo, 1989). Daughters provided more care when needs of parents increased; the activity of sons leveled off despite the incremental needs of their parents. Montgomery and Kamo (1989), however, observed that men and women spent about the same amount of time providing assistance with financial and business matters and, contrary to other findings, concluded they did not differ in overall level of burden.

This research provided an opportunity to determine if the process of guardianship was comparable for these male and female guardians. For example, were their relationships with family members and wards similar? Were they selected as guardians for comparable reasons? Did they express similar needs for support in their role as guardian? In the next sections, we consider some of the differences in the establishment of the guardianship and in the ward-guardian relationship that occurred for men and women. Where it is appropriate in the next sections, we comment on differences between relatives and nonrelatives in becoming a guardian and practicing guardianship.

THE DECISION TO SEEK A GUARDIANSHIP

Literature on decision making about care for older persons in the context of the family is limited. Rather than determine in advance decisions about health care, for example, one sample of older persons believed there was a tacit understanding between them and their family how decisions would be made (High, 1988). Older individuals preferred that family members discuss what should be done, resolve conflicts and disagreements, and base their decisions on the outcome of the discussion (High, 1988). Cicirelli (1981) observed that a most frequent source of conflict involved an attempt by a child to control the activities, including health behavior, of the older person. About 40 percent of aged parents experienced this behavior from their child. Even so, the input of family members is valued and expected.

In response to vignettes, Horowitz, Silverstone, and Reinhardt (1991) found family members were more sensitive to concerns about autonomy than were their elders. Furthermore, participation of family members in decisions for their elders was important. Indeed, researchers observed that support and involvement of family in the decision-making process were related to the quality of the decisions about the care of older persons (Coulton, Dunkle, Chow, Haug, & Vielhaber, 1988). It is important to note that although 79 percent of the guardians were family members, the majority of wards whose guardians were not relative (80 percent) had family members available. So there was opportunity for involvement by family members in the guardianship process even though the guardian eventually appointed was a nonrelative.

Recommendations for Establishment of Guardianship

The decision to petition for guardianship is a determination that most surely will impact the autonomy of the proposed ward. In this section we

Table 6.1
Persons Who First Suggested a Guardian Was Needed

	N[a]	Percent
Family	98	26
Physician or other health professional	82	22
Attorney	57	15
A combination of the above including family	31	8
Nursing home staff	30	8
Social worker	30	8
Proposed guardian	23	6
Hospital staff	20	5
Neighbor or friend	13	3
A combination of the above excluding family	9	2
Police	2	.5

[a] The number of responses exceeds the total number of respondents because some gave multiple responses. Percentages do not total 100 percent.

consider the involvement of family members and others in the decision to seek guardianship.

Guardians indicated on the questionnaire who first recommended guardianship. The persons or organizations who made this suggestion early in the process are shown in Table 6.1. In some instances, guardians mentioned more than one person or representative of an organization who had suggested guardianship. Although guardians were asked who first recommended the guardianship, it is conceivable that two persons may have observed the need for such care at or about the same time. Consequently, in Table 6.1, the number of responses exceeds the number of respondents.

Families of some wards were active in the decision-making process surrounding the establishment of the guardianship. This was illustrated by the part that family members took in identifying guardianship as a possible alternative; they were the most likely group of persons to first suggest that the ward needed a guardian (26 percent). In mentioning more than one person who first recommended guardianship, an additional 8 percent of the guardians included family members in combination with others.

Health personnel, comprising physicians, nursing home, and hospital staff members, also frequently were among the first to suggest that the ward should have a guardian. A little over one-third of the guardians pointed to the importance of health care professionals in bringing the guardianship procedure to their attention. In a few instances, social workers (8 percent) or the proposed guardian (6 percent) were those who first mentioned the possibility of guardianship. Neighbors or friends less frequently (3 percent) called attention to the potential need for additional care for the ward.

Although the family was the single most important group in recommending a guardianship be established, the majority of guardianships were petitioned for initially at the behest of persons other than family members. Certainly families and health care professionals combined assumed the greatest responsibility for observing the need for guardianship and suggesting it as an alternative. It had been anticipated that guardianship for wards whose guardians were nonrelatives might have been suggested first by nonrelatives. The assumption was that wards not ministered to by relatives might have been assisted in large part by nonfamily members who would be in a position to recommend guardianship. But family members were as likely to call attention to the need for a guardianship that in the end was assigned to a nonrelative as they were to recommend a guardianship eventually awarded to a relative.

REASONS FOR SELECTION AS GUARDIAN

As noted in chapter 5, guardians in the total sample were most often family members (78 percent). Spouses and children were guardians for one-half of the wards, and more distant relatives accounted for another 28 percent of the guardians. Even though kin are usually involved, the process entailed in the decision to establish guardianship and to select a guardian is substantially more formal than that usually employed in more informal caregiving.

After the decision was made that a guardian would be sought, families of some of the wards were active in selecting and determining who the specific guardian would be. Family members were involved in the selection of the guardian in 40 percent of the instances described by respondents in the mail questionnaire. However, in 42 percent of the procedures, the choice of a guardian was not discussed among the family members of the ward. Thus, as often as not family members became guardians without discussion of their appointment with other relatives, even when they were available. Any discussion of the appointment of the guardian by family members of the ward was independent of gender of the guardian or whether the guardian was a relative.

One reason family members may not be involved in a substantial portion of the decisions designating the specific guardian is because persons without families may be disproportionately represented in guardianship proceedings. Among these guardians, about one-fifth indicated their wards had no available family members. In some families, naming the specific guardian may have been taken for granted whereas in others there may

Table 6.2
Reasons for Selection as Guardians

Reasons	N[a]	Percent
Involved in the care of the ward before appointed guardian	198	51
Agreement among family members that specific guardian be appointed	124	32
No one else available	105	27
Guardian lived closest to the ward	72	19
Close friend of the ward	44	11

[a] The number of responses exceeds the total number of respondents because some gave multiple responses. Percentages do not total 100 percent.

have been considerable debate. Earlier we noted that 18 percent of those who petitioned for guardianship were not appointed as guardian. This may reflect some instances in which family members intervened to preclude an appointment.

Although there was discussion about the selection of a specific guardian in families of some wards, there are many reasons other than family relationship why persons may be chosen to serve as guardians. Table 6.2 shows reasons why respondents were appointed as guardians. Guardians could select as many of the reasons that applied to their situation as they wanted. Each category was treated as a separate variable, allowing guardians to respond to as many multiple items as applied; therefore, the percentages in Table 6.2 do not total 100 percent.

The majority of guardians were chosen (51 percent) because they were involved in the care of the ward before their appointment as guardian (Table 6.2). Women were a little more likely (56 percent) than men (45 percent) to mention their care of the ward prior to the awarding of guardianship as a salient factor in their appointment ($X^2 = 3.81, p < .05$). But earlier involvement with the ward's care was no more important in the selection of a relative than a nonrelative. Although it might be thought that a sustained caregiving relationship with a family member would be a more frequent reason for the choice of a relative as guardian, this was not supported by the results of the questionnaire.

Agreement among family members (32 percent) and unavailability of anyone else (27 percent) were also factors in the selection of several of the guardians. Agreement among family members was significantly more important in the selection of relatives as guardians (36 percent) than in the choice of nonrelatives (14 percent; $X^2 = 11.18$, 1 df, $p < .001$). Guardians who said they were chosen because "no one else was available" were more likely to be nonrelatives (38 percent) than relatives (25 percent; $X^2 = 4.39$, 1 df, $p < .04$). But even when the ward had family members, their agreement and approval was seen as less important in the selection of a nonrelative as guardian.

Close friendship with the ward and physical proximity figured less often in becoming a guardian for the total sample (11 and 19 percent, respectively) than did other factors. Intimate friendship, however, was an especially important reason for the selection of nonrelatives as guardians (43 percent) compared with relatives (5 percent, $X^2 = 75.24$, 1 df, $p < .001$).

In summary, some factors salient in the selection of nonrelatives as guardians were similar to those that were important in the appointment of family members. Unavailability of others, agreement among family members, and close friendship with the ward, however, differentiated the selection of relatives and nonrelatives as guardians. Intimate friendship was especially instrumental in the appointment of nonrelatives to care for an elder. The comments of guardians in chapter 7 describe how close friendship formed the basis of guardianship selection for some wards.

THE EFFECT OF GUARDIANSHIP ON FAMILIES

While a guardianship may have a profound effect on the life of the ward, it also alters the relationships of some guardians with their families. Seventeen percent of the guardians indicated on the questionnaire that their relationship with family members changed as a result of their becoming a guardian. And for the majority (67 percent) who experienced a change in relationships with their family, the transition was a negative one. As is clear from their comments about the hardships of guardian (see chapter 7), pressure from family members was a common difficulty. For example: "There were disagreements with siblings over my care of the ward. I felt unappreciated. No one else wanted the job, but they all had opinions on my performance." Another guardian noted: "Dealing with relatives was hardest. . . . They made unreasonable demands."

Guardians' concerns ranged from disgruntled family members who criticized their decisions and actions as the caregiver to financial and physical abuse of their ward by relatives. Only 4 percent said that the change in their relationship with their family was both positive and negative.

Male and female guardians did not differ in their experiences of altered relationships with family after establishment of the guardianship. Nonrelative guardians whose wards had families available experienced substantially fewer changes (8 percent) in their relationship with relatives of the ward than did family members (20 percent) who were appointed as guardians ($X^2 = 3.78$, 1 df, $p < .05$). Guardianships established with a member of the family may provide opportunities for historical difficulties to continue, to reemerge, or to generate new conflicts.

Even though family ties may have been altered by the legal action taken, relatives usually agreed a guardian was needed. Indeed, in 77 percent of the families there was agreement a guardianship should be petitioned for, and in 90 percent of them there was consensus on the appointment of the person who eventually became the guardian. Again, the experiences of male and female guardians with their families were comparable in their agreement about the need for a guardian and the choice of a specific person. Selection of relatives or nonrelatives as guardians was not associated with agreement among family members of the ward about the need for the protective service or the preference for the specific person. Thus, in most instances appointment of a nonrelative did not seem to indicate family dissention or an inability to agree on a family member as guardian.

Even with apparently high levels of family support and agreement, still more contact between family members might have improved relationships, and was desired by some guardians. When they were asked whether they would like to talk more with family members about the problems of their wards, one-quarter of the guardians indicated they would appreciate the opportunity. Additional support, then, would be helpful for some even in situations when there was consensus among family members about guardianship arrangements. Men and women did not differ in their preference to have more contact with family members.

RELATIONSHIPS WITH WARDS

Contact between Wards and Guardians

The literature is clear about the close proximity and frequency of contact between older persons and their children (Hess, 1991). Data from the questionnaire used here address the quantitative characteristics of the ward-guardian relationship. No qualitative information is available from wards. Qualitative descriptions about portions of the ward-guardian relationship from the perspective of the guardian are presented in chapter 7.

Guardians noted their proximity to their wards and the frequency of interaction with them. The majority of guardians (85 percent) lived within a drive of one hour or less from the ward. This percentage included those guardians who lived with their wards, which was slightly less than 10 percent. Proximity between wards and guardians was comparable regardless of gender or family relationship.

With the exception of those sharing a household, 13 percent of the guardians visited or phoned their wards daily; 46 percent visited or phoned one or more times per week; 21 percent visited or phoned several times monthly, and 10 percent did so several times a year. About 3 percent saw or

Table 6.3
Factors That Usually Interfered with Face-to-face Contact of Guardians with Their Wards

Factors That Interfered	N[a]	Percent
Difficult communication with ward	151	39
Other obligations	132	34
Nothing interfered	104	27
Nothing needed by ward	73	19
Distance	51	13

[a] The number of responses exceeds the total number of respondents because some gave multiple responses. Percentages do not total 100 percent.

contacted their wards once a year or less. Thus, 87 percent contacted their wards in person or by phone several times a month or more often. For most of these wards, then, there was fairly regular contact with their guardians. Nonrelatives, however, saw their wards significantly less often than did relatives ($t = 2.67, p < .01$), and men maintained substantially less frequent contact with their wards than did women ($t = 2.80, p < .01$).

The amount of time that guardians spent on activities helping their wards varied widely. A little more than one-fifth (23 percent) spent less than one hour per week whereas 12 percent allocated 17 or more hours per week to assisting their wards. The majority (54 percent) devoted between 2 and 7 hours per week to their wards' care. Relatives spent more time on guardian activities than did nonrelatives ($t = 2.54, p < .01$). On the average, relatives allocated between 2 and 7 hours per week on their work as guardians while nonrelatives spent less than 1 hour per week. Men and women spent comparable amounts of time on the duties of guardianship even though women had more frequent contact with wards.

Barriers to Contact

Guardians noted factors that precluded their having more contact with their wards. Table 6.3 includes a number of factors that intervened to reduce contact of guardians with their wards. Guardians indicated all of the barriers that applied to their situation. Because respondents could note as many interferences with contact as were applicable, the percentages do not total 100 percent.

Difficulties in communicating with the ward were most often responsible for limiting contact with them. Conflicts between obligations such as work and family matters were another important barrier to more frequent interaction between wards and guardians (Table 6.3). Distance was substantially less often a reason for limited contact. This is not surprising since most guardians and wards lived within less than a one hour drive from one another. Finally, more than one-quarter of the guardians experienced no barriers in initiating face-to-face contact with their wards. Women more often (33 percent) than men (19 percent) had nothing that interfered with their seeing the ward ($X^2 = 8.60$, 1 df, $p < .001$).

Generally, relatives and nonrelatives experienced similar barriers in maintaining ties with the ward. Nonrelatives (29 percent), however, were a little more likely than relatives (18 percent) to forgo contact with their wards because they needed nothing done for them ($X^2 = 4.23$, 1 df, $p < .05$). The perception that the ward had no unmet needs was a reason for noncontact with the ward given more frequently by men (25 percent) than by women (16 percent; $X^2 = 3.97$, 1 df, $p < .05$). Differences in perceptions of the absence of need could not be attributed to the ward's condition, because women and relatives did not oversee the care of wards who were more impaired. It may be that men and nonrelatives were a little less attentive to their wards or assisted them in different ways.

Being a guardian changed the relationship a minority of the guardians (about one-fifth) had with their wards. Only 6 percent felt their relationships deteriorated, whereas 15 percent of the guardians said their interaction with the ward actually had improved following the establishment of the guardianship.

For most guardians in the sample, however, relationships with wards remained unchanged. In contrast to relationships with family members, which were more apt to have become strained, ties between guardians and their wards more often improved after the guardianship was established. A change in the relationship with the ward was independent of gender and family relationship of the guardian.

RESOURCES PREFERRED AND USED BY GUARDIANS

As caregivers, some guardians in the sample were in a position to need and want help from others. One of the types of assistance guardians requested was informal emotional support. Guardians were asked if they would like to have more persons with whom they could talk over the problems of their wards. About one-third of the guardians indicated they would appreciate having more opportunities to discuss the difficulties of their wards with others. Table 6.4 shows the preferences of guardians for further sources of support.

Table 6.4
Sources of Support Preferred by Guardians

Sources of Support	N[a]	Percent
Social service personnel to arrange services	45	27
Other family members	39	23
Counselor	34	20
Attorney	33	20
Other guardians	32	19
Representative of the court	27	15
Spouse	19	11
Close friends	18	11

[a] This table is based on multiple responses of guardians who indicated they would like more support. Percentages do not total 100 percent.

Guardians who would prefer more opportunity to discuss their ward's problems most often wanted more help from social services personnel, especially in arranging services for their wards. As noted earlier, almost one-quarter wanted more assistance from family members. About 20 percent would appreciate more assistance from counselors, attorneys, and other guardians. Few respondents, however, knew or had contact with other guardians. Representatives of the court were noted by 15 percent of the guardians as persons with whom they would like to discuss problems of their wards. Spouses and friends were less often identified as sources of support from which more help was desired. It is, of course, possible that these persons were already providing as much support as guardians felt they had a right to expect.

Nonrelatives more often than relatives allowed they would benefit by contact with others with whom to discuss their ward's condition. With the exception of counselors, most of the contact preferred by nonrelatives could be on an informal basis. Guardians who were nonrelatives (24 percent) especially preferred to have more conversations about their wards with close friends than did individuals who were relatives (8 percent; $X^2 = 6.60$, 1 df, $p < .01$). Nonrelatives also expressed more interest (35 percent) than relatives (17 percent) in talking with a counselor about their concerns ($X^2 = 4.49$, 1 df, $p < .05$). Nonrelatives somewhat more often than kin would like to discuss problems of their wards with other guardians (31 and 16 percent, respectively; $X^2 = 3.35$, 1 df, $p < .10$). Thus, nonrelatives particularly seemed in need of additional social support, much of which could have been informal. There were no significant differences between men and women in their preferences for further opportunities to discuss the care of their wards.

Explanation of the Duties of Guardianship

Guardians' lack of understanding of their role has been viewed as an impediment to assisting their wards effectively. In their unstructured comments about hardships of their role, guardians called attention to their need for information early in their experience as guardians. One guardian commented: "I believe before a person is given guardianship they should be fully informed of rights and obligations. . . . I had very little information to go on. . . . I'm smart enough to call around and ask for help. I can imagine some poor souls out there are really floundering."

Guardians were asked to identify who was most helpful in explaining the duties of a guardian to them. They chose among an attorney, the ward's court appointed attorney, the judge, the probate office staff, another guardian, and others (to be specified by them). Of these persons, attorneys were viewed as being most helpful by guardians (69 percent). Eight percent found the judge provided the most useful explanation of their duties, and the same percentage identified the efforts of the probate staff as most helpful. Some respondents named more than one of the groups of persons as being equally informative. For example, some identified both an attorney and the judge or the judge and the probate staff as most helpful; however, fewer than 5 percent of the guardians made these observations.

Other guardians rarely provided information about the expectations associated with the role (2 percent). In general, there was some agreement that it would have been helpful to have had more instruction about the expectations of guardians before becoming one. Indeed, in answer to a fixed-response question, almost half (48 percent) "agreed" or "strongly agreed" that some kind of additional information regarding the role of guardian would have been useful. As is noted in greater length in chapter 7, in the response to unstructured questions, guardians also observed they would have liked more training and greater explanation of their duties. One guardian allowed he had "learned by trial and error." Another commented: "No one has helped me; I'm winging it!" It was clear from their comments that additional information would have diminished role strain for several guardians.

Formal Community Services

Often it is suggested that provision and use of community-based services might preclude initiation of the guardianship procedure and serve as an alternative to the appointment of guardians. Indeed, attempts to implement the least restrictive alternative may involve use of one or more of the services listed in Table 6.5. Guardians were asked whether they had used the seven services before guardianship was awarded, after, before *and* after, or if they would have used them, had they been available.

Not surprisingly, there were differences in the services used prior to and after the guardianship was established. Home health care/visiting nurses were most often employed before a guardian was appointed. Indeed, prior to obtaining guardianship, home health care and visiting nurses were the most frequently used services, whereas adult day care was among the least often sought assistance. Nursing home care was obtained before and both before and after appointment of the guardian for about one-third of the wards. A little over 10 percent of the guardians continued their use of home health care and visiting nurses after the guardianship was awarded. There was also use of telephone reassurance by 12 percent both before and after establishing the guardianship.

For most of the guardians, availability of the seven services seemed adequate; no more than 7 percent indicated that they would have used a service if it had been available. Public legal aid and adult day care were most often cited as those services that would have been used more if they had been in place, but the percentages of guardians expressing interest in them were small. Perhaps if alternatives to guardianship had been implemented, the use of many of these services would have been even greater as they augmented other options in lieu of guardianship.

AWARDING OF GUARDIANSHIP: NEW TASKS OR OLD CHORES?

The guardianship process typically culminates with the guardian having significantly more control over the person and/or property of the ward than prior to the establishment of the ward-guardian relationship. As noted earlier, more than one-half of the guardians had substantial contact with the ward prior to the awarding of the guardianship, at least providing sufficient assistance for it to be a reason for their being given the task of protecting the elder. This raised the question of what the guardianship permitted individuals to do on behalf of their wards that they had not done previously. In chapter 5, we discussed the activities of guardians mandated by state statutes and those they engaged in to benefit their wards as noted in the annual reports. In this section we describe some of the activities that guardians indicated they were authorized to do following the establishment of the guardianship that they could not do before.

Guardians were asked: "What did being a guardian enable you to do for the ward that you were not able to do before you became a guardian?" Unstructured responses of guardians were coded into seven closely related categories. There were some combined categories (e.g., finances and health care) because guardians were allowed to undertake activities in more than

Table 6.5
Use and Projected Use of Services to Care for Wards

Services Used	Before		After		Both before and after		Would Have Used if Available	
	N	Percent	N	Percent	N	Percent	N	Percent
Home health care/visiting nurse	73	19	22	6	43	11	18	5
Nursing home care	19	5	135	35	124	32	8	2
Meals on Wheels	55	14	8	2	16	4	10	3
Telephone reassurance	52	13	14	4	47	12	16	4
Public legal aid	17	4	9	2	18	5	27	7
Transportation services for older person	26	7	17	4	28	7	18	5
Adult day care	9	2	11	3	16	4	26	7

one area by virtue of the guardianship or guardianship/conservatorship. As might be anticipated, the majority of the changes in activities related to either legal, financial, personal care, and medical matters, or a combination. Thus, decision making about the physical, financial, legal, and personal affairs of the ward encompassed most of the activities engaged in following the awarding of the guardianship.

Finances

Eighteen percent specifically mentioned taking care of and monitoring finances. The action taken ranged from caring for the individual's finances when the ward could not do so to protecting them from abuse by others, sometimes family members. For example: "The ward was losing money from her purse; she was unable to write checks or count her money too." "I handle the money and all assets so they will not be cheated by certain persons." "I had to stretch her funds to last as long as she did. I just made it too! She was 99." "It (the guardianship) helped me to see that my ward's income was spent on *her* and not used as income to others. Also it helped to preserve the estate—other family members bought her home for about one-third of its value!" "The guardianship helped me make certain she was not taken advantage of by family (distant nieces) and friends." "I had parties charged with theft and the courts got most of the money returned. It (the guardianship) kept other relatives from taking most of her other assets." Thus, guardians in this group especially emphasized finances and protection of assets from the abuse of others.

Finances and Health Care

One-fifth described how their efforts combined financial and physical care activities in ways that they could not have done prior to guardianship. For some, monitoring health care entailed oversight of a professional caregiver while for others it meant providing personal reassurance to the very frail along with financial assistance. For example: "It (the guardianship) helped to pay her bills and to take care of her health care." Another commented that it enabled the guardian to "legally see to her care and preserve her financial resources for her future needs." Additional comments include: "We were allowed to see to her physical and mental needs in addition to the financial needs. We (my brother and I) had been taking care of her as trustees." "I had to manage the monies. I had to see that she received medical help even if she did not want it." "I can be sure her money stretches as far as it can and can make sure of her personal and physical well-being." "I can now assist with finances, assist with medical management, and reassure the ward when he is fearful of death." For others, the guardianship enabled them to emphasize physical protection and to remove the individual from financial abuse. For example, one guardian was able to "ensure her safety and stop exploitation." The guardianship permitted one guardian to "handle financial affairs and keep the ward in a lock-up Alzheimer facility." Another said: "I can take complete responsibility for her welfare healthwise and financially."

One case in particular illustrates the combined financial, physical, and mental health functions that guardianship can permit a caregiver to undertake:

> I did find as my ward grew older that he became more suspicious of everyone—especially me. He kept complete control except for allowing me to write his checks, which he signed. Social Services became involved because he called them to report I was trying to run his life and tell him what to do. After investigating, the social worker insisted I apply for guardianship since his health was getting bad and he refused to see a doctor.

Events such as this related by guardians illustrate factors that prompted the request for guardianship, the roles of other institutions in initiating the petition, and the complexity of the tasks of caregivers before the establishment of guardianship.

Personal Care

Eighteen percent spoke of monitoring personal care, ensuring good care, making decisions about personal care, or assuring safety of the ward. For example, the guardianship enabled one guardian "to determine the best source of care for the ward." It permitted another "to see that she was properly cared for. I was already trustee of her assets." Other responses included: "I have made sure they were cared for properly and have kept people from taking advantage of them." "I was able to see that she was clean and had food to eat."

In a similar vein, another commented:

> [The guardianship assures] that I can make her life as pleasant as can be expected under the circumstances by making sure that all her needs are met physically as well as mentally. That she has everything she needs in clothing and personal products to keep her comfortable and looking well-groomed. Her well-being is number one with me.

The guardianship enabled another person to "place the ward in a skilled nursing home. She did not wish to go but for her safety and physical well-being it was necessary." Guardians in this group, then, felt the guardianship enabled them to ensure the ward's safety and well-being.

Authorization for Health Care

Another 10 percent mentioned specifically that consenting to or authorizing medical care and related decisions were actions they previously could not take. The guardianship made it possible for one respondent to "complete paperwork and make medical decisions." For others the guardianship included "consent for medical treatments and care," or having "a more direct 'say' in the final decisions re health care."

The 12 percent who indicated that with the guardianship they were able "to take charge of the situation" or "to get affairs in order" in a way they had not before were probably implying some financial, legal, and medical activities on behalf of their ward. One person said that basically she "attained control," adding: "My mom is very independent [mentally] and she wouldn't cooperate in various areas." At a general level, this group of guardians emphasized "taking control" and "taking charge" of a situation and seeing it through. For the most part, their comments tended to be somewhat vague and general as to the action they would take on behalf of the ward.

Legal Matters

Eight percent noted legal matters specifically as an area in which the guardianship enabled them to take action that they could not previously. Representative comments were: "I can sign legal documents." "I can make legal decisions without interference from the family." "I can legally take care of the estate." Legal authority and responsibility, however, were implicit in most of the categories of activities described above.

Burdens without Advantages

Finally, 12 percent noted the guardianship did not make it possible for them to do anything for the ward that they had not been able to do prior to the hearing and the decision. This group of respondents revealed frustration about both the lack of any new activities the guardianship enabled them to do on behalf of the ward and the added burdens that were not required previously. In fact, for some persons, circumstances after the guardianship was awarded were more difficult than before. What did the guardianship permit these respondents to do that they had not done previously? Among the comments: "Not one thing! I already had the responsibility—now it is more complicated! Lawyers and courts were more expensive." "Nothing, other than pay attorneys lots of money." "Nothing. It only became more complicated and more expensive in legal fees in order to file reports with the court." "Nothing specially. The courts required the guardianship." "I see no difference." "Nothing. It placed a burden by requiring financial reports every six months and requiring approval of the court to sell assets for care. I obviously resent the whole procedure of guardianship." "I did it all before although now I have to report to the court once a year." "Nothing, but at least I know what I do is legal."

Obviously, in most instances, the reason for a guardianship is to permit action on behalf of the ward that previously would not have been undertaken. There were two types of responses indicating that guardians could do nothing for the ward they had not done before. First, there was frustration on the part of those for whom no positive change had occurred with the establishment of the guardianship. Second, some experienced added burdens. Some of those for whom nothing had changed likely experienced less strain than guardians who recounted what they judged to be added obligations and hindrances.

SUMMARY AND CONCLUSIONS

Although most literature has focused on the legal process of establishing guardianship and the consequences of guardianship for wards, in this chapter we considered some of the characteristics and experiences of individuals who were appointed as guardians. We described how a group of individuals came to be selected as guardians, how they managed some problems, and the effect of guardianship on relationships with their ward and family members.

For many, family loomed large in the process of guardianship, whether by their presence or their absence, by their appreciation and agreeableness, or by their criticism and hostility. Comments on family ties ran the gamut from saying they were very supportive to "I felt unappreciated. No one else wanted the job, but they all had opinions about my performance."

Although families were important in determining the need for guardianship, a substantial proportion were not actively involved in selecting the specific guardian. In general, these guardians were not strangers to caregiving, and many had some responsibility for the care of the ward before their involvement in a formal protective service.

The majority of guardians seemed responsive to their wards and maintained close contact with them. In this way, guardianship resembled the frequency of interaction that occurs in other types of relationships between individuals and the aged. Communication difficulties on the part of the ward limited contact with them for a substantial minority of the guardians. Work and family obligations were also factors in limiting the amount of time persons might spend with their wards. Strain ensuing from work and family responsibilities is more completely described in chapters 7 and 8.

Much has been written about the preeminence of women in caregiving to the aged. There is also some evidence that when men and women care for others, they do so somewhat differently, and possibly with divergent personal outcomes (Dwyer & Coward, 1992). We found the circumstances of male and female guardians were quite comparable in the guardianship process. For example, they observed similar reasons for their selection as guardians, and they held comparable perceptions of the role of family members in the process of establishing guardianship. Furthermore, they cared for wards who had similar levels of capacity and similar levels of assets. Women, however, noted fewer interferences that precluded their contact with their wards, and they interacted with wards more frequently by phone or in person than did men. But men and women spent comparable amounts of time on guardianship duties. That guardianship is a formal and legalized form of caring may have accounted for some of the similarities in the experiences of men and women. A more formal process may not lend itself as readily to gendered caring. Moreover, much of the caring took place out of a family setting. Or by the time a ward is relatively incapacitated and cared for by others, any variability in masculine or feminine approaches to guardianship may be somewhat neutralized.

The tasks of guardianship for some would be easier with increased formal and informal support. One-third of the guardians would like to discuss some of their questions and problems with others. Social services personnel were most often identified as those from whom guardians would like to receive more help in arranging services and perhaps in case management. This preference, combined with the need for greater information about management of the guardianship process, suggests a possible point of intervention. In chapter 7, guardians identify specific types of assistance that would have made them more effective in their roles.

Having cared for the ward previously was the single most important factor in later appointment as a guardian, irrespective of a family relationship. It would have been tempting to conclude that because close family members (e.g., spouses, children) as well as more distant relatives were often guardians, the salience of prior assistance in later guardian selection would hinge on family ties. But prior caring was as important in the appointment of nonrelatives as it was for the selection of relatives. The significance of close friendship as a basis for selection of nonrelatives as guardians, however, was almost as important in the choice as prior provision of care to the ward. For these nonrelative guardians, close friendship may have been a surrogate for family ties. In chapter 7, the depth of friendship expressed by some of the guardians about their wards is evident: "She was my friend. I loved her." Such expressions of affection for wards were common and for several persons were a reason for undertaking the task of guardianship. In chapter 7, we learn more about the qualitative features of the ward-guardian relationship.

7

Themes of Meaning in the Guardianship Experience

In this chapter we consider individuals' unstructured descriptions of their experiences as guardians. In their own words, guardians expressed various meanings of guardianship. Our interpretation of the guardianship experience was based on accounts by those most involved in either direct or indirect care. Many guardians provided indirect care and ensured the ward received personal aid from others. The range of guardians' views was considerable. Perceptions of their involvement as guardians ranged from high satisfaction to manifest hostility and extreme dislike of the tasks. In between the extremes were those who construed and assessed the role of guardian primarily as being responsive to and empathetic with the one they served.

Individual responses to guardianship are the focus of this chapter and chapter 8. In these chapters, perspectives from social science provide a context in which to interpret the views of guardians. The useful frameworks were role strain and themes of meaning in caregiving. (Hasselkus, 1988; Voydanoff, 1988). Chapter 8 comprises two studies: a quantitative analysis of correlates of role strain, and the development of profiles of four types of guardians. Some of our queries about correlates of role strain originated from guardians' descriptions of their work contained in this chapter.

THE CONTEXT OF STRAIN: GUARDIANSHIP AS CAREGIVING

Researchers have examined extensively the influence of caring on the lives of those who care for the aged (Dwyer & Coward, 1992; Pearlin, Mullan, Semple, & Skaff, 1990; Walker, Martin, & Jones, 1992). Stress, role overload, and altered relationships have been especially salient. Caregivers, for example, have considerable financial and emotional strain as well as physical health problems (Clipp & George, 1990; Scharlach & Boyd, 1989; Zarit, Todd, & Zarit, 1986). Even so, individuals continue to provide a variety of types of assistance, ranging from transportation of an elder to 24-hour care.

The circumstances of guardianship, however, may differentiate it from other kinds of caregiving. Guardianship, as legalized caregiving, entails a formalized relationship established at a court hearing, more visible oversight, and greater monitoring than most other types of assistance to the aged. Guardians are required to make certain decisions for their elderly wards. Compared to informal caregiving, decisions and behavior of guardians are open to greater scrutiny. The heightened sense of visibility, perhaps more diverse expectations and enlarged duties, and a lack of information about the guardianship procedure may contribute to strain. Activities previously carried out with anonymity in the context of the family may be monitored and reviewed by others. Furthermore, guardianship entails finding of incapacity of the ward. Formal acknowledgment of incapacity of the ward by the court system may prove stressful for the ward and the guardian. Such a decision by the court involves a clear, formal role reversal, especially if the ward and guardian are parent and child. Thus, certain aspects of the unique activities required of guardians likely will generate strain particular to them, while other demands of guardians, such as those reflected in overload, may be similar to those following from responsibilities of other caregivers as well. From guardians' accounts in the questionnaire it was clear that many of them endured considerable strain as they tried to meet the needs of their wards.

Guardians' attitudes toward their tasks enabled us to speculate about the long reach of caring as it may have affected conceptions of their own lives as guardians and as aging persons. Some of the themes of meaning of caregiving described by Hasselkus (1988) were informative in thinking about the outcomes of guardianship.

THE MEANING OF CAREGIVING

In an ethnographic study, Hasselkus (1988) elicited information on the meaning of the family caregiving experience. Meaning referred to those "values, beliefs, and principles that people use to organize their behavior and to interpret their experience" (Hasselkus, 1988:686). Drawing on ethnographic interviews, Hasselkus described five themes of meaning in caregiving: sense of self, sense of managing, sense of fear and risk, sense of change in role and responsibility, and sense of the future. Themes of meaning typified shared experiences of those who cared for or who protected another. As they relate to guardianship, these themes may entail shifts in conceptions of the self, role strain from the management of the affairs of others, altered and perhaps unanticipated responsibilities, and fears for another and for one's future.

The values and beliefs that guided individuals in their tasks as guardians became clearer as they shared their views on the most difficult aspects of guardianship, positive features of their role, advice for others, and the influence of guardianship on their conceptions of aging. Using their comments, we observe in the following sections how their conceptions of themselves as guardians ranged from the altruistic and humanistic, to the strained, to the instrumental, and lastly to those who would reject the practice of guardianship. Finally, the chapter concludes with the contribution of guardianship to altered images of old age and of their own futures. Throughout, we see some of the beliefs and values guardians used to organize their behavior and to interpret their experiences as they assisted an elder.

HARDSHIPS OF GUARDIANS

Strains of guardianship were revealed in guardians' descriptions of the most difficult aspects of their role. Unstructured descriptions of the most difficult tasks of guardianship, as identified by the majority of guardians, formed five general themes: (1) observation of the deterioration of the ward, (2) management of the guardianship, (3) pressures of decision making, (4) time constraints, and (5) contentious family relationships.

Some of the most stressful aspects of the role emanated from direct contact with the ward or with the family and were reflected in themes such as observation of the decline of the ward and difficulties with family members. Other responsibilities and duties of the guardian role comprised several themes of hardship identified by guardians. These included responsibilities for decision making on behalf of another person, instrumental activities entailed in management of the guardianship, and time constraints. The themes are general and are identified for purposes of understanding the multiplicity of demands placed on guardians. There are no doubt instances of overlapping themes. For example, concern about deterioration of the ward may involve ongoing management by the guardian and finally, may entail grave and stressful decisions. And pressures of decision making are a part of the management of guardianship. Therefore, these categories of hardships of guardians were somewhat overlapping. Even so, we have attempted to enumerate and give examples of five general themes of guardianship strain.

Deterioration of the Ward

Seeing the deterioration of their ward was most frequently mentioned as the greatest difficulty guardians felt in performing their roles (25 percent;

Table 7.1
Hardships of Guardians

Hardships	N	Percent
Deterioration of the ward	78	25
Management of guardianship	61	19
Pressures of decision making	57	18
Time constraints	49	16
Contentious family relationships	29	9
Other (e.g., distance from ward, lack of caring by ward)	26	8
No hardships	17	5

see Table 7.1). Personal contact with wards, some of whom were friends, was especially troubling. One commented, "The visits are sad and depressing." For some, the frequency of visits was affected by deterioration of the ward: "Seeing the decline of a former very smart person is my situation. Just visiting as much as I'd like, but getting depressed when I do visit [is the hardest part]." Among the comments about the ward's deterioration as the most troublesome aspect of guardianship: "Our ward was the most intelligent person I have met. It is hard to see her in the condition as she is now." "Becoming attached to an ill person is difficult when the prognosis is not good." "Seeing the mind and the health go is so difficult." Clearly, some of the behavior of guardians was in response to illness or disability and not guardianship or age per se.

As noted earlier, deterioration often affected friendships, but for some it changed spousal relationships: "I am guardian for my wife; she has Alzheimer's. To see her get worse as time goes by is difficult. She doesn't know me any more." Parent-child relationships also were altered by changes in a ward's condition: "After years of mom's caring for us kids, we now care for her because she is like a child who will never learn for herself to meet life's basic needs."

Some described the procedure of having a parent declared incapacitated or committed to an institution as most difficult. A male guardian commented: "Committing dad was the hardest part." Another observed that "having to testify in open court regarding mother's mental confusion" was very difficult. "Going through the process of having my father declared incompetent was hardest. It should have been done a year before but I didn't want to take his freedom away from him." This formal, very public, and perhaps somewhat shameful declaration of the passage of a parent's capacity was especially painful.

The death of siblings impacted care of some wards and was in the thoughts of their present caregivers. "Seeing her [the ward's] slow decline and the loss of her sister who had taken good care of her" was for one respondent the hardest part of being a guardian.

For others, contending with deterioration of a magnitude that required nursing home care was the most difficult aspect of being a guardian. One respondent, for example, said that "in our case, the fact that we had to put our ward in a nursing home" was the hardest thing about being a guardian. Whereas some were saddened by "memories of better times," others told of a bleak future that included "facing the decision of when the ward can no longer function individually and must be placed in a nursing home." Moreover, the intensity with which guardians experienced their decisions about nursing home placements lingered. One of the most poignant tasks was a parent's placement of a child in a nursing home. A female guardian recalled that "having my son in a nursing home rather than being in our own home" was hardest; "At 85 years, I cannot give him full-time care." This also points to the special circumstances of the very old who may be guardians of the young old or those in midlife.

Helplessness of the guardian to forestall decline of the ward was a hardship. Some guardians said that "watching her go downhill" and "the feeling of being helpless as you see the ward deteriorate" was hardest. Another comment: "First and foremost were the feelings of helplessness in seeing the ward's condition, both physical and mental deteriorate continuously and inexorably and not being able to help or stop it."

Other guardians were able to describe the speed of deterioration: "My ward has been one of my very best friends for about 20 years. She was a very articulate and intelligent woman and since the onset of her illness, she seems to be going downhill fast." Thus, observing deterioration, feeling helpless, and taking action that would deprive individuals of freedom and alter their previous relationship were among the most frequently identified hardships of guardianship. Men and women did not differ appreciably in their propensity to find deterioration of the ward as the most troublesome aspect of guardianship (27 and 23 percent, respectively).

Of course, hardship created by deterioration of the care recipient is not the exclusive purview of guardians. The nature of the care recipient's disability is a determinant of outcomes for those who care regardless of whether they are guardians. Cognitive impairment, for example, undermines previous relationships between spouses more than physical impairment (Stoller, 1992). In comparison to other caregivers, however, the magnitude of deterioration as well as the public declaration of incapacity are likely to be especially marked burdens for guardians. In the estimation of their guardians, both cognitive and physical impairment were prevalent conditions of the majority of the wards studied.

Management of Guardianship

Almost one-fifth of the respondents found management of the guardianship to be the most burdensome of all tasks (Table 7.1). These individuals identified the most difficult aspects of guardianship as completing the paperwork, keeping records, and getting the necessary information to negotiate the court system.

Sometimes difficulties were not directly related to requirements of the court system, however. For example: "Getting all her assets together was hardest—getting seven years of back taxes done for her with no records." Maintaining records needed to file periodic reports for the court was singled out as a difficulty by some. For others, "Medicare and insurance claims and getting the paperwork from those who have provided service" had been hardest. Additional comments: "Negotiating the bureaucracy was the most difficult." "Keeping track of and paying all medical bills, filling out insurance papers and keeping track of everything I spent on her for the monthly court report." "Having to fill out a form once yearly and account for every penny to state authorities." But sometimes management practices, misunderstandings, and responses of others contributed to hardships. For example, one guardian said the hardest part was "being called a thief when her money had run out and the money in question was from my pocket—that could have been used to good advantage for my small children."

For others, difficulties with management of guardianship could sometimes be attributed to limited information about duties, unclear expectations, and a lack of knowledge of the means to attain them. In turn, some persons felt inadequate; for these guardians the hardest part was a "lack of support mechanisms. There was no one to talk to or consult with. This and the unpredictability of events contributed to feelings of inadequacy." In addition, the highly visible nature of guardianship and the periodic monitoring contributed to feelings of insecurity. One guardian commented: "Feeling alone and subject to legal repercussions and worries about the judge's opinions on expenditures are difficult."

Whereas attorneys were identified as most helpful in explaining the duties of guardians (chapter 6), sometimes guardians wanted more complete and timely information from their legal counsel and the court staff. Indeed, 20 percent of the guardians mentioned attorneys specifically as individuals from whom they would have preferred to have had more information. A guardian commented that one of the hardest things was "finding out from the attorney at the zero hour what must be ready for the court. The attorney said in passing, you are entitled to a fee, but never said what it was." Other comments about problems with lawyers: "Having to wait for the court [judge] to approve everything I did." "Having to deal with the probate court and watching lawyers make several thousand dollars a year for nothing." "We never heard a word from the court-appointed lawyer, so we got all our advice from a lawyer friend who was furious because we got no help!"

Still others believed their problems were heightened by agency regulations and practices. "Dealing with social services and other institutions" was hardest for one respondent. "They do not tend to be very cooperative. They would not give information in writing but wanted to give information verbally and face to face. Handling things face to face caused me to miss so much work." (This individual would not be a guardian again because of this hardship.) Others too would have benefited from more information and assistance from professionals: "After we were appointed by the court the social worker never came again."

Guardians commented on the need to monitor their ward's placement in a nursing home as the most difficult aspect of guardianship. One observed: "Overseeing the nursing home responsibility to the patient was hardest. The nursing home responds to complaints by referring to minimum requirements and inspections of nursing homes—prearranged, and the follow-through is terrible." Another described his greatest difficulty as "trying to make sure she got proper medical care in a nursing home setting. She didn't."

The absence of training and the need for it were recognized by some guardians. "My lack of training" was one of the greatest problems. A middle-aged male guardian commented: "I was given very little training and I am sent a financial form one time per year and no one cares or asks (except you) what I might be feeling or what I might be thinking." The need for increased efforts to train guardians has been noted by those interested in improving the functioning of the guardianship system (Schulte, 1989).

Pressures of Decision Making

In the transition from autonomy to dependency, decision making by the ward or on behalf of the ward is an activity that often is altered. Care that is given will be contingent on and adjusted to varying amounts of dependency (Cicirelli, 1992). Dependency is the basis for the adjudication of incapacity and the subsequent care give by a guardian, including decision making.

Eighteen percent of the guardians identified pressures emanating from the need to make decisions on behalf of the ward as their greatest difficulty. Men and women regarded the demands of decision making somewhat differently: 13 percent of the men acknowledged it as their greatest hardship, compared to 21 percent of the women. Some literature suggests that women have greater involvement in care for the most dependent aged (Montgomery, 1992). In chapter 6, however, we noted that the condition of the wards cared for by men and women did not differ. It is possible, of course, that patterns of decision making and worry about them are gender-linked. Women may regard decisions about the care of the ward as somewhat more stressful than do men.

Some of the most difficult aspects of decision making involved issues of health, life, and death: "Making decisions about her health situation—how much life support to continue or increase when the quality of her life is as bad as it is was very hard." "Knowing I may have to make a difficult medical decision which will terminate my ward's life." "To tell the doctor that my father was a 'no code' if his heart stops." "In the very last days of my mother's life, signing to have life support taken off was hard. This was done on the advice of her doctors, and I knew it was right but still it was very difficult." As noted earlier, testifying about a ward's mental health often implied a decision about the future of the ward as well; for example, one guardian said that "having to testify in open court regarding mother's mental confusion" was a great hardship.

The extent of dependency reflected in the magnitude of decision making also took its toll on some—"Knowing that you are responsible *all of the time* for one who is completely dependent on another person." For some guardians, the most difficult aspect of decision making involved knowing the preferences of the incapacitated but having to act counter to them: "having to do things that you know if they were in their 'right mind' they would not want done." Others were troubled by efforts to anticipate what the ward would have done if he or she had the capacity. Anticipating the ward's decision had he or she been capable of making "correct" judgments was graphically expressed as a burden. "Thinking for your ward and making their decisions the way you think they would if they could"; "Wanting to do my very best for the ward"; "Not knowing if all of the decisions I make are the correct ones for my loved one"; and "Making decisions about what is best for the ward as well as what they would do if they could make the decision" were among the strains of guardianship. Neither "substituted judgment" nor "the best interests of the ward" were easy concepts to implement.

The pressure of total decision making as the greatest hardship of guardianship was well summarized by these comments: "You have to think for the ward." "Having responsibility for making decisions for another person—in effect living their lives for them was hardest." There also was immense concern about making the "right" decisions, while hoping that the guardians did a good job as they "took control of the life of another."

Time Constraints

As noted in chapter 8, availability of time, and perhaps subsequent overload if tasks of caring exceed the time available, as well as the lack of role clarity are among the cornerstones of role strain theory. Time constraints, in one form or another, loomed large and were the greatest hardships of guardianship for a little less than one-fifth (16 percent) of the sample. Expressions of strain emanating from the allocation of time ranged from feeling that guardianship interfered with other aspects of life to perceptions of guilt because of time constraints. A most extreme reflection on the interface between duties as a guardian and other aspects of life was vividly noted: "You have no personal life!" Others said that "demanding my time worrying about the ward" was an interference, or that "finding time" was the biggest problem, or that the guardian role was "confining." Still others emphasized the unmitigated strain: "There is the constant pressure of responsibility for someone who is totally incompetent."

In between the individuals who expressed irritation at the interference from guardianship and those who felt guilt because they did not do more were individuals who described many demands from work and family. Comments include: "Finding the time to do the work (for the guardianship) while maintaining my own job, family etc. was hardest." "Time is a problem; I have a full-time job and a family to care for." "Time is the biggest hindrance; I work full-time and have a family." "Time—working full-time and family demands just spread a person too thin. I feel like a rubber band stretched to the breaking point." A male guardian said that "thinking I may be taking too much time away from my own family of four" was the most difficult aspect of guardianship. Others noted the time spent on worry, the record keeping for guardianship, and time spent in travel if wards were located a distance away from the guardian. For example, one guardian said that "worry, time spent on paperwork, and traveling 1,100 miles to visit and tend to her needs" were the greatest obstacles.

Some individuals specifically noted occupational and personal costs. For example: "Taking care of the ward's needs without harming my business was hardest. The time away cost me jobs and accounts." The life of another guardian was shaped enormously by her caring role:

> I quit a job to stay at home with father. I missed the contact with peers and the 'hustle and bustle.' I also found it very hard to be responsible for someone else. I never had children—never married—never wanted to. It was very hard to switch roles with father.

Feelings of guilt were troublesome for some guardians. Distance or institutionalization sometimes enhanced feelings of guilt and made the relationship between ward and guardian less comfortable: "Being able to reassure her she is not alone and keep her from being lonely is a problem. I sometimes feel guilty that I can't have her at home with me." "I felt guilty that I did not have time or energy to make the trip to see the ward." "There are feelings of guilt for not doing as much for my ward as I should have."

Despite gender differences in caring observed in the literature, and popular conceptions of women's conflicts between paid work and family activities, men and women were equally likely to identify time constraints and subsequent strain as their greatest difficulty. Even though female guardians spent more time with their wards, it was not reflected in their perceptions of overload as a difficulty in their role. Time constraints as the primary hardship of guardianship distressed men and women comparably.

Contentious Family Relationships

In reflecting on the greatest difficulties of guardianship, 9 percent described pressures emanating from interaction with family, complaints from family, or neglect by the family. More women (12 percent) than men (5 percent) spoke of constraints and intrusion from family members.

These respondents described various forms of interference from family members as the most difficult thing about being a guardian: "Having family members trying to tell you to do this and that when you were doing the best that you could while not fully understanding what a guardian was or what it meant." "I received much harassment by phone from three sisters of the ward who wanted to change residency to another nursing home nearer them. I was treated with discourtesy from the family." "Dealing with her [the ward's] relatives." "She [the ward] was their main topic of conversation whenever I was around and they made unreasonable demands." "Putting up with relatives." "There was constant complaining [by family]—distrust of me, which was constantly available to her [the ward] by phone." Another noted: "There were accusations and lies about me by family members." There was the "worry about whether you are satisfying other members of the family by what you are doing." For one respondent the greatest difficulty was "the dissension among some distantly related family members about my being named guardian and conservator and the battle they waged—pointlessly and unsuccessfully to take over those duties."

Specific decisions by the guardian often evoked negative responses from family members. One guardian said the hardest thing was "putting up with my sister and sister-in-law's criticism when I could no longer care for her [the ward]. She could not walk well, bathe, or dress herself."

Demoralization was often the outcome of contentious family relationships and a strained relationship with the ward. This view was summarized by a 46-year-old female guardian: "The most difficult thing about guardianship was disagreements with my siblings over the care of the ward and feeling unappreciated by the ward; no one else wanted the job, but they all had opinions on my performance!"

Thus, disagreement and conflict with family members primarily stemmed from disparate expectations for the role of the guardian among relatives of the ward and/or the guardian, complaints from family about performance, and for some, distrust among relatives. These comments from guardians support Iris's (1988) conclusion that family history and interpersonal dynamics impact the outcomes of the guardianship process, including future family relationships. Greater role strain fostered by family dissonance especially plagued female more than male guardians.

These, then, were among the greatest hardships of guardianship. Five percent of the individuals, however, noted they found nothing hard about being a guardian. Some of those who managed their guardianship with ease regarded it as an exchange for earlier favors or an expression of love. "I found nothing hard about my job. It was a very small thing to do for someone who spent his 'good' days earlier in life doing his best for me." Another said, "There was nothing hard about it because I loved this person." Men, however, were more likely than women to find nothing difficult about guardianship (8 and 4 percent, respectively). As established earlier, the differences in perceptions of difficulty by men and women were not attributable to variation in their ward's condition. We observed in chapter 6 that women spent more time, either personally or by phone, with their wards. This closer contact and women's greater reluctance to let anything interfere with their contact with the ward may have enhanced their perception of difficulty in the guardian role. For the most part, though, men and women described similar hardships in their roles as guardians.

BENEFITS OF GUARDIANSHIP

The hardships of guardians noted in the earlier section were not experienced independently of benefits and satisfactions. Indeed, the majority of guardians described hardships but also enjoyed benefits and satisfactions. It is not unusual to find high levels of satisfaction with caring accompanied by elevated amounts of stress (Miller, 1989; Walker, Shin, & Bird, 1990). In research on family caregiving, two explanations have been suggested for the presence of high satisfaction and high stress among some individuals. One suggestion is that accomplishment of a difficult and stressful task such as caregiving may be satisfying in its own right (Miller, 1989). The successful accomplishment of tasks, even though stressful, may provide satisfaction. Another interpretation of this counterintuitive relationship is that greater involvement and perhaps greater stress may diminish feelings of guilt and contribute to increased satisfaction (Noelker & Townsend, 1987). In the earlier section, we observed that guilt was a factor in the hardships described by some guardians.

Table 7.2
Benefits of Guardianship

	N	Percent
Opportunities to help another	159	49
Personal gratification	91	28
Legal and financial oversight	36	11
No positive features	34	11
Other	3	1

To understand the benefits of guardianship, individuals were asked to discuss some of the positive things about being a guardian. Despite their sometimes graphic descriptions of the hardships of guardianship, guardians found many benefits from their roles as well. Views of guardians about the positive aspects of their work were grouped into the general types shown in Table 7.2. These benefits were categorized as: personal gratification, the opportunity to help another, and protection of the financial and legal concerns of the ward. Some found no positive features of guardianship.

Personal Gratification and the Opportunity to Help Another

Expression of feelings of personal gratification from helping someone and a view of guardianship as an opportunity to improve the care and subsequently the life of another were the two most frequently noted benefits. Over one-quarter of the guardians described examples of personal gratification derived from assisting a ward, while half of the guardians spoke more specifically of opportunities to help another person. Sometimes opportunities to assist were an occasion for repayment of prior aid or favors received from the ward. In some instances, it was difficult to distinguish between the two categories, that is, personal gratification from service and gratitude for an opportunity to see to the best interests of the ward. Seeing to the best interests of the ward often involved ensuring that care was improved.

Personal gratification sometimes reflected feelings of being needed, as in the following comments: "Guardianship satisfies the altruistic needs of the guardian and provides educational experiences and serves the community." "Feeling I am doing a good deed." "I felt good doing this (guardianship)." "I could love and care for her (the ward)." "You feel needed." Some wards responded well to their guardians, and the latter benefited accordingly. For example: "I enjoy him!" "The ward's positive reactions to my visits were rewarding, especially when I brought my family." An active response from a ward contrasted with experiences of guardians whose wards neither knew nor cared what was being done for them.

Some guardians evaluated their benefits with reference to the magnitude of the need: "To be able to help when it was badly needed is a benefit to me." Further illustrative comments were: "Feeling that I am meeting an important need and sometimes being able to protect the ward from exploitation." "Being able to provide love during a time of need." "The feeling of being able to help a friend in need." In addition, "the feeling you are helping someone who cannot help themselves" and "the knowledge you are helping someone who can't help himself/herself" were noted as benefits. Another guardian said that "knowing you are helping someone who is unable to make decisions affecting their lives" was gratifying.

Closely related to direct statements about benefits of personal gratification were observations about positive consequences for guardians when they "saw to the best interests of the ward" or arranged for improved care. For example, ensuring that the wards were not exploited or knowing that they were well cared for translated into benefits for the guardians. Almost one-half of the guardians found satisfaction in knowing the ward was protected and in many instances better cared for than before.

Sometimes guardianship was seen as the end of victimization: "It gives me peace of mind that the ward is being properly cared for and not in a position to be taken advantage of." Another guardian commented: "She is a very close friend and I didn't like to see her being treated as her children were treating her. This is not what is happening now and physically she appears better."

For others, whose wards may not have been exploited earlier, there was also peace of mind and a sense of closure about their care: "For me, I knew for sure my sister was being taken care of and loved." "I know someone is better off because of me—not many can say that. I can help him help himself, watch him gain." "I felt good knowing that I made her last four years of life a little better. She was my good friend and I loved her." Finally, a female guardian, age 26, found the greatest benefit in "knowing that my ward is in capable and caring hands with me as his guardian. It gives me a sense of security and safety for him. (Rather than his having a guardian that he is unfamiliar with or who is unfamiliar with him.)"

That several guardians drew comfort from the current circumstances of their wards was evident; for these guardians, "the accomplishment of what was best for the ward" was the most positive part. "I believe he was being taken care of the best I could possibly do. No one else was willing to do this for him."

Some guardians were more specific in articulating the aspects of care that gratified them. For example: "My ward has regular meals, health care, baths, and a clean home." "I know they are taking care of him as best as he can be. They (the caregivers) can anticipate his needs." "At least I know she is taken care of and has enough to eat." "I have the satisfaction of knowing she will have attention from the nursing home." "I know he is getting the care I feel he should have. I have the power to change it if it is unsatisfactory."

Some developed a closer relationship with their wards. As was related in chapter 6, if changes occurred in relationships of wards and guardians, they were usually positive. One described the most positive aspect of guardianship for him as "bonding with the ward, a feeling that there is someone protecting the ward and advocating for her." Others found satisfaction in giving "love to people, some who have not experienced it." "I feel I am honest and fair and in so being have the opportunity to make her remaining years comfortable and stretch her money as far as it will go. There is no family." This is an illustration of the suggestion in chapter 6 that friends who become guardians may serve as surrogate family members. Another commented, "It is both a joy and privilege to serve in such a responsible position as to help transform the quality of life of those often more frail, neglected, and at risk."

Included in the description of gratification and beneficial outcomes were perceptions of equity and exchange. It was observed that guardianship provided people an opportunity to repay a relative or friend for previously rendered services or help. "He spent his good days earlier doing his best for me!" "This person had been like a father to me most of my life." For some, then, serving their wards was not without reward: "Wards give love and affection." The hoped-for equity extended into the future:"I know my time is coming; I hope my kids will take care of me." Indeed, parents were often the recipients of the exchange. For example: "It was the last thing I could do for my father. He had always helped me and I appreciated the chance to help him." For another guardian the greatest benefit was "being with mom. She took care of me so I just returned her love." Another noted, "It was a comfort to know I would be giving mother her wish to be with me. We always were very best friends and had a close relationship."

For some, friendship was the basis of the exchange: "The ward had helped me years before, so I wanted to help her." "The ward and I had been the best of friends for 20 years; she is very articulate and intelligent." "I could help her who helped me in the past." For some friends, guardianship was an opportunity to reciprocate earlier assistance and to attain closure on a relationship. A 65-year-old female guardian summarized it well: "I finally feel that I have been able to repay her [the ward] for her many kindnesses over the years. She really paid in advance for my help now."

These, then, were features of some of the benefits and personal gratification derived from helping others and improving their care.

Legal and Financial Oversight

Eleven percent of the guardians found special benefits from being able to handle the legal and financial affairs of the ward (Table 7.2). Male and female guardians differed little in finding the legal and financial aspects of guardianship as the greatest benefit (13 and 10 percent, respectively).

One guardian, for example, said the greatest benefit was to have "accurate record keeping, bills paid on time, bank accounts balanced, and deposits made promptly." Another mentioned "being able to see that her finances were safeguarded for her personal care." Others spoke of the more general advantages of their authority, such as having the "authority to advocate for one who cannot exercise his rights." "No one questions my authority to act on his behalf." "If the ward becomes very ill, it won't be a hassle trying to get medical and financial things done." Another respondent said the guardianship "provided stability in handling financial/legal matters. It provided continuity of care for the ward. It relieved other family members from worry." Finally, one guardian found this as his greatest benefit: "I could do things for her without worrying her."

The Absence of Benefits

Whereas some individuals experienced no hardships, other guardians were unable to think of any positive aspects of guardianship. Indeed, 11 percent found nothing positive in their experience of caring for the ward. Although they were in the minority, those who could find no benefits to their role as guardian were clear about their negative views. Two guardians noted, "There are no 'positives'!" and "It's an obligation to the ward, and I hate all of it!" When asked about the benefits of guardianship, still another commented: "None! It cost the estate over $5,000 in legal fees to file reports covering care of the ward." Another noted he was misinformed about the process: "Nothing (positive about guardianship). I was misinformed and inadequately informed by legal counsel." Persons expressing these thoughts were often angry about the entire experience of guardianship and would not be guardians again.

There were few differences in the benefits derived from guardianship by men and women. Men were a little more likely to mention personal gratification than were women (31 percent compared to 26 percent), while women (52 percent) found somewhat greater rewards in seeing to the interests of the ward than did men (45 percent). Men and women also were much alike in finding no benefits from their efforts on behalf of their ward (10 and 11 percent, respectively). Therefore, any advantages that accrued from performance of the duties of a guardian for the most part were quite comparable for these men and women.

ADVICE FROM GUARDIANS

Guardians were asked: "If you could give advice to others who are or will be guardians, what would your advice be?" With the exception of one guardian who said, "That is a legal question and I would give advice only for a fee," the vast majority of persons who were queried provided suggestions for fellow caregivers. Their advice ranged from an affective and humanistic focus, to highly instrumental suggestions, to the recommendation not to be a guardian. We discuss advice offered in five general areas: (1) compassionate and practical admonitions, (2) management of guardianship, (3) anticipated role strain, (4) professional expertise, and (5) alternatives to guardianship.

Compassionate and Practical Admonitions

The largest group of guardians (29 percent) gave advice about how to think and act, and advocated compassion, calmness, and patience. Men and women were equally likely to give compassionate admonitions. The advice of the compassionate contrasted with those who addressed the more specific instrumental and managerial aspects of guardianship, described in the next section.

Advice categorized as compassionate included admonitions based on religious tenets. For example, a 75-year-old male commented, "It is our Christian duty to help the less fortunate and it is most gratifying." Another paraphrased the Golden Rule; "Do for the person as you would want a person to do for you." Still another asked that guardians "treat the person and their caregivers as you would like to be treated in the same position." Another advised, "Put yourself in the ward's position. Would you like you as a guardian? Do for them what you would expect for yourself—the very best!"

A second group emphasized love, both given and received by guardians: "Guardians can receive more affection than they will know from their wards. They give love." "Volunteer with love." "You have to love the one whom you are guardian of." "Be a loving caregiver." "Administer care and duties with love and respect for that person's dignity."

Patience and tolerance were called for by several. A male guardian, age 42, urged: "Be patient, this is a thankless job; someone has to do it." Other comments included: "Patience." "Be human and accept other people as they are. Be patient. Have feelings." "Be understanding, have compassion, and be willing to be very patient." "Learn to be patient and giving—put yourself last!"

Some advised kindness and helpfulness: "Be kind. You could end up the same way." "Don't try to do what you want but only what is best for the ward." "Be as helpful as you can." "Keep calm, cool, and collected; be thankful you can help." "Gain the confidence and trust of your ward and strive to the utmost to be worthy of it." "If you have plenty of room, keep the ward in your home and make him/her a part of your life."

There were others who urged common sense along with other virtues: "Be practical, use good judgment and common sense, and above all be kind, loving, and compassionate." Some admonished guardians that there would be difficult times: "Have much patience. There is much time and effort involved—many times on a moment's notice. You can become tired and discouraged, but you cannot give up!" And in another vein, one advised, "Relax, don't have a cow!"

Guardians also were urged to look ahead and anticipate the tasks of guardianship as well as to remember when their ward was different. For example: "Build a bond of love and confidence with elders before guardianship becomes an issue." Another noted, "Remember the person's feelings for you before they lost their capabilities and their personality changed." Still others urged that persons become guardians to provide opportunities for psychic benefits to the ward: "Do it. For the minimal responsibility you actually have, the trust and security your ward feels is more than worth it."

About 8 percent of the guardians gave admonitions specifically mentioning action to meet the needs of the ward and to maximize his or her welfare: "Take the responsibility and do the best job you can for the welfare of your ward." "Take care of the ward as you would yourself or your own child." The guardian as a protector was emphasized by some: "All decisions you make can be positive and rewarding for that person; know all you can about what interests that person. Stay in close contact, protect them in all ways." "Guard and protect the abilities and desires of the person cared for." "Try to keep the ward in usual and customary residence and schedules. Make things as simple as possible with as little negative interference as possible from others." Male and female guardians did not differ in their tendency to give these types of advice.

Management of Guardianship

Several of the guardians gave pragmatic, instrumental suggestions for managing guardianship (18 percent). Instrumental suggestions were offered equally by men and women.

Without noting specific tasks, some recommended taking action quickly. For example: "Take charge!" "Don't wait until it has to be done on an emergency basis." Another acknowledged how delay might be linked with psychological responses to the ward: "Do not wait too long to take action.

Attempt to realistically separate the needs of the actual situation from your emotional attachment to the ward. In my case the ward is my mother who hates all nursing homes." Another suggested obtaining the wishes of the ward early on: "If you have family members (in-laws also) who may disapprove for petty reasons, have your ward make a tape stating her wishes or have a letter signed by the ward and witnessed while the ward has a good mental condition."

Some mentioned specific tasks guardians might undertake; often these suggestions took the form of increasing levels of information or knowledge about the process of guardianship. They emphasized gathering significant amounts of information early on in the process: "Do more research ahead of time." "Find out all of your rights as a guardian. I am still finding out." "Find out more about your job. Have an understanding of things as best you can." "Go to the library and do a lot of research. Try to go on the offensive from the beginning to squash any opposition." "Get all of your important papers signed and do not believe relatives." "Be sure you understand what you are agreeing to!" "Make sure you are able to fulfill all of your obligations and understand what they consist of. Don't expect any glory!" These guardians advocated advance planning and information gathering.

Other guardians mentioned specific areas in which more information would have been helpful: "Learn Medicare procedures. Don't be so intimidated by the medical profession!" "Prepare for it with information in advance if at all possible. Contact the Alzheimer's Society for information, if appropriate." One guardian pointed out potential troublesome legal and financial issues: "The (state) courts are most insulting and most disagreeable when auditing books. Also the money belongs to the ward but the ward or guardian can't spend anything until there is court approval (1–2 months)."

Another group of guardians addressed their management tasks by focusing on record keeping and compensation: "Save every receipt you get for things you purchase for your ward. Keep clear books." "Be sure you have an arrangement to be compensated fairly. If there is a fairly large estate, it is a lot of work." One person combined advice about record keeping and potential life strain ensuing from the amount of time required: "Keep an accurate record of the time and expenses and be prepared to put your own life on hold."

Others had suggestions for dealing with organizations and family members to improve conditions of the ward: "Make sure the facility (if applicable) keeps you updated on all phases of the ward's health as well as making sure the ward is receiving all he/she needs to live as comfortably as possible." Another commented about the welfare of wards in nursing homes that "it may improve the ward's care if you show an interest in it." In conclusion, guardians whose advice encompassed the management of guardianship contrasted with the expressive emphases of the previous group. Those who advised about management of guardianship recommended action, research, education, and planning.

Anticipated Role Strain

Another group commented especially on the time constraints guardians may face (14 percent). Women gave somewhat more advice about role strain and time constraints (17 percent) than did men (11 percent). Portions of this advice grow out of some of the hardships described in an earlier section. Many focused on the amount of time required and conflict between work and family: "I found this to be a very stressful time in my life." "It's a lot of work and worry and not for everyone." "It is too much responsibility if you lead a busy life as I do." Some equated guardianship with parenting: "It's like having children—a lot of responsibility." "It takes a lot of time like having another child." "It is a bigger job than one would anticipate."

Others spoke of the extensive amounts of time and the intrusiveness of the interruption. "Prepare for a long-term commitment—7 days a week—24 hours a day!" "Be prepared to have a lot of your time taken up by the guardianship." "Be prepared for a semipermanent volunteer nonpaying job." "Give much thought to the fact it is a huge responsibility." "Have lots of time, patience, and a car!" "If the ward is in an institution and you are dealing with Social Security, most of the contact will be during working hours. It can cause conflict with work." But the allocation of time was not without benefit. "It is a lot of work at times but also very rewarding."

Earlier in this chapter pressures of decision making were identified as one of the most difficult aspects of guardianship. Therefore, it is not surprising that advice would address the uncertainties of decision making as a component of strain in the guardian role. One guardian commented: "You will have to make some very tough decisions about someone else's life and care. Talk with others, it will help with the feelings of guilt and anxiety. It's not an easy job!" Some of the persons who cautioned about the amount of time required for guardianship duties also warned, "Be sure you have the time to devote to this and that you are willing to make the decisions that have to be made."

While they commented on time constraints, some guardians alluded to the extreme amount of work with minimal or no reimbursement: "Plan on a lot of work and no thanks. The lawyer gets paid for a lot of work I've had to do. Plus he gets paid a lot more." "Be prepared for frustration and excessive legal expense even if you are trying to take care of a parent who cannot take care of him or herself."

Wards were not always grateful for the assistance of their guardians. A guardian warned, "Be sure you can take abuse from the ward." Another advised, "Be prepared to endure negative comments and attitudes. Believe strongly in what you are doing. The guardianship responsibility must be a key priority in your life."

Some cautioned about serving as a guardian for a family member: "Being a guardian is a large responsibility. Do not be a guardian for a family member especially if they live with you." Other advice: "Don't be one for a family member or a close friend." "Make sure community resources are there to meet the ward's need before agreeing to accept a guardianship." Only one person remarked on the importance of knowing the ward well: "I don't think I could be a guardian for someone that I did not know well."

Professional Expertise

The advice of 13 percent of the guardians was to secure professional assistance, and men and women did not differ in this recommendation. Guardians were most frequently urged to seek professional help from attorneys. In the previous chapter, attorneys were cited frequently as being most helpful in explaining the duties of a guardian. And a substantial minority of guardians would have liked to have talked over their ward's problems with attorneys more often.

When guardians gave advice, however, attorneys were maligned, recommended, and commended. Guardians commented: "Have a first-class attorney. Keep an accurate record of all monies spent." "Have an attorney who has knowledge of the probate court. Expect rejection by the ward." "Get special legal help." "See your lawyer first before you are railroaded by the county social worker." Others were more guarded: "Be cautious of lawyers. They are greedy and could care less. You can do a lot without me." One person suggested assistance from court staff: "Speak in depth with a probate staff person and get to know your ward well." On balance, guardians were more positive than negative about their interaction with attorneys and legal staff.

Recommended expertise was not restricted to legal matters: some advised psychological counseling. "I would talk to a counselor for guidance and for someone to talk out frustrations. Also, I would follow my own heart and do what I feel is best not what other people want you to do."

Alternatives to Guardianship

Earlier it was observed that the majority of guardians had not considered alternatives to guardianship. A minority of guardians (8 percent), however, advised others not to seek guardianship. This advice was of two types. Most of these guardians suggested alternatives, while others recommended rejection of involvement of any sort. Representative advice from those presenting alternatives to guardianship was: "Don't do it. It is not necessary and benefits only the lawyers." "Have none at all. An attorney can do it better." "Get a power of attorney. Don't waste estate funds on attorneys and court costs. (I'm in the legal profession.)" "Obtain a durable power of attorney with joint checking, etc. and do not go through an expensive conservatorship/guardianship." "Check to find another way that would be less expensive. I had to have an attorney and also pay for a court-appointed attorney and court costs which were over $2,000." Generally, this type of advice included recommended alternatives that were thought to be less costly.

A few persons advised that careful thought take place before accepting the role of guardian. Some were very direct: "Don't do it unless you have a strong back and a weak mind." One guardian cautioned, "Think twice before agreeing to be a guardian." Another advised, "Think twice about becoming a guardian and then don't do it!" Men and women did not differ in their advice to seek an alternative to guardianship or to refrain from involvement altogether. Regardless of whether individuals "followed their own hearts" or abjured the practice of guardianship, the experience shaped their conceptions of old age and of the future.

DEFINING THE FUTURE: GUARDIANS' VIEWS OF OLD AGE

In this section we consider the contribution of guardianship to the views of old age held by guardians. Following Hasselkus (1988), we focus on the beliefs and values individuals used to organize their behavior and to interpret their experiences as a guardian with reference to their own aging. Research about those who care for the aged often does not link their experience with the elder to the caregiver's management or anticipation of their own aging. In this research, the interpretation of the guardianship experience shaped the sense of the future held by several guardians. The sense of the future generally was one of gloom, often focusing on the decline in the ward's condition and its implications for the guardian's own prospects. As guardians shared their views of how guardianship had influenced the meaning of old age for them, several of Hasselkus's themes of meaning were illustrated. These included a sense of managing as it related to planning, a sense of fear and risk, and a sense of the future. The sense of managing was reflected in awareness of the need to plan, and the sense of fear and risk was sometimes recounted as personal concerns and worry.

Presumably, guardianship is usually awarded only in instances of extreme vulnerability, either physical, mental, or functional. Therefore, guardians most often will have contact with and responsibility for the aged with the greatest frailties. This experience with fragility undoubtedly was reflected in guardians' conceptions of aging.

Table 7.3
The Effects of Guardianship on Guardians' Views of Aging

	N[a]	Percent
Personal concern and worry	78	44
Concern for the aged	41	23
Awareness of the need to plan for old age	32	18
Importance of health and quality of life	11	6
Importance of social support	6	3
Resistance to aging	6	3
Other	5	3

[a] This is based on responses of 179 persons who described how guardianship had affected their views of aging.

Guardians were asked first whether being a guardian had changed their thinking about old age. Then, if their duties as a guardian had changed their views of later life, they described the ways in which their thinking about old age had altered. A little more than one-half (51 percent) agreed that guardianship had changed their perspective on old age. Men and women did not differ in their tendency to change their thinking about aging as a consequence of guardianship. But relationships with their wards shaped male and female guardians' perceptions of age in slightly different ways.

Personal Concern and Worry

The largest proportion of respondents for whom guardianship had shaped their views of aging expressed worry and concern about their own aging and about what would happen to them (44 percent; see Table 7.3). Men and women were similar in their propensity to discuss worries and concerns about aging as outcomes of their guardianship experiences. Their concerns had two main themes: first, the hope and expectation that someone would be available to care for them, and second, expression of a personal but sometimes general fear of aging.

Hoped-for Future Assistance. Among the comments: "Mother was the fourth elderly person I cared for until death. I hope someone will be kind to me when and if I need it in my last years." "I know my turn is coming and hope my kids take care of me." "I hope that someone will be there to help me when I get old! But we live in a world of 'paper,' 'forms,' etc., and it is too much for older adults. In critical decisions, they need help." Others had thought about the possibility that no one would be available to assist them should they need it: "What will happen to me if there is no one for me?" "Old age is frightening if your health is impaired. Who will take care of me? I hope I get as good care as my mom has." In summary, some guardians with these views articulated exchanges they expected to receive from their children. Others who were more tentative and perhaps less sure of such future assistance expressed the hope that someone would be available to help them.

Fear of Aging. Concerns were not always couched in terms of hoped-for assistance from others, rather, they were more global expressions of worry and sometimes fear: "Since I am 71 years old, it causes me to worry about my own future." "Since being a guardian, old age scares me more." "It's more scary than I thought. I see the vulnerability." "Old age scares me silly."

Still others articulated their fears more specifically: "Guardianship has made me fearful of being confined to a nursing home, either myself or my spouse." "I am afraid my personality will change." "I have been left with a fear of growing older and ending up that way." Other comments included: "There is the fear that it could happen to me." "I fear for my prospects." "I have become very aware of the last days of the elderly." "I just pray I am not incapacitated to the point I have to be in a nursing home!" "I do not want to go to a rest home; I'd rather be run over by a truck." "I am discouraged by the long drawn-out deterioration." "It (guardianship) has made me dread the process of aging." "It scares me to age and not to have means of self-support." Thus, the prospect of aging with the possibility of prolonged disability requiring residence in a nursing home, or the threat of aging without support, were specific troubles evoked by the experience of guardianship. The personal concerns and worries about aging were shared by men and women equally.

Concern for the Aged as a Group

Although the most frequent influence of guardianship was on individuals' conceptions of their own aging, about one-quarter expressed their concerns for older persons as a group. Men and women equally interpreted their experiences as a guardian in light of their personal aging. But women somewhat more often (26 percent) than men (18 percent) observed that guardianship had made them sensitive to the needs of the aged in general.

They commented on the negative attitudes toward aging, the help older persons may need, and the sympathy they had developed for their elders. Responses included general expressions of their growing awareness about the circumstances of some of the aged. Unlike the earlier comments, these statements were not directed toward respondents' own aging. The views of these guardians reflected concern for the welfare of others. For example:

"Since being a guardian I am far more concerned about older persons' well-being." "I've learned that sometimes it's very hard to become old." "Old people need more care and help than I realized on all aspects of their lives." "It (life) is too much for older adults; they need help with critical decisions." "Life gets too complicated for old people to handle." Beyond the mechanics of guardianship, there was also expression of the importance of affection and caring; for example, "I saw how much an older person needs someone who loves them to watch over them and their care and welfare."

In their concern for the aged, still others mentioned those whom they believed could assist, or observed flaws in the help currently provided. One guardian comments: "I am much aware of the problems the elderly have, and you *can* help." Others commented about physicians and health care: "The medical profession doesn't want to be bothered by giving good care to the elderly. They have very little understanding of aging and know almost nothing about nutrition." "I did not like the way hospital personnel treated him (the ward); I definitely feel that society in general does not treat the elderly with any respect or caring." "There should be some way of stopping people out to take advantage of older people." For these guardians, then, their contact with the ward provided them insight into difficulties confronted by some older persons. Their observations were general and did not necessarily characterize their ward or reflect specifically on their own aging.

Awareness of the Need to Plan

Another group of guardians (19 percent) concluded they should begin to plan for old age. Men (21 percent) a little more than women (16 percent) observed that guardianship had made them realize the importance of planning for later life.

Among the comments: "Prepare—prepare—prepare!" "I am much more aware of the need to plan more carefully toward the day that I may need a guardian." "It's better to get things in order before you get old." In this context they spoke of living wills and powers of attorney. The objectives of planning ranged from easing the burden for others to ensuring one's wishes were carried out: "You should have a plan so doctors and hospitals don't take all of your money." "People should realize the importance of making their wishes known—such as living wills, what to do with family heirlooms, etc."

Some cited specific reasons for their admonition to plan. For example: "Observing Alzheimer's at close hand has made me realize I should prepare for this possibility myself." "I will make a living will so as not to be put on life-sustaining equipment or a food tube as my grandmother is." Thus, the third most frequent change in thinking about old age attributable to guardianship was to engage in advance planning in the event of incapacity.

Importance of Support and Health Maintenance

That guardianship had evoked for them the importance of social support was noted only by women, and then by just a few (3 percent). For example: "It's important, if at all possible, to have a trustworthy friend or relative." About 6 percent indicated guardianship had made them think of the importance of health as an aspect of aging. The salience of health maintenance was reflected in comments such as, "I will do all things in my power to maintain emotional, spiritual, and physical independence." Another noted, "I will try to take care of myself and conscientiously try to be mentally alert."

Resignation and Resistance to Aging

A few persons noted the major influence of their activities as guardians was to make them want to avoid old age and to die early. Conditions that may or may not accompany old age (i.e., illness, disability, and/or dependency) were explicitly mentioned by some and were probably implicit in the responses of others. These views, for example, are illustrated in statements from two persons: "I don't particularly want to get there (old age)." "I don't want to get there, especially in a nursing home."

Men (6 percent) somewhat more than women (.9 percent) observed they did not want to become old. This category of responses included the following comments: "I hope I never get old. It's terrible being dependent on others." "The more I see of it the less I like it (old age)." "I don't want to be that old!" "I don't want to live until I have to have someone take care of me." "It would be much easier and better for all to die younger." "I hope I never grow old." "I hope I go quick and not linger helplessly." "Die younger!" "Don't get old—especially if you have no family." "Live it up before it all goes." In one sense, these responses were polar opposites to those advocating advance planning and self-help to avert crises.

Apparently the influence of contact with wards on perceptions of aging, in part, is reflected in responses to disability or incapacity. Aging per se generally has not been viewed as negatively as disability. Braithwaite, Gibson, and Holman (1985–86), for example, observed that 15 percent of youth rated active older persons negatively compared with 65 percent who assessed disabled older people negatively. Disability is associated with reduced expectations for growth, continued development, and decision making (Atchley, 1991). The image of older disabled persons as passive may contribute to stereotypes held by social service and medical personnel, and further restrict potential autonomy (Cohen, 1988).

The majority of these guardians who contemplated old age differently than they had prior to assuming their roles were influenced by the incapacity of their wards rather than by their age per se. For some, it was reflected in references to their personal situation, whether through the need for planning or worry and fear for their own future. Among others there was concern for older persons in general and an empathy for the difficulties the aged confront. A few, either facetious or sincere, expressed a desire not to grow old, which perhaps meant not to be disabled as their ward was. In any case, it was possible to ascertain some of the beliefs and values that caregivers used to interpret their experience with special reference to their own future aging.

In this chapter, guardians' descriptions of the benefits and hardships of their roles were presented in some detail. In a subsequent step, multivariate analyses of role strain were conducted to determine the most salient factors in fostering distress of guardians. These results are presented in chapter 8, along with the multivariate analysis of a typology of guardianship.

8

Role Strain of Male and Female Guardians: Tests of Two Models

This chapter comprises two multivariate studies of strain in the guardianship role. Both studies are based on guardians' responses to a questionnaire about their tasks, as reported in preceding chapters. The first study tests a model of correlates of role strain among male and female guardians. The second study considers how family relationships and role strain differentiated among four patterns of managing guardianship.

As documented in previous chapters, because of the intrusion of guardianship on individual liberties, much recent attention has been given to enhancement of procedural safeguards on behalf of the ward. In contrast, the impingement of guardianship on the lives of guardians has received less attention. Rather, with some exceptions, when the work of guardians has been addressed, the focus has been on increased oversight and monitoring, with perhaps less concern for providing help and assistance with their participation in a complex legal system. A portion of the emphasis on monitoring and accountability of guardians completes a popular stereotype of them as sometimes unscrupulous, abusive, and a threat to the well-being of the ward. Yet, except for the limited information in the court records, little is known about guardians. From earlier research of others and the findings in chapters 5 and 6, we know they are most often family members of the ward (Peters, Schmidt, & Miller, 1985), usually adult children (Bulcroft, Kielkopf, & Tripp, 1991; Grossberg, Zimny, & Scallet, 1989). An objective of the first study was to investigate correlates of role strain experienced by guardians of older wards and to make suggestions for diminishing the discomfort felt by them.

STUDY I: CORRELATES OF ROLE STRAIN

Role Strain

Role strain refers to the felt difficulty in complying with role expectations (Menaghan, 1983). That is, strain may be defined as "inadequacy or difficulty in performing role obligations" (Voydanoff, 1988:749). These difficulties may range from unclear expectations for a particular role to a lack of skills or information to carry out tasks successfully. A study of correlates of role strain, then, may include identification of barriers thwarting role performance such as overload, ambiguity, or lack of information and skills. In chapter 6, we discussed the context of strain in guardianship. We concluded that compared to informal caring, decisions and behavior of guardians are usually open to greater scrutiny. Perhaps the context of guardianship, with its more diverse expectations and enlarged duties, greater visibility, and paucity of information about procedures, contributes to role strain. Along with those unique to guardianship, there are common factors that may generate strain for many types of caregiving. One of these shared factors is role overload.

Role Overload. Overload may be linked to perceptions of difficulty in role performance. Role overload refers to the imbalance existing when too many demands exceed the amount of time available to fulfill them (Coverman, 1989). Overload can be thought of as multiple demands exceeding resources (Lewis & Cooper, 1987). Time is a primary resource and an integral aspect of measures of overload. Earlier inquiry included the implications of the amount of time spent at work for role strain (Keith & Schafer, 1991). Much research has found a positive relationship between the number of hours persons spend at work and their work-family strain (Voydanoff, 1988). In this research, the number of hours per week persons spent on guardianship matters was considered in relation to role strain. It was anticipated that higher strain would be associated with a greater amount of time spent on tasks related to the guardianship.

A much-asked question in studies of role strain is whether occupying multiple roles benefits or disadvantages individuals relative to the amount of strain they experience. Conflicting expectations and multiple demands are two of the possible outcomes of performing several roles (Keith & Schafer, 1991). But accumulated roles actually may provide flexibility to manage multiple demands, not to mention their contribution to status enhancement, privileges, personality enrichment, and ego gratification (Sieber, 1974). Employment, for example, can serve as a respite from other roles as well as providing an opportunity for social interaction (Baruch & Barnett, 1986). As a whole, occupying multiple roles seems beneficial for both men and women, and the quality of experiences in given roles is salient to well-being, as is the amount of diversity.

Although research on caregivers to the aged informs us about some of the possible outcomes of employment outside the home, it has yielded inconsistent observations about the relationship between work outside the home and strain. Scharlach and Boyd (1989) recommended increased attention to the positive functions of combining caregiving and employment. Occupational involvement may provide benefits to caregivers (Stoller &

Pugliesi, 1989), make caring easier, and may diminish stress (Scharlach & Boyd, 1989). In this research we expected that involvement in employment would be associated with less role strain among guardians.

Characteristics of Experience in the Guardian Role. Baruch and Barnett (1987) confirmed the relationship between the quality of role experiences and well-being of women. They observed that mere occupancy of a role, independent of the response to it, was not associated with well-being. Therefore, satisfaction derived from the quality of the experience in a given role was linked with well-being (Baruch & Barnett, 1986). Role satisfaction has been found to increase general life satisfaction, as well as to foster better physical health (Coverman, 1989). A role viewed as benefiting the occupants and having positive effects on their lives likely will be perceived as one accompanied by less strain. It was hypothesized that perceived benefits from being a guardian would be associated with diminished strain.

In addition to the satisfaction and benefits derived from roles, the roles may differ in their salience and level of importance in the lives of individuals (Keith, 1989). In this research, we hypothesized there would be a significant interaction effect between the importance of the role of guardian and benefits derived from it. It was expected that role strain would be elevated when the role of guardian was viewed as very important but was found to have few benefits.

Roles also vary in the degree to which they are anticipated and planned for (Seltzer, 1976). Socialization implies roles are expected and intended. Anticipatory socialization facilitates role transitions and performance. It is clear from the accounts of guardians that guardianship is a role for which there is little anticipatory socialization. When socialization for a role is not planned and not carried out at an expected time in the life course, then acquisition of information and skills must be derived through some means other than a normative pattern of education and instruction. Comments of guardians suggested that acquisition of knowledge of the procedures used in the guardianship system may be a critical factor in managing role strain.

Thus, in addition to the potential benefits of strain reduction provided by multiple role occupancy, access to resources and programs is an important part of an analysis of the context of stress and strain (Pearlin, Mullan, Semple, & Skaff, 1990). Having access to resources and deriving support from them should mitigate strain. Earlier we documented guardians' preferences for assistance. The expressed need for further information about the expectations and activities of guardianship were studied in relation to role strain. It was hypothesized that possession of sufficient information about the tasks of guardianship would be associated with diminished strain.

Guardianship is not carried out in isolation. As shown in chapters 6 and 7, for some guardians the behavior of family members, whether it was intrusive or supportive, was key in determining the quality of the guardianship experience. Behavior of other members of the role set, including the ward and family members, may ease or thwart the work of the guardian. Expectations of wards may be seen as unrealistic and requiring too much effort on the part of the guardian. In addition to elevated expectations of their guardians by wards, family relationships may undergo change, sometimes shifting toward less support for the guardian. In this research the demandingness of the ward and a consistent relationship with family members were investigated in relation to role strain. A demanding ward may undermine his or her relationship with a guardian. Demanding wards and altered relationships with family members were expected to be stressful for guardians.

Hypotheses

The following exploratory hypotheses about the relationship between aspects of guardianship and strain were investigated:

1. A greater amount of time spent on matters related to the guardianship will be associated with higher strain.
2. Employment outside the home will be associated with lower strain.
3. Perceived benefits from being a guardian will be related to lower strain.
4. There will be a significant interaction effect between the importance of the role of guardian and benefits derived from the role, so that when the role of guardian is viewed as important but with few benefits, strain will be higher.
5. Sufficient information about the process of guardianship will be associated with lower strain.
6. Perception of the ward as demanding and altered family relationships will be accompanied by higher strain.

PROCEDURES

Sample and Measures

In Study I, we analyzed information from the sample of guardians described in chapter 2. The analyses were based on the responses of guardians to the mail questionnaire. Demographic characteristics of guardians, including age, sex, education, marital status, employment status, and health, were reported in chapter 6.

Role Strain. A scale to measure role strain was used in Study I and Study II. The role strain scale (alpha, .80) included six items, with response categories ranging from "strongly agree" (5) to "strongly disagree" (1). Representative items were: "As a guardian, I sometimes feel that I give much more than I receive"; "I sometimes feel that being a guardian conflicts with what I should be doing for my family or friends"; "Being a guardian causes some financial strain for me." Mean scores ranged from 1 to 5 ($\bar{X}$ = 2.69, sd = .87), with higher scores indicating greater strain.

Role Demands of Guardians. Guardians noted the number of hours per week they spent on guardian activities. These were coded as less than one hour (1), two to seven hours (2), eight to sixteen hours (3), and seventeen or more hours per week (4). Employment outside the home, used as an indicator of a more diversified role set, was coded as employed (1) or not employed (2).

Quality of Experience in the Guardian Role. Guardians observed the extent to which being a guardian had a positive effect on their lives ("strongly agree" [5] to "strongly disagree" [1]). Salience or importance of the role of guardian was assessed by responses to the statement, "Being a guardian is very important to me" ("strongly agree" [5] to "strongly disagree" [1]).

The perception that wards are often demanding and the need for more instruction about expectations for guardians prior to assuming the role were assessed, using the same five-point scale. A higher score indicated wards were seen as demanding and that the guardian would have found more instruction about the role helpful. Guardians noted whether relationships with family members had changed as a result of their becoming a guardian ("yes" [1] or "no" [2]). Respondents indicated the extent to which their own health had interfered with duties to their ward ("strongly agree" [5] to "strongly disagree" [1]).

Assessments of age, education, and marital status of guardians were included in the analyses. Higher scores indicated older ages and more education. Marital status was coded as 1 (married) or 2 (unmarried).

RESULTS

Gender and Guardianship

Male and female guardians were of similar ages, but men more often were married than were women (86 and 63 percent, respectively; Table 8.1). Male and female guardians did not differ in employment status, although men had substantially more education than did women. Ratings of health were comparable for men and women.

Men and women spent somewhat comparable amounts of time on the tasks of guardianship. When there were differences, women spent a little more time. One-half of the guardians spent seven hours per week or less on guardian activities while the remainder devoted more time to these efforts. Males and females did not differ in proximity to their wards (Table 8.1). Three-quarters or more lived within a one-hour drive of the ward.

Table 8.1
Characteristics of Male and Female Guardians

	Males	Females	T or X^2 Values
Age ($\bar{X}$ yrs., t)	59.7	57.8	1.41
Education (%, t)			
Less than high school	5.6	6.8	3.11**
High school	31.9	43.9	
Some college or vocational/technical	62.6	49.3	
Four year college degree or more			
Employed (%, X^2)	58.2	53.6	.79
Marital status (%, X^2)			
Married	86	63	22.96**
Not married	14	37	
Hours per week spent on guardian activity (%, t)			
-1	21.13	24.14	1.90
2-7	62.8	48.1	
8-16	9.0	12.0	
17 or more	6.9	15.5	
Proximity to ward (%, t)			
Shared same household	6.2	10.7	1.23
Less than 1 hour drive	78.1	75.2	
More than 1 hour drive/ less than 4 hours	10.3	9.8	
More than 4 hour drive	4.8	4.3	
Relationship to the ward (%)[a]			
Spouse	9.3	7.4	
Daughter	---	32.	
Son	45.8	---	
Two or more children	6.8	7.5	
Other relative	28.0	28.2	
Nonrelative	10.2	22.3	
Dept. of Human Services	0	1.5	
Others	0	.5	
Health (%, t)			
Excellent	29.9	35.7	.57
Good	53.5	46.2	
Fair	14.6	16.0	
Poor	2.1	2.1	
Very Poor	0	0	
Length of guardianship ($\bar{X}$ yrs., t)	2.0	2.2	.60
Strain ($\bar{X}$ yrs., t)	2.7	2.7	.62
Positive effect of the guardian role ($\bar{X}$, t)	2.83	2.80	.23
Importance of Role ($\bar{X}$, t)	2.30	2.02	2.41*
Demandingness of ward ($\bar{X}$, t)	2.87	2.71	3.36*
Need instruction ($\bar{X}$, t)	3.17	3.04	.92
Health interference ($\bar{X}$, t)	1.93	2.07	1.25
Change in family relationship (%, X^2)			
Yes	20.0	14.50	1.93
No	80.0	85.50	

* $p<.05$
** $p<.01$
[a]No chi square test was used because of the number of empty cells.

Being a guardian was a more important role to women than to men, and men found wards to be more demanding than did women. But they were equally likely to derive positive benefits from their efforts with their wards. Changes in family relationships occurring as a result of the guardianship were not associated with gender of the guardian. Among the total samples, 17 percent observed their relationship with family members had changed as a consequence of their assuming guardianship. Interference from their own health difficulties, a need for further instruction in the role of the guardian, length of guardianship, and role strain were not associated with gender. About 14 percent observed their health was a barrier to performing tasks of guardianship, and 58 percent noted instruction on the tasks expected of guardians would have been helpful to them.

Multivariate Analyses

Separate multiple regression analyses for men and women were used to investigate the correlates of role strain among guardians. In the analyses, age, education, employment status, marital status, and proximity to the ward were entered as an initial block of variables. Following this, the amount of time spent with the ward, salience of the role, the positive effect of guardianship, demandingness of wards, changes in family relationships, needs for instruction, and health of the guardian were examined in relation to role strain (Table 8.2).

Role Strain of Men. Age was the only demographic characteristic linked with role strain of men (Table 8.2). Older male guardians reported less strain than their younger counterparts. As hypothesized, men who devoted more time to guardian activities and who saw their wards as more demanding were also more strained. And if guardianship was unimportant to them, they reported greater strain. Supporting the hypothesis, men who needed more instruction about expectations for guardians also had greater role strain. Interference of their personal health in the conduct of guardian duties also was a source of strain for men. These factors accounted for 36 percent of the variance in role strain among men.

Contrary to our hypothesis, positive effects on their lives as a consequence of guardianship were not associated with diminished strain among men. A second unsupported hypothesis was that a change in family relationships attributed to the guardianship would be a source of strain. Neither benefits from guardianship nor a change in family relationships were important factors in the role strain of these men. Thus, benefits from guardianship did not offset strain associated with it, and altered family relationships found to be a source of stress for women were benign among men.

Role Strain of Women. None of the demographic characteristics were linked with role strain of women (Table 8.2). In contrast to the hypothesis,

Table 8.2
Summary of Multiple Regression Analyses for Role Strain among Guardians

	Men		Women	
	r	B	r	B
Age	-.17	-.20*	-.07	-.05
Marital status	-.02	-.06	.02	-.02
Education	.00	.00	.09	.07
Employment	-.04	.06	-.04	-.04
Proximity to ward	.01	-.02	-.05	.02
R^2	.04		.01	
Demandingness of ward	.32	.22**	.35	.27**
Positive effect	--	--[a]	.27	.27**
Need instruction	.43	.35**	.28	.23**
Change in family relationship	--	--[a]	-.18	-.13*
Hours per week	.15	.19**	.21	.20**
Health interference	.22	.15*	.22	.18**
Importance of role	.25	.19**	--	--[a]
Total R^2	.36		.35	

[a] These variables did not enter the equations.
* $p<.05$
** $p<.01$

role strain of women was independent of their employment status, but as anticipated, more hours spent per week on guardian activities contributed to higher strain. In contrast to men and in support of the hypothesis, women who had a positive guardianship experience were less strained.

As hypothesized, perceiving wards as demanding and experiencing a change in their relationship with family members were troublesome for women and were reflected in strain. A lack of instruction about guardianship and interference by personal health problems contributed to difficulties for women in performing the guardian role. These variables accounted for 35 percent of the variance in role strain of women. In contrast to findings for men, the salience of the guardian role for women was not linked to their level of strain.

The hypothesized interaction effect between the quality of the guardianship experience and the importance of the role on strain was not significant. The expectation that strain would be enhanced when the role was seen as important but unsatisfying was not supported for either men or women.

SUMMARY

The multivariate models considered here suggest that, for the most part, men and women found similar situations contributed to strain in their roles as guardians. Some of the differences, however, likely reflected the centrality of women in caring for the aged and maintaining family relationships. In general, women more than men have been involved in caregiving to the aged (Spitze & Logan, 1989). Perhaps indicating greater acceptance of caregiving as a female role, guardianship was more important to these women than to the men. Despite the greater salience of their role, they did not enjoy a higher quality of guardianship experience. Yet, corroborating other literature on well-being (Baruch & Barnett, 1987), role strain of women was mitigated by the quality of their experience as a guardian. Men did not benefit similarly from the quality of their experiences in the role of guardian. When the role was more important to men, they were more strained. But both sexes who described wards as demanding experienced greater strain. Other research has shown the condition of the care recipient may contribute to the well-being of those who care (Stoller, 1992). And behavior that guardians may define as demandingness of a ward may be linked to the ward's deteriorating condition.

Traditionally, women more than men maintain family networks (Spitze & Logan, 1989). Consequently, circumstances changing the relationship with the family may be experienced differently by men and women. Guardianships, which are legalized caregiving, sometimes are a source of family disagreement and lingering conflict. For these female guardians, changes in family relationships were associated with higher levels of role strain, suggesting that difficulties in carrying out duties of guardianship may be enhanced for women when ties with relatives undergo change. Altered family relationships of men, however, did not affect how they viewed the role of guardian.

Among these guardians, being a relative of the ward was not associated with strain. Rather, guardianship accompanied by altered family relationships seemed to contribute directly to strain of women. Being a relative of a ward was not a critical factor; instead the relationship with the family of the ward, whether the guardian was a relative or not, was important to the well-being of women. In Study II, we investigate how family involvement and family relationships differentiated among the types of guardianship.

In the literature, employment outside the home has been viewed as both a potential stressor and an activity that may diminish and deflect some of the troubles associated with caring for others (Scharlach & Boyd, 1989). Employment was neither a stressor nor a positive force in the lives of these guardians as reflected in role strain. For these men and women, intrinsic benefits of employment did not limit strain ensuing from guardianship duties. An assessment of the amount of time spent on employment comparable to the measure of the amount of time spent on guardianship would have been a more sensitive indicator than the categories of employment versus nonemployment.

Insofar as the amount of time spent on guardian activities represented overload, it increased strain for both men and women. For example, as presented in chapter 7, they clearly described the intrusion of guardianship in both work and family relationships: "It interferes with other parts of my life." "It's too much responsibility if you have a busy life." "I thought it was taking too much time from my family." "It is all-consuming." "I found this to be a very stressful time of my life." "I have no personal life." "Taking care of the ward's needs without harming my business was difficult. Time away cost me jobs and accounts."

In addition to the strain fostered by role overload and conflict between obligations, problems with physical health were a factor in the distress of both men and women. The connection between stressful aspects of roles and health has a long tradition (Franks, Campbell, & Shields, 1992). One line of thinking is that chronic strains may adversely affect health. In another kind of model and the one tested here, Montgomery and Kamo (1989) used caregiver health as a predictor of subjective burden. Corresponding to our findings they observed that less healthy caregivers, both sons and daughters, reported being more burdened by their tasks.

In summary, demandingness of the ward, role overload, personal health problems, and an expressed need for additional instruction about guardianship procedures were factors that contributed to strain of both men and women. At the end of the chapter suggested implications of these findings for practice are presented.

STUDY II: FAMILY RELATIONSHIPS, ROLE STRAIN, AND TYPES OF GUARDIANSHIP

In Study II, we investigated the relative importance of family relationships, role strain, and characteristics of wards and guardians in differentiating four patterns of guardianship. We examined whether family relationships, including disputes over the guardianship, and role strain differentiated the ways in which guardians conceived of their roles.

Earlier, we noted that research on the importance of family relationships and decisions about guardianship is timely because increasing numbers of older persons likely will need assistance with decision making and caring for their person, their property, or both. And family members are usually pivotal in decisions that are made. In this section we study how personal attitudes of wards and guardians and characteristics of family relationships differentiated among four types of guardianship.

Maclean (1989:79) described the care of the aged at the societal and community levels as disputed territory: "Even a territory of field work and professional practice which is generally despised and neglected can become a cause for boundary disputes once it is a matter of deciding upon the appropriate division of power and public resources." But disputes over care can take place at the individual and family level as well. By now it is well known that most care of the aged, much of it invisible, occurs in the home and community. Perhaps guardianship more than some other forms of caring may lend itself to becoming disputed territory among family members. Because guardianship involves legalized relationships ensuing from a court hearing, it is a more formalized type of caring. As such, it is likely to be subject to more formal oversight and monitoring. Furthermore, any disputes regarding appointing a guardian, removing a guardian, or restricting powers of a guardian may be handled formally and hence be quite visible. Therefore, the disputes and troubles of guardianship may be both highly public and formal. Yet, much of the routine of being a guardian is very private, tedious, and for many families it is carried out without adequate preparation and information. Clearly, guardians may respond to their roles in very different ways, but it is our position that their work is often quite stressful.

In this research a typology was developed to reflect some patterns individuals manifested in response to managing their work as guardians. This work builds on the unstructured comments of guardians described in chapter 7. Types of guardianship were identified as the tough, the sympathetic, the sad, and the challenged. A model of role strain, family relationships, and personal characteristics was investigated to determine how these factors might differentiate among the four types of guardianship.

Family Relationships and Guardianship

That the family is the linchpin in the care of the aged is indisputable (Dwyer & Coward, 1992). Determination of incapacity entails a clear, formal reversal of tasks and renegotiation of a relationship, particularly if the ward and guardian are parent and child. It may be especially stressful for both parents and children to redefine a parent as dependent, vulnerable, and incompetent. Yet, as noted earlier, information on decision making about care for older persons in the context of the family is limited. Because guardians are most often family members and because guardianship is more drastic than many types of informal arrangements for care, relationships between family members may be altered by the decision. Relationships between the elder and those who help may change (Blieszner & Hamon, 1992), but relationships with other family members may change as well. Former disagreements and conflicts may reappear, remain unresolved, or even intensify. Of all types of caregiving that represent disputed territory, guardianship is likely a prototype of high visibility and formalization.

Earlier, we suggested that unique activities of guardians would be expected to generate strain peculiar to their roles, whereas some other strains experienced by guardians (e.g., role overload) may be shared with a variety of caregivers. In turn, perceptions of both kinds of strain may influence how persons regard their work as guardians. In Study II, it was hypothesized that contention and disagreement in the family surrounding the decision to seek guardianship and selection of the specific guardian, change in family relationships, and role strain would differentiate among the types of guardianship. The contextual variables and background characteristics were included in the multivariate model.

PROCEDURES

Sample and Measures

In this analysis, as in Study I, we employed the sample of guardians described in chapter 2. Some of the demographic characteristics of wards and guardians were drawn from the court records.

Characteristics of the Ward and the Guardian. The sex of ward and guardian was coded as female (1) or male (2). The ward and guardian were coded as relatives (1) or nonrelatives (2). The length of the guardianship ranged from less than 1 year to 18 years, with a mean of 2.10 years.

Family Relationships and Role Strain. Guardians indicated whether there was disagreement among family members about the necessity for a guardian, discussion among family members about who should be guardian, disagreement about who should be guardian, and whether their relationship with the family changed as a result of becoming a guardian ("yes" [1] or "no" [2]). The role strain scale, described in chapter 2 and used in Study I, was employed in the multivariate analysis of a typology of guardianship.

Typology of Guardianship

A typology was developed to reflect responses to and styles of managing guardianship employed by guardians. A goal of the typology was to distinguish broad patterns of the ways in which guardians regarded and carried out their tasks. The four patterns or types were based on guardians' written descriptions of the most difficult aspects of their roles and how they

Table 8.3
A Typology of Guardianship

Types	Percentages
The tough	15
The sympathetic	35
The sad	25
The challenged	25

managed guardianship. Restricting the analysis to difficulties of being a guardian, however, does not mean that positive aspects of guardianship described earlier were not significant for guardians. Rather, in this exploratory effort to develop a typology the decision was made to limit the purview of the analysis to the hardships and management of guardianship. It was then possible to conduct a multivariate quantitative analysis using a typology based on guardians' descriptions of their roles, which were presented in more detail in chapter 7.

The literature provided direction in the initial inspection of the descriptions of difficulties of guardianship. Orientation to providing support, caring, or coping has been variously described as instrumental-expressive, instrumental-emotional, or emotion-focused/problem-solving focused (Berrera & Ainlay, 1983; Bhagat, Allie, & Ford, 1991; Pattison, 1973). Initially it was possible to group responses or orientations to the hardships of guardianship in one of two general categories—instrumental or affective. Open-end responses were classified by two coders. The goal, however, was not to reduce the number of types to the smallest number. If this had been the objective, the broad distinction between instrumental and emotional orientations (Pattison, 1973) could have been used. Although these two general distinctions were apparent in the conceptions of guardian hardships, it was quickly evident that responses were somewhat more complex. In the end, four general patterns were derived from the descriptions (Table 8.3).

Instrumental conceptions may include what others have described as material aid and behavioral assistance (Berrera & Ainlay, 1983). But provision of material aid and assistance was approached differently by these guardians. For example, although individuals with responses eventually labeled the "challenged" and the "tough" both seemed to address their tasks in instrumental ways, the latter approached their work with extreme negativism toward the process, the courts, and the ward. They exhibited an emotional response to the instrumental tasks involved in guardianship with their descriptions of the difficulties that were harsh and critical. Open-end responses of 317 guardians were classified into four general patterns of managing guardianship and labeled as the tough, the sympathetic, the challenged, and the sad (Table 8.3). Agreement between coders was 96 percent. When there were differences in the classification, raters reviewed the responses and arrived at consensus on the categorization. Some of the quotations used to illustrate the types were initially presented in chapter 7.

The Tough. The first pattern was described as the tough. These guardians disliked the paperwork associated with guardianship, sometimes expressed hatred and distrust of lawyers and the courts, and found being a guardian was not to their liking. They seldom indicated they would be a guardian again. Their advice to others included comments such as: "Don't do it!" "This is a thankless job!" "Think twice and then do not do it." "Do not become emotionally involved." "Make up your mind that anything you do the relatives will not like!" "Expect mental strain and don't expect appreciation from the family." "Don't expect glory!" They cautioned to "Test the waters before you dive in too deep." "Be sure that you can take abuse from the person." "I hated going to court and resent the whole procedure." "The courts are most insulting and disagreeable."

Thus, the tough described negative feelings about the guardianship. A persistent theme reflected a harshness in their judgments about others connected to the guardianship and toward the process. About 15 percent of the guardians responded in this way to their roles.

The Sympathetic. The perceptions and recommendations of the tough were in sharp contrast to those of the sympathetic, whose comments on managing guardianship included: "Volunteer with love." "Relax, don't have a cow!" "Do for people as you would want them to do for you." "Do not try to do what you want; do what is best for the ward." "Try to gain the confidence and trust of the ward and strive to the utmost to be worthy of it." "Be human, be patient, and have feelings." "And pray without ceasing." "Have patience, compassion, and empathy." "You are thinking for your ward; treat them as you want to be treated." The sympathetic not only focused on the needs of the ward but also emphasized the positive affective dimensions of their relationship.

The largest group of guardians (35 percent) were defined as the sympathetic. These guardians were sensitive to the needs of others and emphasized wanting to do more for the ward, hoping they made the right decisions in the best interest of the ward, and wanting to be sure they were doing the best job for the ward.

The Sad. About one-quarter of the guardians were described as the sad. These persons cited observing the decline of the ward, depressing visits with the ward, and the suffering of the ward as the most difficult aspects of their guardianship.

These were individuals who seemed to suffer greatly as their wards deteriorated: "It is so sad to watch my aunt deteriorate." "The visits are the most depressing." "The saddest thing was having my father declared incompetent." Furthermore, the sad interpreted old age in terms of what it might portend for them and recounted how the guardianship had altered their thinking about their own aging, although they were not alone in this sentiment. At the same time some reflected a need for resources to address the needs of the ward. The sad lacked the aggressive anger of the tough as they railed against the system and its functionaries, but unlike the challenged, they did not seem to take hold, grasp the task, and garner resources to assist them in their efforts. Finally, the sad lacked the more optimistic spirit, the emotional support, and perhaps the hope of the sympathetic, who relied greatly on love, patience, and taking the other into account.

The Challenged. Those who were called the challenged (25 percent) spoke of managing resources so the ward would be cared for, developing strategies so the ward would not be abused or taken advantage of, and acting as advocates for their ward.

The challenged were highly task-oriented as they addressed the needs of the ward. Some examples of their efforts were working closely with the courts to have stolen items returned to wards, attempting to stop fiscal and physical abuse, and affiliating with organizations designed to serve older persons. They advised: "You need to be concerned with time management; know when further investment of time will be unproductive." "Be on the offensive. . . . Go to the library and do a lot of research." "Prepare yourself." Preparation and use of resources were the tools of the challenged. They spoke of being able to meet an important need and of being able to protect wards from exploitation. Solving multiple problems of wards was viewed as challenging and, in turn, rewarding.

The hallmarks of the challenged were feelings of competency, of efficacy, and of carrying out their tasks as guardians with dispatch. They took guardianship seriously: "The guardianship responsibility must be a big priority in your life." But some were sensitive to those guardians who were less adept in their work with wards. One who was challenged and judged his efforts to understand and manipulate resources a success observed there are "some poor souls (guardians) out there who are really floundering." Although the challenged had the interests of the ward in mind, theirs was perhaps the most instrumental approach. In one sense, these four patterns of managing the needs of wards represented coping styles and the means used to approach a potentially stressful relationship.

Statistical Analyses

Bivariate analyses of the association between the typology and characteristics of the ward and the guardian were conducted using X^2 and F tests.

Discriminant analysis was used to assess the model of family relationships and role strain. Discriminant analysis is a multivariate statistical technique that may be employed to identify characteristics that differentiate between two or more groups. Standardized discriminant function coefficients indicate the relative contribution of a particular variable to the function. The interpretation of these coefficients is similar to that given to beta weights in multiple regression. Coefficients, then, represent the relative discriminating power of a variable when others are simultaneously examined in the same model. Thus, the four patterns of managing guardianship—the tough, sympathetic, sad, and challenged—were categorical variables, and discriminant analysis was employed to determine whether family relationships, role strain, and selected characteristics of guardians and wards differentiated among them. This statistical procedure aided in developing a profile of the approaches adopted by guardians.

RESULTS

Bivariate Analyses

In this section, bivariate relationships between the typology and characteristics of the guardian and the ward are considered (Table 8.4). As noted, some literature on caregiving suggests differential involvement of men and women in the tasks related to caring for older persons (Abel, 1990) and differences in the tendency to feel they are not doing enough (Stoller, 1992). These male and female guardians, however, had comparable responses to managing guardianship as reflected in the typology (Table 8.4). That is, men and women were equally likely to be defined as tough, challenged, and so on. Age, marital status, income, and education of guardians also were not related to the typology of guardianship (Table 8.4). Thus, selected demographic characteristics of guardians were not associated with the types of guardianship and were excluded from the multivariate analyses.

Inspection of measures of family relationships used to test the model indicated several differences at the bivariate level among the four types. Guardians described as tough had more often than their peers participated in discussions with family members about the guardianship prior to its establishment, disagreed about the need for a guardian, disagreed about the selection of them as guardian, and experienced a change in their relationship with their family (Table 8.4). Finally, the tough reported higher levels of role strain than those in the other patterns.

The tough tended to be guardians of male more often than female wards and to have been guardians for the shortest period of time, whereas the sad had served as guardians for the greatest amount of time. The family relationship (relative/nonrelative) of the ward and the guardian was not significantly associated with the typology. The sad, however, tended to

Table 8.4
Ward and Guardian Characteristics by a Typology of Guardianship

Guardian Characteristics	Sad	Sympathetic	Tough	Challenged	F or X^2 Values
	Types of Guardianship				
Sex (%, X^2)					
Male	41.0	32.7	31.2	44.9	4.11
Female	59.0	67.3	68.8	55.1	
Marital status (%, X^2)					
Married	67.9	73.3	62.5	79.5	4.87
Unmarried	32.1	27.7	37.5	20.5	
Employment (%, X^2)					
Yes	48.7	61.1	52.1	57.7	3.24
No	51.3	38.9	47.9	42.3	
Income ($\bar{X}$, 1-5[a], F)	4.0	3.9	3.6	3.9	1.02
Education ($\bar{X}$, 1-6, F)	3.3	3.5	3.6	3.4	.34
Age ($\bar{X}$ yrs., F)	59.4	57.0	56.4	59.1	.96
Ward/Guardianship Characteristics					
Sex of ward (%, X^2)					
Male	21.8	29.2	35.4	29.5	8.75
Female	78.2	70.8	64.6	70.5	
Relationship of ward and guardian (%, X^2)					
Family	78.2	93.2	89.6	93.3	2.75
Nonfamily	21.8	16.8	10.4	16.4	
Length of guardianship ($\bar{X}$ yrs., F)	2.55	2.01	1.60	1.99	1.71
Capacity of ward ($\bar{X}$, 5-15, F)	12.65	12.75	12.27	12.94	1.04
Proximity of ward and guardian ($\bar{X}$, 1-4, F)	2.0	2.2	2.4	2.1	.54
Guardianship Characteristics/ Role Strain					
Disagreement/Need for guardian (%, X^2)					
Yes	7.7	5.4	18.8	3.8	10.87***
No	93.3	94.6	81.3	96.2	
Discussion about guardianship (%, X^2)					
Yes	35.9	44.2	50.0	25.6	9.93**
No	64.1	55.8	50.0	74.4	
Disagreement/selection of guardian (%, X^2)					
Yes	10.5	5.4	27.1	5.1	20.56***
No	89.5	94.6	72.9	94.9	
Change in relationship with family (%, X^2)					
Yes	15.8	18.9	31.9	9.1	10.75***
No	84.2	81.1	68.1	90.9	
Role strain of guardian ($\bar{X}$, 1-5, F)	2.6	2.7	3.1	2.6	4.14***

* p <.10
** p <.05
*** p <.01
[a] This refers to the range of values.

Table 8.5
A Discriminant Analysis of Family Relationships, Role Strain, Ward/Guardian Characteristics, and the Typology of Guardianship

	Typology of Guardianship (Standardized Discriminant Function Coefficients)
Family Relationships	
Disagreement about need for guardianship	.14
Discussion about guardianship	.24
Disagreement/selection of guardian	.45
Change in relationship with family	.10
Role Strain Scale	.45
Ward/Guardian Characteristics	
Length of guardianship	.12
Sex of ward	.14
Sex of guardian	.35
Relationship of ward and guardian	.06
Capacity of ward	.29
Proximity of ward and guardian	.20

Canonical Correlation	.37
χ^2 (df = 33; p<.001)	61.27

have wards who were nonrelatives a little more often than those in other patterns. The tough more often than other guardians were adult daughters or co-guardians with another sibling.

Multivariate Analysis

What was the relative importance of family relationships, role strain, and personal characteristics of wards and guardians in distinguishing among the four patterns of guardianship? Discriminant analysis was used to investigate the ways in which family relationships, role strain, and personal characteristics differentiated among the four styles of guardianship (Table 8.5).

In the multivariate analysis four items were included to assess family relationships: disagreement about the need for a guardian, disagreement about selection of the specific guardian, discussion of the guardianship, and change in the relationship among family members. In addition, the role strain scale and six characteristics of wards (sex and capacity) and guardians (sex, length of the guardianship, proximity, and family/nonfamily relationship of the ward and guardian) were included. Guardian characteristics such as age, education, and income, and age and income of the ward were not included in the multivariate analyses because they were not related to the typology.

There was one significant function indicating that disagreement among family members about who should be guardian and level of role strain were most important in differentiating among the four types (Table 8.5). Thus, when other variables were included in the analysis, disagreement among family members and role strain distinguished between the tough and the other three types. The tough experienced the greatest role strain (Table 8.4). A least significant difference test indicated the tough were the most strained of the four groups, and their family relationships were most contentious. More than one-quarter (27 percent) of the tough encountered disputes over their appointment as guardian compared to 11 percent of the sad and 5 percent of the sympathetic and the challenged. Examination of the canonical discriminant functions at the group means (group centroids) indicated the tough were located farthest (-.85) from the challenged (.32) and closest to the sympathetic (.01) and sad (.24). In the test of the role strain model, strain and disagreement about selection of the specific guardian differentiated the tough from the other types. That is, on characteristics reflecting role strain the sad, the challenged, and the sympathetic were more similar to one another than they were to the tough.

What factors were of little or no importance in differentiating between the types? Personal characteristics of the ward (e.g., sex, age, family relationship) and of the guardian (e.g., age, sex, marital status, education) generally were not associated with the way in which guardians addressed their tasks. Guardians' regard for their work with wards as expressed in the typology was independent of these indices of social stratification.

SUMMARY

This research has demonstrated the centrality of family interaction related to decision making in the formation of guardians' definitions of their roles. The quality of the interaction between family members was salient in differentiating among the types. Measures both of family relationships and of role strain implicated stressful aspects of family ties as influences on guardians' views of their work. Among the aspects of family relationships studied disagreement among family members about the selection of a particular person as guardian was most important in differentiating the types. Such conflict might be mitigated by providing to guardians and their families more complete information about the expectations, duties, and skills of guardians.

Guardians' responses to unstructured questions indicated that family relationships were among the difficult aspects of being a guardian, and they amplified other findings about family relationships. Female guardians, for example, commented on their relationships with family members: "Contending with relatives was most difficult. The family made unreasonable demands" (female, age 54); "Disagreements with siblings over the care of the ward are the hardest" (female, age 46); "Family members were discourteous to me" (female, age 65). Although women seemed to elaborate disproportionately on difficulties with family members, for some men as well, the conflict was sustained. One male guardian, age 57, recounted an attempt to remove him as guardian. There were disagreements among family members about his being appointed guardian. Some guardians described harassment from relatives. Iris (1988) noted that selection of the individual to be guardian fosters more difficulty than the initial decision to petition for guardianship.

For some others, family concerns and dissention only compounded the lack of knowledge of guardianship: "A hard thing about guardianship was having family members trying to tell you to do this and that when you were doing the best that you could and not fully understanding what a guardian was or meant" (female, age 42). These, then, were some of the qualitative descriptions of family troubles experienced by guardians.

Little quantitative research is available about decision making by families of older persons, including those of older wards. Yet, families are crucibles for much of the work that is done for older wards. And our research demonstrated that when family relationships go awry, guardians are directly affected, and are more strained and negative toward their activities. The tough and the other types were graphically different in their attitudes toward their tasks.

The limited literature suggests that little thought is given by families beforehand to decisions about health care for their older members. The norms for such processes are not clearly articulated, either by older persons or their relatives. For most older persons in the study, advance decisions about care were not in place. Prior agreement on decisions about guardianship and related issues should have alleviated or at least diminished strain for guardians, wards, and members of their families. As noted earlier, the wisdom of having family members involved is supported by some research. Support and involvement of family members in the decision-making process were associated with higher quality decisions about the care of older persons (Coulton, Dunkle, Chow, Haug, & Vielhaber, 1988). In our research, data were not available about the quality of decision making in families, but certainly contentiousness in the decision-making process figured in guardians' views of their tasks. We would speculate that the ward also was impacted negatively by family strain.

The model tested informed us about the lives of guardians who responded to their tasks in particular ways. Even though literature has suggested there may be differences in orientation to caregiving by sex (Abel, 1990), by educational levels, or by employment status (Scharlach & Boyd, 1989), demographic and personal characteristics of guardians and wards tended to be unimportant in determining the ways in which the guardians addressed their task. These findings correspond to those of other recent research in which situational characteristics were more important than demographic factors in affecting outcomes for caregivers (Walker, Martin, & Jones, 1992). For these guardians circumstances related to the guardianship (e.g., the nature of the involvement of their families in the guardianship or exchanges with their wards) were more closely linked with views of their tasks than were demographic characteristics.

IMPLICATIONS OF STUDY I AND STUDY II

What are the implications of the findings from these two studies for assisting guardians and their families? From the perspective of intervention and practice, what might have diminished the strain experienced by these men and women, and what might alleviate the strain of guardians in the future? First, knowledge about aspects of guardianship that other guardians have found problematic should be of use to persons as they go about deciding whether to undertake the particular duties of caring for an elder.

Recognition that more instruction and information about expectations for guardians would have been helpful prior to assuming the role was associated with greater role strain among both men and women. As noted in chapter 7, several guardians clearly articulated their desire for more knowledge of the guardianship system; indeed, 58 percent indicated they needed more instruction. Some of their advice for others was specific, while some was more general: "We needed help." After one respondent was appointed guardian the social worker never met with them again. This guardian also never was contacted by the court-appointed attorney. Other comments included: "I believe a written booklet and calendar on reports detailing and explaining the duties would be of help." "Make sure you receive strong training from strong legal mentors." "I was given very little training." "I believe before a person is given guardianship they should be fully informed of rights and obligations. I had very little information to go on." "Make sure you know exactly what it is you are doing—it may be more complicated than you think."

Provision of more systematic instruction to guardians is much needed and should correspondingly reduce role strain. Completing the paperwork, keeping records, scheduling reports, and acquiring information to negotiate the court system, for example, have been identified as difficulties. Guardians believed they could have benefited from more instruction on the court system and how to negotiate it, more information from their probate staff, greater discussion of available social services, increased knowledge about alternatives to guardianship, additional information on Medicare and Medicaid procedures, and assistance with bookkeeping and paperwork. In addition to alleviating stress through greater role clarity, conceivably access to more instruction prior to assuming the guardianship might diminish the amount of time necessary to carry out the duties and thereby reduce strain related to overload as well.

Among the correlates of role strain, the expressed need for opportunities to obtain more information about the guardianship system seems most amenable to intervention. Furthermore, such a strategy should impact role strain both directly and indirectly by reducing the amount of time spent on the mechanics of guardianship. It should diminish some of the false starts and perhaps free up time that could be spent more profitably with the ward or members of the family. Other literature has suggested guardians would benefit from additional information and education about guardianship procedures (Eekelaar & Pearl, 1988). Some of the pressures involved in decision making on behalf of the ward might be diminished with the provision of more instruction for guardians and their families.

Guardians identified as the challenged and the sympathetic, who seemed most similar, might make the most successful use of additional opportunities to secure both information and personal assistance. The challenged already were resourceful and skilled in preparing ahead to serve their wards. The sympathetic highlighted their concern with making "right" decisions on behalf of the ward. For all of their bravado and sharp criticism of others and of the system, to be a tough guardian was difficult and stressful. For these guardians the role was more disputed than for others. As reflected in the strain scale, lives of tough guardians were accompanied by greater conflict with family or friends, more financial strain, and the belief that needs of guardians are overlooked.

Those guardians among the tough who found the court system troublesome also might have benefited from the availability of services that could direct them through the procedure more closely. In turn, as guardians increase their skills, family members may have more confidence in their performance. The tough, however, may be the most resistant to receiving help even though their levels of stress and hostility would seem to warrant attention.

Other research has demonstrated an association between the quality of caregiving relationships and the occurrence of stress (Scharlach, 1987). Some of the flawed family relationships and lack of knowledge that fostered greater strain among guardians should be addressed through more systematic education and training of guardians and their families. In chapter 12, some efforts to assist guardians that are currently underway are noted.

The final section of the book, beginning with chapter 9, shifts from the micro-level analysis of wards and their guardians to the societal level in which guardianship legislation is formulated and implemented. First, specific legislation in selected states is reviewed, with attention to guardianship practices at various stages in the process. This is followed by analyses of the impact of statutory change on outcomes for proposed wards (chapter 10) and the effect of implementation of recommended practices on guardianship decisions for older persons (chapter 11).

9

The Context of Guardianship Legislation in Selected States

Legal reforms are said to derive from changing social attitudes and the desire to have the law reflect those attitudes (Handler, 1978). Indeed, law is mobilized and subsequently created when desires, preferences, and wants are transformed into a demand for change (Jenkins, 1980). The movement to change the treatment of wards (most of whom were older wards) under the guardianship process occurred at a time when societal attitudes about aging and older adults in general were also changing. Gerontological research in the last 20 years has attempted to change many of the negative stereotypes and myths about older adults and the aging process. These myths include a belief that growing old will inevitably result in senility and dependency due to mental and physical frailty, all culminating in a "second childhood." Since laws reflect contemporary societal attitudes and beliefs, it is not surprising that these myths were also embedded in early guardianship statutes. The laws controlling the appointment of a guardian supported a benevolent, nonadversarial judicial process, where the appointment of a guardian was seen as beneficial and perhaps inevitable. Just as the attitudes about old age began to change slowly, legal scholars and gerontologists began to call for legislative reform of guardianship laws.

Handler (1978) suggests that when a specific law has been targeted for change, the change in the law will bring about both the symbolic and instrumental goals of a particular social movement. Specifically, statutory changes reflect a symbolic change in attitudes about a social phenomenon or relationship, as well as an instrumental change in how individuals are treated under a given law. Changing guardianship statutes is an effort to alter symbolically assumptions about older adults (e.g., old age inevitably brings mental and physical decline) by requiring the process to be adversarial, requiring judicial safeguards for the proposed ward, and judging incapacity by individual functioning rather than by physical or mental status. Changes in guardianship law also have an instrumental function and in theory, should result in: (1) an improvement of the treatment of older adults throughout the judicial process; (2) a reduction in the number of unwarranted guardianships; (3) an increase in the number of limited guardianships awarded; and (4) an increase in the scrutiny given to the guardian's activities by the court. Specifically, those calling for a reform in guardianship laws have sought changes in the definition of incapacity, changes in the judicial procedure (e.g., notice of hearing, obtaining legal representation), more involvement on the part of the proposed ward, and closer regulation of the guardian's activities (American Bar Association, 1989). How successful have advocates been in changing the symbolic nature of guardianship law?

In this chapter we review guardianship statutes in nine primarily midwestern states. The three states that are the focus of our detailed investigation, Iowa, Missouri, and Colorado, were included in this nine-state analysis. The other states chosen for review were Illinois, Kansas, Minnesota, Nebraska, South Dakota, and Wisconsin. These additional states were selected for analysis because of the high percentage of older adults residing in these areas, and because they represent diverse ways of implementing guardianship reforms. Comparison of the three states that are central to this book with other states can reveal the degree to which these three states have reformed their guardianship laws in relation to the other states selected. We will note the extent to which these state statutes reflect the symbolic changes desired in the judicial treatment of the proposed wards.

METHODOLOGY

Statutory provisions of each state were analyzed separately according to each step in the guardianship process. Statutes were analyzed based on the degree to which they conformed to recommended statutory reforms appearing in the literature. Criticisms of the guardianship process, discussed in detail in chapter 3, will be mentioned briefly here to highlight the specific areas targeted for reform. Key provisions of the statutes that were selected for analyses are presented below.

AREAS OF GUARDIANSHIP REFORM

Definition of Incapacity

The statutory definition of incapacity is the standard used to judge evidence presented to support the allegation that the proposed ward is in need of a guardian. Statutory definitions of incapacity have been criticized because many simply require the existence of a mental or physical impairment, rather than using as a test of incapacity the degree to which the impairment prevents the individual from meeting daily needs (Mitchell, 1978; Sherman, 1980). The more progressive statutes should contain language that defines incapacity based on functioning rather than on physical or mental status.

Petition and Notice of Hearing

The guardianship petition is the document that initiates the guardianship process. The petition, which is typically completed by the proposed guardian, states the basic facts about the proposed ward (age, location, living family members), information about the proposed guardian (relationship to the ward and their address), and in some instances the reason why a guardianship is sought. The notice of hearing provides information about when and where the hearing will be held. Both the petition and notice of the hearing are to be given to the proposed ward prior to the hearing.

Advocates have argued that petitions should provide concise reasons or allegations of incapacity rather than merely reciting the statutory definition of incapacity (Sherman, 1980). Requiring specific allegations to accompany the petition allows time to prepare a defense prior to the hearing. Furthermore, it has been suggested that the petition should contain a clear explication of the proposed ward's rights, such as the right to be present at the hearing and to be represented by an attorney (Mitchell, 1978) and that it should be served personally by someone who can explain the purpose and ramifications of a guardianship (Atkinson, 1980; Mitchell, 1978). These three aspects, whether the petition contains alleged reasons for incapacity, whether the petition contains a list of rights, and how the notice was served to the proposed ward, were selected for analysis.

Finally, many advocates suggest that prior to the hearing, the court should take an active role in obtaining additional information about the prospective ward. One suggestion has been to establish court visitors, who would act as the eyes and ears of the court by interviewing prospective wards and guardians and reporting back to the court (Atkinson, 1980). Whether or not a court visitor or other professional is used was noted.

Guardianship Hearing

Other criticisms of the guardianship process point to the lack of due process rights provided to the proposed ward prior to and during the hearing. Three due process rights have been identified as critical in the process and found to be lacking are the right of proposed wards to be represented by legal counsel, the right to be present at the hearing, and the use of a more strict standard of evidence (Horstman, 1975; Mitchell, 1978; National Senior Citizens Law Center, 1974).

With regard to the appointment of legal counsel for the proposed ward, statutes can either direct the court to appoint legal counsel to represent the ward, give the court the option of appointing counsel, or remain silent and not direct the court to appoint representation. In some cases, statutes direct the appointment of a guardian ad litem (GAL) in lieu of legal counsel. GALs are supposed to represent the best interests of the proposed ward, and therefore are less likely to act simply as an advocate for the ward's wishes. GALs can, however, play an important role by investigating all aspects of the proposed ward's physical, mental, and social situation.

Another important aspect of the hearing is the presence of the prospective ward at the hearing. In the past, wards were seldom present at their own hearings. Advocates have argued that the ward should be present in order to be able to play an active part in the process. Statutes should therefore direct the court to require the ward be present at the hearing if at all possible.

A final concern regarding the guardianship hearing is the amount of evidence required to prove incapacity. According to legal scholars and researchers, the amount of evidence needed to prove incapacity has been scant (Associated Press, 1987; Mitchell, 1978; Peters, Schmidt, & Miller, 1985). As a result, any amount of evidence provided by the petitioner has, in many cases, been sufficient to prove the need for a guardian. Advocates have called for the use of a tougher standard to prove incapacity, such as the clear and convincing standard of evidence, and an inquiry into the ward's decision-making capacity (ABA, 1989).

Progressive statutes should therefore require the ward to be present, appoint legal representation or a GAL on behalf of the proposed ward, require the use of the clear and convincing standard to evaluate the evidence presented to prove incapacity, and inquire into the decision-making capacities of the proposed ward.

Scope of Guardian Powers

If the court finds that the proposed ward is in need of a guardian, the guardian is given legal authority to make a variety of personal decisions on behalf of the ward. Observers of the guardianship process have noted that courts are more likely to grant plenary powers (the most extensive) to guardians, without regard to any competencies that wards may retain in some aspects of their lives (Sherman, 1980). Such an appointment of plenary powers may be unwarranted, and the appointment of a limited guardian may be a more appropriate match for the ward's level of capacity. When the powers given to the guardian match the ward's incapacities the number of inappropriate plenary guardianships should decline. In addition, once the guardian has been appointed, unless statutes indicate to the contrary, guardians have the power to make a number of decisions for the ward, including residential placement, and medical and surgical decisions. Finally, there has been a push for guardianship statutes to ensure that the scope of powers given to the guardian is the least restrictive to the ward as possible.

In short, the guardianship statutes should have a limited guardianship available, should contain language that directs the court to match the powers given to the guardians with the needs of the ward, should require the guardian to seek court approval before making decisions that could hold serious personal ramifications for the ward, and should specifically direct the court to use the least restrictive alternatives when decisions for the ward's care are made.

Reports on Guardian Activity

Critics of the guardianship process argue that the activities of the guardians are rarely monitored by the court, and that the reports that are provided focus on financial accounting of the estate as opposed to the ward's status or condition (Horstman, 1975; Peters, Schmidt, & Miller, 1985; Ratcliffe, 1982). Unless the court requires guardians to file reports describing the activities conducted on behalf of the ward, it has no way of knowing what has happened on behalf of and to the ward, or if the ward's condition requires the continuation of the guardianship. Guardians' activities should be reported to the court annually, and should provide information about the ward's living arrangement, physical and mental condition, any medical treatment obtained, the nature of the contact between the guardian and the ward, and whether the guardianship is still needed.

The criticisms of the guardianship process and the concern about potential abuse of individual liberties have prompted many states to revise their guardianship statutes. If the statutes are indeed reflective of the symbolic changes desired by advocates, they should contain all of the provisions recommended above. We now examine nine state guardianship statutes and compare each with the criticism previously discussed.

RESULTS

Definition of Incapacity

Definitions of incapacity have been criticized in the literature because of the focus on physical or mental status rather than on a determination of the lack of functional capacity to meet daily needs. A review of statutory definitions of incapacity for each of the nine states revealed that Nebraska, Kansas, and Minnesota rely on a finding of functional ability to meet essential needs rather than using the old standard of physical or mental status as a basis for incapacity (Figure 9.1). The Missouri statute, while

Figure 9.1
Statutory Definitions of Incompetency[1]

<u>Colorado</u>
...means any person who is impaired by reason of mental illness, mental deficiency, physical illness or disability, advanced age, chronic use of drugs, chronic intoxication, or other cause (except minority) to the extent that he lacks sufficient understanding or capacity to make or communicate responsible decisions concerning his person....[CRS §15-14-101 (1)]

<u>Illinois</u>
...because of mental deterioration or physical incapacity is not fully able to manage his person or estate...[IRS §110½ 11a-2]

<u>Iowa</u>
...by reason of mental, physical or other incapacity is unable to make or carry out important decisions regarding the proposed person or affairs...[IC §633.552(2)(a)]

<u>Kansas</u>
...whose ability to receive and evaluate information effectively or communicate decisions or both is impaired to such an extent that...lacks capacity to manage financial resources to meet essential requirements for physical health, safety or both...[KSA §59-3002(a)]

<u>Minnesota</u>
...impaired to the extent that he lacks sufficient understanding or capacity to make or communicate responsible decisions concerning his person and who has demonstrated deficits in behavior which evidence his inability to meet his needs for medical care, nutrition, clothing, shelter or safety...[MSA §525.54(2)]

<u>Missouri</u>
...unable by reason of any physical or mental condition to receive and evaluate information or to communicate decisions to such an extent that he lacks the capacity to meet essential requirements for food, shelter, clothing, safety or other such that serious physical illness, injury or disease is likely to occur...[MRS §475.010(8)]

<u>Nebraska</u>
...lacks sufficient understanding to make, communicate or carry out responsible decisions concerning his or her own person...[NRS §30-2619.01(a)]

<u>South Dakota</u>
...when it appears necessary or convenient, may appoint a guardian...of a person who is mentally ill or for any cause mentally or physically incompetent to manage his own property (may be appointed for a recipient of public assistance where it is found such recipient is wasteful and unable to manage assistance payments for the purpose to which they were intended...)[SDC §30-27-6, §30-27-7]

<u>Wisconsin</u>
...substantially incapable of managing his property or caring for himself by reason of infirmities of old age, developmental disabilities or other like impairments. Physical disabilities without mental incapacity is not sufficient to establish incompetence. [WS §880.01(4)]

[1] Statutes referred to in Figures 9.1-9.6 may have been revised since the analyses were conducted.

Figure 9.2
Statutory Provisions for the Petition, Notice, and the Court's Investigative Role in Guardianship Hearings

State	Personal Service of Notice of Hearing and Petition	Petition Includes Reasons for Alleged Incapacity	Petition Lists Rights Available to Prospective Ward	Court Authorization of an Investigation of Ward's Condition	
				Visitor Program	Other Professional
Colorado	X	X		X[f]	X[g]
Illinois	X	X[c]			X[g]
Iowa	X				
Kansas	X[a]	X[d]			X[g]
Minnesota	X[b]	X[e]	X		
Missouri	X	X	X		X[g]
Nebraska	X	X	X	X[g]	X[g]
S. Dakota	X	X			X[g]
Wisconsin	X	X			X[h]

[a] Court may appoint a professional to serve petition
[b] Petition must be read to proposed ward if requested by the proposed ward
[c] Report must accompany petition outlining condition, what the scope of powers should be
[d] May require physician's statement to accompany petition
[e] Proposed ward may request a bill of particulars specifying factual information
[f] Visitor is appointed unless proposed ward has his/her own counsel
[g] Discretionary rather than mandatory
[h] If requested by the proposed ward or anyone on behalf of the proposed ward

retaining language that cites the reason for impairment, does focus on functional ability as well. Kansas, Minnesota, and Missouri have listed specific functional outcomes to be used to determine functional capacity (e.g., ability to meet safety, shelter, medical, and nutritional needs). The Wisconsin statute contains language that prohibits a finding of incapacity based on physical disability alone, but along with Colorado, retains a reference to using infirmities of aging or old age as a reason for incapacity. The South Dakota definition of incapacity differs from others in that a guardian may be appointed if the court deems it necessary or convenient, and those receiving public assistance may have a guardian appointed if they are found to be wasting money and unable to manage assistance payments.

Petition, Notice of Hearing, and the Court's Investigative Role

Figure 9.2 presents different statutory provisions of each of the nine states regarding requirements of the petition and notice of the guardianship hearing. Also noted is the court's statutory authority to appoint an independent investigation of the ward's condition.

All states require personal service of the petition and notice of hearing. A few states have attempted to improve the manner in which the information about the hearing and its consequences are presented to the proposed ward. For example, the Missouri statute requires that the petition and notice be in simple language, clearly state the reasons why the appointment is sought, and provide a list of rights of the prospective ward. In Kansas, the court allows for personal service of the petition by a professional (e.g., mental health worker, health officer) rather than by a police officer or service processor.

A few states require that the petition contain reasons why the ward is thought to need a guardian. While all states, with the exception of Iowa, require that petitions include reasons why the prospective ward is thought to be incompetent, the Illinois statute requires a report regarding the condition of the ward to accompany the petition. In Kansas and Minnesota, the court may require additional information regarding the allegations. Only three states, Minnesota, Missouri, and Nebraska, require that the petition contain a list of rights available to the prospective ward in the guardianship process.

In some jurisdictions, courts are authorized to take an active role in obtaining further evidence of the ward's alleged incapacity. Additional information is usually obtained either through a court visitor or by appointing independent professionals to make physical or mental evaluations. All states, with the exception of Iowa and Minnesota, may order independent evaluations of the mental or physical condition of the proposed ward. For example, the Kansas courts have discretionary powers to order an investigation covering the character, family relationships, and past conduct of the proposed ward; whether the proposed ward is likely to injure him or herself or others; the character and past conduct of the proposed guardian; and the property of the proposed ward. The Wisconsin statute permits an independent medical or psychological evaluation of the proposed ward. However, such an evaluation occurs only if the proposed ward or anyone on his or her behalf requests it.

The Nebraska and Colorado statutes authorize the use of a court visitor during the guardianship process. The two states differ, however: use of the court visitor is optional in Nebraska, while in Colorado, the visitor is required in each case, unless the proposed ward has legal counsel. In Nebraska, the court-appointed visitor conducts an evaluation that includes interviews with the proposed ward and guardian and with the agency that provided care to the prospective ward, a visit to the current residence of the proposed ward, and, if a change in residence is recommended, a visit to the future place of residence. Regarding the specific issue of incapacity, the visitor assesses the prospective ward's ability to make, communicate, or carry out responsible decisions in the following areas: (1) selecting a place of residence; (2) arranging for medical care; (3) protecting personal effects; (4) giving consent; (5) arranging for training, education, or other habilitative services appropriate to him or her; (6) applying for government benefits;

(7) entering into contractual agreements; and (8) receiving money and applying it to personal expenses. The Nebraska statute also requires the visitor to be trained in such areas as law, nursing, social work, mental health, gerontology, or developmental disabilities.

The role of the visitor in Colorado is similar. The visitor must meet with the proposed ward and explain the nature and purpose of the proceeding; ascertain the proposed ward's views about the proposed guardianship and guardian; and inform him or her of the right to have an attorney. The visitor must also interview the proposed guardian and health care provider. Finally, the visitor is to describe to the court the proposed ward's degree of incapacity; provide an evaluation of the fitness of the proposed guardian; inform the court if the proposed ward requests an attorney; and provide a recommendation as to whether a guardian ad litem or physician should be appointed to represent or examine the proposed ward.

Guardianship Hearing

A frequent criticism of the guardianship process is the routine absence of the proposed wards from the hearing (Horstman, 1975). Illinois, Kansas, Minnesota, and Wisconsin require the prospective wards to be at the hearing unless there is evidence that it would be injurious to their health (Figure 9.3). Colorado, Iowa, Missouri, Nebraska, and South Dakota require the

Figure 9.3
Statutory Provisions for the Guardianship Hearing

State	Proposed Ward's Presence at the Hearing	Representation of Proposed Ward		Guardian Ad Litem Appointed	Use of Clear and Convincing Evidence	Must Inquire into Capacity of Decision-Making Ability[1]
		May be Appointed	Must be Appointed			
Colorado	X[a]	X[d]		X[e]		X
Illinois	X[b,c]	X		X[e]		X
Iowa	X[a]	X[d]				
Kansas	X[b,c]		X		X	X
Minnesota	X[b]		X		X	
Missouri	X[a]		X		X	X[g,h]
Nebraska	X[a]	X		X[f]	X	
S. Dakota	X[a]					
Wisconsin	X[b,c]			X	X	

[1] While all courts have the option to require additional evidence, these states specifically address this by statute
[a] Statute states ward has the right to be present
[b] Attends hearing unless it would be detrimental to prospective ward's health
[c] May be held at a more convenient place
[d] Proposed ward is notified of right to have an attorney appointed
[e] May appoint if deemed necessary by the court
[f] May be appointed if proposed ward doesn't have counsel or doesn't request counsel
[g] Examines alternatives to guardianship which are least restrictive
[h] If respondent can meet basic needs, then guardianship is denied

prospective wards be advised that they are entitled to be present at the hearing. The court in South Dakota may order the proposed ward to be present at the hearing. In an attempt to ensure that the proposed ward is at the hearing, Illinois, Kansas, and Wisconsin statutes authorize the court to hold the hearing at a more convenient location for the proposed ward if needed.

With regard to the appointment of an attorney to represent proposed wards, all states, with the exception of South Dakota, inform proposed wards that they are entitled to have an attorney appointed to represent them. Only the Kansas, Minnesota, and Missouri statutes require the court to appoint an attorney to represent proposed wards, unless they already have an attorney. The Colorado, Illinois, Iowa, and Nebraska courts may appoint an attorney for the proposed ward if they believe legal representation is needed. In addition to, or in place of, the appointment of an attorney to represent the proposed ward, courts may appoint a guardian ad litem. Colorado, Illinois, and Nebraska have the option to appoint a GAL, whereas in Wisconsin GALs are appointed for the proposed wards.

As previously mentioned, any evidence (including evidence that some may consider anecdotal or hearsay) provided by the petitioner to support the proposed ward's incapacity has often been considered adequate when courts use a less strict legal standard of proof. Kansas, Minnesota, Missouri, Nebraska, and Wisconsin have explicitly instructed the courts to use a more strict standard of evidence—that of clear and convincing evidence (Figure 9.3).

Finally, four states—Colorado, Illinois, Kansas, and Missouri—require that the court, in making its determination of incapacity, inquire into the decision-making ability of the proposed ward. Inquiring into the decision-making capacity of the proposed ward protects the proposed ward from a determination of incapacity based solely on a physical diagnosis. The Missouri court must consider any less restrictive alternatives to a guardianship when considering the appropriateness of the appointment of a guardian and, if the court determines that the ward can meet basic needs, the guardianship is denied.

Scope of Guardian Powers

Almost every state has the option of limiting the scope of the guardian's authority by having a limited guardianship available (Figure 9.4). A handful of states also require that the powers given to the guardian match the incapacities of the ward. For example, Illinois requires courts to make a determination of the nature and extent of the ward's intellectual and physical functioning, capacity for decision-making, and management of financial assets, and courts are to limit the powers of guardians accordingly. The Kansas statute requires that courts must find the extent to which

Figure 9.4
Statutory Provisions for the Scope of Powers Available to the Guardian

State	Limited Guardianship Available	Powers Given to Guardian Match Needs[1]	Specific Reference to Use of Least Restrictive Alternatives for the Ward	Must Obtain Court Order for Certain Actions
Colorado	X	X	X	X[b]
Illinois	X	X		X[c]
Iowa	X			X[d,e,f]
Kansas	X	X		X[b,c,d,f]
Minnesota		X	X	X[c,d,g]
Missouri	X	X	X	X[b,d]
Nebraska	X	X[a]		
S. Dakota				X[g]
Wisconsin	X			X[h]

[1] Makes specific reference to guardianship orders matching incapacity needs of protected person
[a] Order may specify responsibilities of guardian and ward
[b] Institutional care for mental illness, alcoholism
[c] Residential placement
[d] Surgical procedures
[e] Change of residence
[f] Withholding of life-saving medical procedures
[g] Sale of personal or real property
h Permanent protective placement

disabled persons are able to make their own decisions and when appropriate, appoint a limited guardian. Similarly, the guardianship orders from the Nebraska court must specify the responsibilities of both the guardian and the ward.

The Colorado, Minnesota, and Missouri statutes are notable in that they make specific reference to providing the least restrictive outcomes for the ward. The Minnesota statute states that if no appropriate alternatives that are less restrictive than a guardianship are available, the guardian is granted only the powers that are necessary for the needs demonstrated.

Finally, in most jurisdictions, guardians are given the authority to take control of almost all aspects of the ward's life. There are, however, certain activities for which the guardian must seek the court's permission before they are conducted on behalf of the ward. In some instances, guardians must obtain the court's permission before selling the ward's personal or real property, consenting to certain intrusive medical procedures, or placing the ward in a mental health facility. Each state differs with regard to the specificity of the limitations on guardians' activities. Kansas requires the guardian to seek a court order for activities concerning residential placement, surgical procedures, institutional care, and the withholding of life-sustaining procedures. All other states, with the exception of Nebraska, mention at least one activity for which the guardian must seek the court's permission.

Figure 9.5
Statutory Requirements for the Guardian Reports

State	Frequency of Guardian's Report to the Court	Information That Must Be Included in Guardian's Report				
		Visits with Ward	Living Arrangements	Ward's Condition	Medical Treatment	Recommendation of Need for Continuation of Guardianship
Colorado	Determined by the Court[a]					
Illinois	Determined by Court[a]	X	X	X	X	X
Iowa	Annual[b]	X	X	X	X	X
Kansas[1]	Annual[b]			X		
Minnesota	Annual[b]		X	X	X	X[d]
Missouri	Annual	X		X	X	X
Nebraska	At Least Every 2 Years					
S. Dakota	Annual					
Wisconsin	Annual		X[c]	X		

[1] Within 3 years after appointment, the court conducts a review of the continued need for guardianship
[a] This information is required if the court orders the guardian to file a report
[b] Unless determined otherwise by the court
[c] Statement required indicating whether the ward is living in the least restrictive environment consistent with needs of ward
[d] Guardians must provide wards with a notice that informs him/her of the right to petition to have the guardian removed

Reports on Guardian Activity

Once a guardian has been appointed, she or he must file reports as often as the court instructs. Six of the state statutes reviewed require the guardian to submit an annual report outlining the ward's condition (Figure 9.5). In three of these states, however, the court has the authority to alter the frequency of the report. Minnesota requires that with every annual report submitted to the court, the ward is to receive notice of his or her right to petition for the removal of the guardian. Perhaps the most notable is the Kansas statute, which requires the court to conduct a review every three years of the appropriateness of the continued need of the guardianship and the powers granted. In contrast, Colorado, Illinois, and South Dakota allow courts to determine if and when guardians must file a report of their activities.

The information contained in the guardian's report to the court also varies widely by state. Iowa, Minnesota, and Missouri require annual reports that provide more information about the condition of the ward than do other states. Illinois also requires the guardian to report on numerous aspects of the ward's condition, but the frequency of the report is left up to the court, as it is in Colorado. Nebraska and South Dakota do not specifically mention the type of information required to appear in the guardian's report.

COMPARISON OF KEY STATUTORY PROTECTIONS

Although the states selected for analysis were all located in the same region of the country, they represent examples of both comprehensive and limited protections of wards. A final comparison of the nine states was conducted, using key protective provisions of the guardianship process as the basis of the analysis. The eight provisions selected as points of comparison were: (1) a definition of incapacity using functional status as an indicator of incapacity; (2) a notice and/or petition that provides an explanation of the ward's rights and the nature of proceedings; (3) required appointment of an attorney to represent the ward; (4) use of a court visitor to gather additional evidence for the court; (5) use of the "clear and convincing" standard of evidence; (6) specific reference to the use of least restrictive alternatives when determining the outcomes for the ward; (7) instructions to match the powers given to the guardian with the ward's needs; and (8) requirement that the guardian file a detailed report (defined as requiring an annual report on multiple aspects of the ward's condition). States are listed on Figure 9.6 in descending order, based on the extensive nature of the protections afforded to the ward.

Based on these criteria for comparison, the states whose statutes provide the highest degree of protection for proposed wards are Missouri, Minnesota, and Kansas (Figure 9.6). The next group of states that are somewhat less comprehensive in their statutes, yet provide several key protections, are Wisconsin, Colorado, and Nebraska. The states that have fewer of the protections designated are Illinois, Iowa, and South Dakota.

In a sense, these nine states selected for study represent the diverse ways in which the guardianship process is implemented in each jurisdiction. The three states selected for in-depth study, Missouri, Iowa and Colorado, represent distinctively different approaches and degree of protections provided to the proposed ward throughout the guardianship process; yet each is representative of other states in the amount of protections provided.

CONCLUSIONS

The criticisms expressed about the guardianship process have been addressed by many of the state statutes considered here, but the degree to which these symbolic changes have been made vary. At least three states require the court to consider the functional capacity of the ward, to use clear and convincing evidence when weighing the evidence presented to prove incapacity, and to limit the powers of the guardian to those that are least restrictive and match the proven deficits of the ward. Eight of the nine states

Figure 9.6
Comparison of Selected Guardianship Provisions in Nine States

State	Uses Functional Status as an Indicator of Incapacity	Provides an Explanation of Rights/Nature of Proceedings	Appoints an Attorney for Proposed Ward	Court Visitor	Uses Clear and Convincing Evidence Standard	Specific Reference to the Use of Least Restrictive Alternatives	Powers Given to Guardians Match Ward's Needs	Requires Detailed Report of Ward
Missouri	X	X	X		X	X	X	X
Minnesota	X	X	X		X	X	X	X
Kansas	X		X		X	X	X	X
Wisconsin		X[a]	X (GAL)		X			X
Colorado		X[a]	optional	X		X	X	
Nebraska		X	optional	optional	X		X	
Illinois		X[a]	optional				X	
Iowa		X[a]	optional					X
S. Dakota								

[1] "Detailed report" is defined as requiring an annual report on multiple aspects of the ward's condition.
[a] An attorney, GAL, or court visitor, if appointed, is to provide an explanation of rights.

have sought to limit in some way the powers given to guardians. Seven states provide for a limited guardianship, whereas six states direct their courts to limit the powers of the guardian to match the limitations of the ward. Only Minnesota, Colorado, Kansas, and Missouri make mention of ensuring that least restrictive alternatives are used in the care of wards. Yet, ensuring that the least restrictive alternative is sought should enhance the match between needs of the ward and the extensive nature of the guardianship. Overall, our analysis revealed that three states have enacted the majority of suggested reforms; of the other six states, three have made moderate changes, while in the other three a great deal of statutory changes are needed to meet suggested reforms.

Indeed, although many of the statutes symbolically change the process, much of the language states that the court *may* employ certain protections. For example, the use of a court visitor has been advocated as a way for courts to obtain independent evidence as to the need for a guardianship. The use of a court visitor is mandatory in Colorado, while in Nebraska the court visitor is optional. Similarly, six of the nine states have the option of ordering an independent physical or mental examination of the proposed ward. In each of these states, obtaining an additional evaluation is discretionary, not mandatory.

Another example of the court's discretionary power seen in many of the statutes is the appointment of an attorney to represent the proposed ward and the monitoring of guardian activities. Although eight of the nine states reviewed provide the proposed ward with the information that he or she is entitled to be represented by an attorney, only two states *require* the court to appoint counsel if the proposed ward has not obtained representation. Monitoring the guardian's activities is an important function of the court, but our investigation revealed that three statutes allow the court to determine if and when guardian reports are to be filed. Our investigation of the Colorado records revealed that guardians are seldom required to file any reports. When statutes do require the guardian to file reports, many of them are again silent regarding the kind of information that should be contained in the report. Only four of the nine states specify the type of information that must be reported to the court, again leaving the court with the option of deciding the level of specificity required in the guardian reports.

In conclusion, symbolic changes in legislation are needed before any instrumental changes can be made in the treatment and outcomes for the proposed ward. Symbolic changes, however, are no guarantee that the actual treatment of those individuals who enter the system will be radically different than it was before statutory changes were made. This is especially true in those states with minimal changes or that allow the court great latitude in implementing the protections afforded to the proposed ward in the statutes. As a result, our investigations of the guardianship process must examine the effectiveness of guardianship legislation in each state.

For example, are differences in legislation reflected in the types of guardianships that are awarded? This question will be addressed in chapter 10.

10

Guardianship Reform: Do Revised Statutes Make a Difference in Outcomes for Prospective Wards?

Frolik (1981:629) observed: "Although there is no dearth of guardianship reform proposals, there is a lack of critical examination of the efficacy of such programs." More recently, Dejowski (1990) reflected on the need for systematic assessments of guardianship legislation and practices. In this chapter we investigate the guardianship decisions for older proposed wards prior to and following changes in state statutes in Iowa, Missouri, and Colorado. In earlier work we compared outcomes of hearings in two states (Keith & Wacker, 1993). In this chapter a longitudinal view of guardianship decisions for older persons in three states is provided. An objective of this chapter was to determine whether court decisions about guardianship differed following passage of legislation that included increased procedural safeguards for proposed wards. The findings of the hearings reported in this chapter were linked to actual changes in legislation, while outcomes described in chapter 11 were correlated with the implementation of recommended practices irrespective of the revision of state statutes.

The ultimate test of reform should be in the variation in outcomes following implementation of revised statutes. For if laws are not put into practice, revisions will have no effect (Wang, Burns, & Hommel, 1990). First, we assume that the impetus for statutory revision originates from a change in attitudes toward the rights of the aged and in perceptions of current guardianship statutes. These perceptions may prompt the call for and passage of revised legislation. Revised statutes are implemented and followed by changes in outcomes for individuals under the law. If revised guardianship statutes reflect a shift in attitudes, then outcomes of hearings for older persons are indicators of instrumental change, and may demonstrate how individuals are treated with respect to a particular law.

THE CONTEXT OF REFORM

As late as 1980, commenting that changes in guardianship legislation had been bypassed in the sweeping changes in mental health law, Sherman (1980:351) observed: "Surprisingly, the procedural and substantive inadequacies of guardianship have aroused little concern from either commentators or the law reform movement." As is evident in previous chapters, such an oversight is not the case today. Chapters 3 and 9 provide confirmation that in the intervening years, the procedural and substantive inadequacies of the guardianship system have been the basis of considerable legislative reform. As we have seen, calls for reform of guardianship legislation have occurred in Europe, Canada, and the United States (Eekelaar & Pearl, 1989). Some of the conditions leading to reform and the substance of suggested legislative changes are similar from country to country and state to state.

By now, the reasons for the substantial attention recently given to the process and outcomes of securing guardianships, as described in earlier chapters, should be clear. The great concern, of course, rests with the profound ramifications of being found incompetent. Traditionally, guardianship has represented a dramatic intrusion on individual liberties. Perhaps this is most graphically illustrated by noting common areas in which wards have been found to be incapacitated, and guardians have been authorized to act. Barnes (1988), for example, cited the results of a survey of 114 guardianship cases in New Hampshire. The following is a sampling of areas in which wards were found to be incapacitated: "Travel, or deciding where to live; refusal or consent to medical treatment, counseling services, or other professional care where consent is legally necessary; making contracts, possession or management of real or personal property or income from any source, making gifts; initiating, defending or settling lawsuits; lending or borrowing money; paying or collecting debts; managing or operating a business; waiving the provisions of a will . . . and accessing and releasing confidential records and papers" (Barnes, 1988:972). There also may be loss of liberties that cannot be delegated to another, such as the right to vote, marry, drive, or perhaps to gather with others either publicly or privately. Finally, there is the stigma of being found incapacitated, which may be foremost among the grave outcomes of a declaration of incapacity. Because the majority of aged wards previously acted as autonomous adults, appointment of a surrogate decision maker will constrain long-held rights and expectations (Barnes, 1988). As the scope of a guardian's authority is increased, the liberties of the ward decline.

In an effort to ensure erroneous findings of incapacity do not occur, implementation of several safeguards has been suggested. The recommended procedural safeguards noted in earlier chapters indicate that reforms should address all stages of the guardianship proceedings (Wang, Burns, & Hommel, 1990). Aspects to be addressed include, for example, specific information in the petition, notice of the hearing, standards used to assess competency, the nature of evidence, legal representation for the proposed ward, the scope of powers granted to the guardian, court supervision of the guardian, and provision for termination of guardianships (Eekelaar & Pearl, 1989).

The intent of recent legislative reform has been to seek the least restrictive alternative forms of assistance for proposed wards. Barnes, however, concludes that "in many cases, both traditional and reform guardianship concepts remove more of the ward's rights than required to compensate for the ward's diminished capability" (1988:969). Barnes maintains that the concept of the least restrictive alternative should be a part of the competency determination because both society's values and guardianship itself have changed. Historically, in guardianship proceedings, due process standards and specification of a least restrictive alternative were not viewed as necessary to attain a fair and accurate result. In an earlier chapter, we noted that under a benevolent and nonadversarial judicial process, the appointment of a guardian was seen as beneficial, if not inevitable. But in the past 25 years due process standards have been adopted to address the strain between individual liberties and benevolent assistance (Barnes, 1988). Despite legislative changes, there is still an inherent conflict between the perception of the need to help and the rights of the elderly (Dudovitz, 1985).

In addition to the changing conception of guardianship, Barnes (1988:970) suggested that today guardianships are established for persons who are "far more aware and capable than wards of the past." Consequently, consideration of the least restrictive alternative is especially timely because of changes both in the conception of guardianship practice and in the level of the capacity of wards.

In the search for a least restrictive option, existing services that might be used in lieu of guardianship should be explained carefully to the older person, the petitioner, and those who care for them. Most of the guardians we studied, however, had not been apprised of alternatives to guardianship. As noted in chapter 4, because the extent of impairment in decision-making capabilities may vacillate over time, the variability should be taken into account in arranging for assessment of capacity and in determining needs.

As Barnes explains, "Limited guardianship . . . limits the guardian's authority to decisions the ward is incapable of making, by defining areas of the guardian's powers that correspond to the ward's incapabilities" (1988:972). Because of the ward's presumed partial incapacity, authority not given to the guardian is retained by the ward. "However, the limited guardianship concept fails to identify the least restrictive form of assistance because it considers only assistance provided through guardianship" (Barnes, 1988:972).

A decision to implement the least restrictive alternative outside of the guardianship system would be identified in our analysis of court records only as a denial of the petition for guardianship. In the event of denial, information was not available on the alternative that was selected or on plans, if any, that were set in place. The outcomes of hearings for wards for which data were available were full (plenary) guardianship or full guardianship/conservatorship, limited guardianship or limited guardianship/conservatorship, or denial. Consequently, our focus on the least restrictive alternative within the guardianship system is represented by limited powers.

The general hypothesis of this research was that implementation of revised legislation instituting some of these safeguards should result in greater use of least restrictive alternatives (e.g., limited guardianship or denial). A second hypothesis was that more explicit and stringent state statutes would be associated with the awarding of more limited guardianships or with denial of a greater proportion of the petitions. With this in mind, states with quite different statutes were selected for study.

CHANGE IN STATUTES: CONTRASTING LEGISLATION IN THREE SAMPLES

Although the statutes in Missouri, Iowa, and Colorado have been changed, they differ in the degree of explicitness of their protective language for safeguarding individual liberties (Figures 10.1, 10.2, and 10.3). These statutory differences are graphic enough that we might expect them to be reflected in differential outcomes for proposed wards. The differences in state statutes are mentioned in some detail because more generally they represent varying approaches to the process of awarding guardianship.

The revised Missouri statute generally reflects a more detailed process that gives specific directions to legal representation, advocates least restrictive alternatives, and sets forth specific individual rights afforded to the prospective ward (Figure 10.1). The court must find the prospective ward lacks the capacity to meet essential requirements of daily living (i.e., food, clothing, shelter), but the mere presence of such an incapacity is not enough. An additional finding, that physical injury or harm is likely to occur as a result of the incapacity, must be present. Also, the statute allows the court to make a distinction in the degree of incapacity, thereby making it possible to adjudicate "partial incapacity." Additional provisions instruct the court to deny any petition for guardianship if it finds the prospective ward has the capacity to meet the essential requirements of daily living.

Another important safeguard in the Missouri statute is the specific authorization of the use of the least restrictive alternative when a finding of incapacity is present. Under this ideology, the least drastic means for providing for the needs of the ward should be employed (Sherman, 1980).

Figure 10.1
Comparison of Missouri Guardianship Statutes before and after Legislative Changes

	Pre	Post
Definition of Incapacity	"...any person who is incapable by reason of insanity, mental illness, imbecility, idiocy, senility, habitual drunkenness or other incapacity...of either managing his property or caring for himself or both..."	"...unable by reason of any physical or mental condition...to such an extent that he lacks capacity to meet essential requirements for food, clothing, shelter or safety or other care such that serious physical injury, illness or disease is likely to occur..."
Application for Guardianship	"Such petition shall state:...the fact that the person...is incapable by reason of insanity, mental illness, imbecility, idiocy, senility, habitual drunkenness or other incapacity...of managing his property or caring for himself...[and] the reason why the appointment is sought..."	"Such petition shall state...that the person...is unable by reason of some specified physical or mental condition...to such an extent that the person lacks the capacity to meet essential requirements for food, clothing, shelter, safety...such that serious physical injury, illness or disease is likely to occur..."
Notice of Hearing	"...shall be notified of the proceeding by written notice stating the nature of the proceeding, the time and place...and that such person is entitled to be present...and to be assisted by counsel..."	"...shall be served with written notice stating the time and place of the proceeding...the name of the appointed counsel, the names and addresses of the witnesses who may be called to testify in support of the petition...a copy of the respondent's rights..."
Appointment of Counsel	"If no licenses attorney appears for the alleged incompetent at the hearing the court shall appoint an attorney to represent him at the proceeding..."	"Upon filing the petition...the court shall immediately appoint an attorney to represent the respondent...the attorney shall visit his client prior to the hearing...shall obtain from the client all possible aid..."
Hearing	"When a petition is filed...the court...shall order that the facts be inquired into by a jury..[or]...by the court..."	"The court may direct the respondent to be examined by a physician or licensed psychologist or other professional..." "The petitioner has the burden of proving incapacity, partial incapacity...by clear and convincing evidence." "The respondent has the right to be represented by an attorney..have a jury trial...present evidence...cross-examine witnesses...remain silent...have the hearing open or closed to the public...be present at the hearing..." "If the court finds that the respondent possesses the capacity to meet his essential requirements...it shall deny the petition.
Order	"If it appears that a guardian should be appointed...the court shall make such an appointment..."	"It shall make...in its order detailed findings...stating the extent of his physical and mental incapacity to care for his person [and] his finances [and] whether or not he requires placement in a supervised living...and if so, the degree of supervision needed." "...in determining the degree of supervision necessary shall apply the least restrictive environment principle...and shall not restrict his personal liberty...to any greater extent than is necessary..."
Limited Guardianships	not mentioned	"If the court...finds that a person is partially incapacitated, the court shall appoint a limited guardian..[and]...specify the powers and duties of the limited guardian so as to permit the partially incapacitated ward to care for himself commensurate with his ability..." "...the court shall impose only such...restraints on personal liberty that are necessary to promote and protect the well-being of the individual..."

Figure 10.2
Comparison of Iowa Guardianship Statutes before and after Legislative Changes

	Pre	Post
Definition of Incapacity	"...the proposed ward is...incapable of caring for his own person."	"...by reason of mental, physical or other incapacity lacks sufficient capacity to make or carry out important decisions concerning the proposed ward's person or affairs."
Application for Guardianship	"...the petition shall state...name, age and address of the proposed ward...that the proposed is incapable of caring for his own person...the name and address of the proposed guardian and that such person is qualified to serve..."	"...the petition shall state...name, age and address of the proposed ward...by reason of mental, physical or other incapacity to make or carry out important decisions concerning the proposed ward's person or affairs...the name and address of the proposed guardian and that such person is qualified to serve..."
Notice of Hearing	"...notice of the filing of such petition shall be served upon the proposed ward..."	no change
Appointment of Counsel	not mentioned	"...the court shall determine whether under the circumstances...the proposed ward is entitled to representation and if so appoint an attorney..." "The court shall ensure that all proposed wards entitled to representation have been notified of the right..."
Hearing	"...the cause shall be tried as a law action, and either party shall be entitled to a jury trial..." "If the allegations of the petition as to the status of the proposed ward and the necessity for the appointment are proved, the court may appoint a guardian."	no change
Order	"Unless otherwise directed by order of court, the guardian shall have general supervisory responsibility for the care of a ward..."	"A guardian may be granted the following powers which may only be exercised upon court approval: changing the ward's permanent residence if the proposed new residence is more restrictive of the ward's liberties; arranging...major elective surgery..."
Limited Guardianships	"...the court may take into account all available information concerning the capabilities of the ward...and may direct that the guardian have only a specially limited responsibility for the ward..."	no change

The Missouri statute instructs the court to use this doctrine when determining the degree of supervision necessary, and not to restrict the personal liberties or freedom to manage finances beyond what is necessary (Missouri Revised Statutes, 1986). In addition, the court must consider various least restrictive options available before issuing the guardianship as an alternative of last resort.

After the petition is filed, the court appoints an attorney to represent and meet with the prospective ward. In addition to attorney representation, the court may appoint an appropriate professional to examine the respondent.

Throughout this process, the rights of the ward are specifically set forth. For example, when interviewing the prospective ward, the professional

Figure 10.3
Comparison of Colorado Guardianship Statutes before and after Legislative Changes

	Pre	Post
Definition of Incapacity	"...impaired by reason of mental illness, mental deficiency, physical illness or disability, advanced age, chronic use of drugs, chronic intoxication or other cause to the extent that he lacks sufficient understanding to make or communicate responsible decisions concerning his person..."	no change
Application for Guardianship	"The incapacitated person or any person interested in his welfare may petition for a finding of incapacity and appointment of a guardian."	"The incapacitated person or any person interested in his welfare may petition for a finding of incapacity and appointment of a guardian or other protective order."
Notice of Hearing	"Notice shall be served personally on the alleged incapacitated person and his spouse and parents...waiver of notice by the alleged incapacitated person is not effective unless he attends the hearing or the waiver of notice is confirmed in an interview with the visitor..."	no change
Appointment of Counsel	"...[the court] may appoint an appropriate official or attorney to represent him in the proceeding and shall have the powers of a guardian ad litem..."	"The person alleged...to be incapacitated is entitled to be present by counsel..." "If at anytime in any court proceeding the allegedly incapacitated person requests that an attorney be appointed to represent him or expresses a desire to contest the petition...or proposed guardian...the court shall appoint an attorney to represent him..." "If at any time in any court proceeding, in the opinion of the court, the rights and interests of the allegedly incapacitated person cannot...be adequately protected...the court shall appoint an attorney to represent such person..."
Hearing	"The person alleged to be incapacitated may be examined by a physician appointed by the court..." "...may be interviewed by a visitor sent by the court..."	no change "...unless the allegedly incapacitated person had counsel...it shall appoint a visitor
Order	"the court may appoint a guardian as requested if it is satisfied that the person for whom a guardian is sought is incapacitated...and that the appointment is necessary or desirable as a means of providing continuing care and supervision...the court may dismiss the proceeding or enter any other appropriate order." "A guardian may give any consents or approvals that may be necessary to enable the ward to receive medical or other professional care, counsel or treatment..."	"...shall determine the nature and extent of the care, assistance, protection, or supervision which is necessary or desirable under all the circumstances." "The court shall consider less restrictive alternative means of providing the necessary protective services..." "...the court shall consider the wishes of the incapacitated person...[his] views concerning the selection of the guardian, the scope and duration of the guardianship and any limitations or restrictions the guardian shall have..." The court shall determine the extent to which a guardian shall be permitted to give any consents or approvals that may be necessary to enable the ward to receive medical or other care..."
Limited Guardianships	not mentioned	"The court may limit or restrict any of the powers or duties of the guardian or the scope or duration of the guardianship..."

examiner must inform respondents of the reason for the examination and their right to remain silent. The notice served to the respondent has a clear delineation of the respondent's right to be represented by an attorney, have a jury trial, present evidence and cross-examine witnesses, and be present at the hearing.

At the hearing, the burden of proving incapacity rests with the petitioner, and the evidence substantiating the allegation must be clear and convincing, which is a stronger requirement than those set forth for most guardianship proceedings. From a review of the Missouri Revised Statutes it is clear that numerous safeguards and limitations have been specifically set forth to provide direction to the court.

The current Iowa statutes reflect a somewhat different approach to the guardianship process (Figure 10.2). An individual is considered to be incapacitated if "by reason of mental, physical, or other incapacity is unable to make or carry out important decisions" concerning the proposed ward's person or financial affairs. The scope of this definition is less narrow than the Missouri definition stated above. The proposed ward is entitled to representation if the court deems it necessary. The attorney then becomes responsible for ensuring proper notice is given, providing representation, interviewing the prospective wards, and informing them of their rights and potential effects of the guardianship. In addition, the court may take into account all information available and may have additional evaluations performed in order to direct a limited scope of responsibility given to the guardian.

The statutory changes in Colorado made the court visitor mandatory rather than discretionary (Figure 10.3). The legislative changes also required the court to consider least restrictive alternatives for provision of protective services, created language authorizing limited guardianships based on the least restrictive doctrine, and required consideration of the wishes of the incapacitated person regarding the choice of guardian and alternatives to the guardianship.

Statutes of the three states represent different approaches to the guardianship process and include changes made to ensure the rights of the prospective ward are upheld. The Missouri statute, however, is the most specific. It may be useful to classify legislation according to the degree of specificity or generality it exhibits: "Legislation which is general with regard to its provisions, objects of reference and service to be given, would seem to offer the possibility not only of multiple interpretation but it is also likely to give rise to procedures and policies with a more permissive orientation" (Grace & Wilkinson, 1978:278). Therefore, as a general proposition, we expected that narrower and more explicit legislation would be associated with the appointment of more limited guardianships and more denial of petitions.

Based on the variation in revised legislation, two types of hypotheses were suggested: hypotheses specifying differences in decisions found prior to and following legislative changes, and hypotheses regarding variation in outcomes under the differing state statutes. The hypotheses address the nature of the powers requested, powers granted, difference between the powers requested and those granted, presence of a medical statement, and length of guardianship in relationship to legislative change.

HYPOTHESES

Upon implementation of legislation supporting greater attention to the least restrictive alternative, it was anticipated that a larger proportion of limited guardianships would be requested. All three states included the provision for limited guardianship. Iowa specifically mentioned limited responsibility for the ward prior to the enactment of new legislation; the addition of limited guardianship represented a change in the Missouri and Colorado statutes.

Because of an increased emphasis on employment of the least restrictive alternative, it was anticipated that more limited guardianships would be requested in petitions following legislative change in the three states. It was expected that not only would more limited guardianships be requested, but also more would be awarded following revision of the statutes.

Because of the increase in safeguards included in the newer legislation, it was also hypothesized that a larger proportion of petitions would be denied and the cases dismissed following the changes in legislation.

There is always the possibility that while a petition may request guardianship with a particular level of powers, the powers awarded to the guardian may be modified in some way. For example, a request for a plenary (full) guardianship may be modified to a limited one or, of course, a petition for a limited guardianship may be awarded full powers. Or the petitioner might request a full guardianship/conservatorship and receive a limited guardianship/full conservatorship. Along with a greater emphasis on the least restrictive alternative, however, it was anticipated that following adoption of new legislation, more petitions requesting plenary guardianships would be modified to limited guardianships or in some other way the powers would be narrowed.

Because a finding of incapacity is central to determining the need for a guardianship and because some of the changes in legislation advocate the use of more explicit evidence of incapacity, it was expected that at least a statement from a medical or health professional would be included in the records of the three states more often following the adoption of legislation. The revised Missouri statute, in particular, provides the most explicit definition of incapacity.

If the safeguards called for in the newer legislation are employed, we might expect to find that only individuals most in need of care had become wards in the later period. Earlier, persons less in need of care may have been awarded guardianships. An outcome of this may have been that in earlier years individuals with greater capacity spent longer periods of time as wards. The length of guardianships before and after legislative changes was examined. Guardianships established under legislation less attentive to safeguarding individual liberties may have continued over longer periods of time. Therefore, it was hypothesized that length of guardianship would be shorter in the period following statutory changes in the three states.

A final hypothesis concerned differences among the three states. Because legislative changes were more extensive and stringent in Missouri than in Iowa and Colorado, it was anticipated that outcomes for wards would reflect Missouri's greater use of the least restrictive alternative. In part, because the definition of incapacity in Missouri was far more explicit than those in Iowa and Colorado, it was expected that more limited guardianships would be awarded and more petitions dismissed in Missouri than in Iowa and Colorado following enactment of revised legislation. We anticipated that following statutory changes, the proportion of decisions for limited guardianships and for denials in Colorado would rank between those granted in Missouri and Iowa. The reason for this hypothesis was that the mandatory visitor reports and consideration given to the ward's preferences in the revised Colorado statutes were expected to contribute to greater attentiveness to the least restrictive alternative and limitation of powers.

METHODOLOGY

Data used in this chapter were obtained from 1,160 court records of guardianship petitions from Iowa, Missouri, and Colorado. These states had quite different revised legislation.

In Iowa, 152 records dated before May 24, 1984, the time of enactment of revised statutes, and 208 following this date were selected. In Missouri, 199 records dated prior to October 1, 1983, and 207 after this date when new legislation was enacted were chosen. In Colorado, 97 records filed prior to 1979 and 297 records compiled after implementation of the revised statutes were studied. (See chapter 2 for a discussion of the difficulty in accessing the records in Colorado prior to 1979, which contributed to the inclusion of a disproportionately smaller number of records dated before the revised legislation.)

Table 10.1
Powers Requested before and after Legislative Changes by State

Powers Requested (Percentages)	Iowa Pre	Iowa Post	Missouri Pre	Missouri Post	Colorado Pre	Colorado Post
Full	100 (N=152)	99 (N=207)	99 (N=199)	97 (N=201)	100 (N=97)	99 (N=294)
Limited	0	1 (N=1)	0	3 (N=6)	0	1 (N=3)

RESULTS

Were more limited guardianships *requested* following revision of legislation? Table 10.1 shows the percentages of the petitions filed for guardianship both prior to and following changes in legislation by state. No limited guardianships were requested prior to changes in legislation; following revision of statutes, seven, or about 1 percent of the total number of petitions, requested limited powers. Of these, the majority (n = 6) were requested in Missouri; because the number of cases is small, only limited support is provided for the hypothesis.

Were more limited guardianships *awarded* following the changes in legislation? In hearings held prior to changes in legislation, only one petitioner in Iowa and four in Colorado were awarded limited guardianships (Table 10.2). Subsequent to the change in legislation, 51 of the guardianships awarded involved limited powers, with 45 of the total appointed in Colorado. Therefore, there was some support for the hypothesis that more limited guardianships would be awarded following statutory changes.

Was denial of petitions more frequent following statutory changes than prior to implementation of new legislation? Only 24 petitions were denied across the entire time period studied (Table 10.2). Although there was a slight increase in Iowa and Missouri following the change in legislation, the number of petitions denied in Colorado declined by 1 percent. There was little variation by state in the change in the proportion of petitions denied following passage of the revised statutes.

Were petitioners awarded the powers they requested? That is, how often were the requests for powers by petitioners modified? In a cross tabulation of the powers requested in the initial petitions and those eventually granted by the courts, data for the three states were combined (Table 10.3). The most common pattern was for petitions for full powers to be granted both before and after statutory changes; 98 percent of requests for full guardianships were granted prior to revised legislation, compared with 90 percent after

Table 10.2
Powers Granted before and after Legislative Changes by State

Powers Granted (Percentages)	Iowa		Missouri		Colorado	
	Pre	Post	Pre	Post	Pre	Post
Full	98 (N=149)	95.5 (N=199)	99.5 (N=198)	96 (N=199)	93 (N=90)	83 (N=245)
Limited	1 (N=1)	1 (N=2)	0	2 (N=4)	4 (N=4)	15 (N=45)
Petition Denied	1 (N=2)	3 (N=7)	.5 (N=1)	2 (N=4)	3 (N=3)	2 (N=7)

Table 10.3
Powers Requested by Powers Granted before and after Legislative Changes

Powers Granted (Percentages)	Powers Requested			
	Pre		Post	
	Full	Limited	Full	Limited
Full	98 (N=437)	0	90 (N=633)	100 (N=10)
Limited	1 (N=5)	0	7 (N=51)	0
Petition Denied	1 (N=6)	0	3 (N=18)	0

the alteration in statutes. In some instances, full powers were granted, but the type of guardianship that was petitioned for was changed; for example, a full guardianship may have been requested but a full guardianship/conservatorship was granted.

Ironically, of the ten petitions for limited guardianships, all were granted full powers. None were limited or denied. Although the number was smaller, requests for limited guardianships were more likely to result in the appointment of plenary guardianships than requests for plenary ones were. Limited guardianships awarded were in response to initial requests for another type of powers. In Colorado, for example, the 49 limited guardianships that were awarded were initially requests for plenary powers.

Was a specific statement about the medical condition of the proposed ward by a health professional more likely to be included in the records following changes in legislation? Table 10.4 shows the percentages of cases

Table 10.4
Inclusion of a Medical Statement by a Health Care Professional before and after Legislative Changes by State

Medical Statement (Percentages)	Iowa		Missouri		Colorado	
	Pre	Post	Pre	Post	Pre	Post
Yes	59 (N=90)	73 (N=152)	90 (N=179)	89 (N=185)	66 (N=64)	76 (N=225)
No	41 (N=62)	27 (N=56)	10 (N=20)	11 (N=22)	34 (N=33)	24 (N=72)

for which evidence about the medical condition of the proposed ward was provided by a health professional. The presence of a statement by a health professional about the medical condition of the proposed ward increased more following legislative revisions in the two states with the least stringent legislation, Iowa and Colorado. However, the observed differences in compliance among the three states is due to the high frequency of inclusion of statements of medical condition in Missouri both prior to and following statutory revisions. For two of the three states, then, the hypothesis of increased inclusion of statements by health professionals following revised legislation was supported.

Were more recent guardianships likely to be of shorter duration than those granted prior to the change in legislation? The average number of years guardianships were open was calculated for closed guardianships both before and after the passage of legislation. Prior to the enactment of legislation, guardianships averaged 2.86, 3.36, and 3.36 years in length in Iowa, Missouri, and Colorado, respectively. Following the change in legislation, the length of guardianships was 1.69, 1.54, and 1.54 years in Iowa, Missouri, and Colorado. Guardianships administered prior to changes in legislation were significantly longer than those awarded following alteration of the statutes (t = 5.30, 5.07, and 5.07, $p < .001$, respectively). This finding may provide some support for the thinking that safeguards in newer legislation contributed to awarding guardianships to those who were most in need. In the earlier years, persons who were more able and had greater mental, physical, and functional capacity may have been wards for longer periods of time.

SUMMARY

More than a decade ago, Frolik (1981) observed that use of the plenary guardianship should be ceased and replaced with limitations on the powers of guardians: "The time has come to abolish plenary guardianship as a relic of the past. . . . Both the individual and society can be served better by flexible, limited guardianships that are tailored to the needs and capabilities of the individual" (Frolik, 1981:660). In the intervening years, widespread reforms in legislation have occurred. An explicit preference for limited guardianships is incorporated in many revised statutes (Wang, Burns, & Hommel, 1990). In a limited guardianship the guardian is awarded only the powers necessary to meet the needs of the ward, and then only for the amount of time necessary to address the concerns of the ward.

Writing, advocating, passing, and implementing the new legislation has been costly. Wang, Burns, & Hommel (1990:561) remarked: "Changes in the law will, however, have no practical effect unless the legal profession makes certain that the laws now on the books are put into practice." Were changes in legislation associated with differences in outcomes for proposed older wards? Despite legislation establishing limited guardianships as an option and encouraging their use by reformers, Frolik's admonition to replace plenary guardianships was heeded in only a minority of the 1,160 cases studied. In the three states studied, once a petition was filed requesting particular powers for the petitioner, usually plenary powers, it was likely to be approved. Modification of the type of powers requested in the petition usually was not ordered at the hearing, and there were few petitions for limited guardianships.

In summary, across the total sample of petitions initiated both before and after changes in legislation, the overwhelming majority were awarded some level of guardianship rather than being dismissed or denied. Slightly more petitions were denied following the changes in legislation compared to those prior to statutory change. However, the proportion of those denied once they got to a hearing was quite small both before and after the legislative changes.

To the extent that changes occurred following revised legislation, they tended to support the general hypothesis that least restrictive alternatives as reflected in limited guardianship would be employed. Even though it happened infrequently, modification of the type of powers occurred more often following statutory revision.

Under revised legislation, powers requested were most often modified in Colorado, where they resulted in appointments of more limited guardianships. Indeed, the most graphic change was observed in Colorado, and it was even more marked because changes in the other two states were substantially smaller. The major feature distinguishing revised Colorado statutes from previous ones for the time period studied was the mandated court visitor program. Although these data permit only conclusions based on correlational data, the implementation of the mandatory visitor program was related to the decision for the least restrictive alternative within the guardianship system. The visitor program was associated with strikingly different decisions than were observed in Iowa and Missouri, even though the latter had quite explicit revised safeguards in place. In chapter 11, we report that visitors' recommendations about guardians were associated with decisions for limited powers. Thus, there is the suggestion that conclusions of visitors may have had a greater impact on the outcomes for these older wards than implementation of some other practices (e.g., presence of the ward at the hearing).

Furthermore, the more explicit state legislation regarding evidence tended to be associated with greater use of statements by health professionals about the condition of the proposed ward. Was presentation of statements about the capacity of proposed wards associated with outcomes of the hearings? More explicit indications of capacity were not mirrored in greatly disparate decisions in the three states. Even with differences in explicitness and stringency of evidence required to establish incapacity of proposed wards, there was little variation in outcomes for wards by state.

The small number of limited guardianships requested and subsequently awarded in the petitions studied corroborated findings from other research. Moreover, the rights and capacities of wards are rarely broadened (Friedman & Savage, 1988). Why are so few limited guardianships requested and awarded? What may be some of the reasons for the seeming discrepancy between the use of options of least restrictive alternatives suggested in revised legislation and the eventual practices? Why are the policies of reform not reflected in a more diverse set of outcomes for a greater proportion of proposed wards? There are several possible reasons for the tendency toward homogeneous decisions regarding guardianship.

It may be that limited guardianships are not requested because petitioners do not know the extent of powers available, those that can be requested, or services and arrangements that might be used in lieu of guardianship. Schulte (1989) observed that guardians often lack information about resources to aid them in carrying out their tasks. Petitions for guardianship may be filed because community resources are limited (Coleman & Dooley, 1990). There is a need to inform petitioners and proposed wards about least restrictive alternatives external to and within the guardianship system, including limited guardianships. As it is now, the majority of guardians are not presented with any alternatives to guardianship.

It also may be that implementation of some of the safeguards (e.g., informing the proposed ward about the hearing, the appointment of counsel) or the way in which they are carried out is not sufficient to protect the proposed ward. For example, wards often are not represented by an attorney, or the appointed counsel does not act as an advocate for the ward, with the result the hearing is nonadversarial. Wang, Burns, & Hommel (1990:565) further observed that vigorous advocacy by attorneys representing proposed wards is often absent, and that without adversary counsel "the prospective ward is destined to lose."

Another possible reason for the small number of requests for limited guardianships could be that the more specific, stringent requirements for evidence of incapacity have diminished the number of petitions warranting the limitation of powers of the guardian. That is, some petitions that might have been filed and brought to a hearing before legislative changes may have been withdrawn or discouraged much earlier in the process prior to adjudication under revised statutes.

The apparent discrepancy between policy and practice may, in part, reflect confusion regarding the assessment of capacity. "Incompetency or incapacity is the threshold determination in any guardianship hearing" (Coleman & Dooley, 1990:48). Changing definitions of incapacity represent one of the major reforms in guardianship legislation (Wang, Burns, & Hommel, 1990). Newer conceptions of capacity focus on the individual's ability to function independently.

Much hinges on the initial evaluation of capacity and the continued monitoring of the functioning of wards. Statutes should direct the court to assess capacity as it specifically relates to the ward's social, legal, and medical functioning. The more specific the assessment, the more specific the guardian's powers can be. The responsibility lies with the court to investigate and determine if the requested powers match the current needs of the proposed ward, rather than needs yet to emerge in the future, if at all. A way to address evolving needs of wards is to have annual reviews of guardianships conducted by the court, or to have guardians indicate their needs for expanded powers in their annual reports.

The most stringent legislation may not be sufficient to withstand the application of ageist assumptions about later life. Perhaps it is in the assessment of evidence about capacity that opportunities for decisions based on ageist thinking may occur most frequently. There is a continued call for education of attorneys and judges about the needs of the aged and disabled (Stiegel, Mason, Morris, Gottlich, & Rave, 1993).

Limited guardianships, for example, may not be requested, in part, because petitioners may reason that in a short time the individual will need a plenary guardianship. As one court record noted, "Well, he is 63 years old and even though he does not need one now (a guardianship), he will need one soon anyway so we will just go ahead and do it." A full guardianship was granted. Petitioners may request "everything now" (a petition for a full guardianship) to avoid the time and expense in returning to court. This thinking reflects stereotypic assumptions about the inevitability of incapacity in old age and that the incapacity will be of a magnitude to justify as drastic a measure as guardianship.

Negative attitudes toward aging may have their basis in a cluster of beliefs that can impact the guardianship process. These may include beliefs that physical disability is indicative of mental difficulties in the elderly; the labeling of idiosyncratic behavior as bizarre or aberrant, thus warranting a finding of incapacity; belief in the reversion to a second childhood; and the view that the aged should receive human services emphasizing only minimum or maintenance care (Hull, Holmes, & Karst, 1990). Such perceptions may contribute to the application of different standards for the aged in matters of due process and self-determination: "The elderly are somehow handled with imprecise procedures and obsolete legislation" (Hull, Holmes, & Karst, 1990). Perhaps no amount of statutory reform can alter the tendency for attitudes toward aging to overshadow and shape the interpretation and implementation of legislation.

11

Use of Recommended Guardianship Practices and Outcomes for Older Prospective Wards

In chapter 10, outcomes of hearings for older proposed wards before and after statutory revisions were compared. The analyses focused less on specific practices than on the nature of decisions prior to and following legislative reform. In this chapter we investigate how implementation of recommended practices influenced outcomes for proposed wards, regardless of whether the practices represented a statutory change.[1] Literature cited earlier, as well as some of the data presented in chapter 10, indicate that reform and change in practices may not follow legislative revisions. Our concern in this chapter is not whether changes in behavior follow from statutory reforms, but whether recommended practices have an effect on decisions when they are adopted. This research contributes to the evaluative literature on guardianship practices, a current need identified by scholars (Dejowski, 1990; Iris, 1991).

In this chapter we investigate whether selected procedural safeguards advocated to protect proposed wards were related to the actual decisions about guardianship for older persons. That is, when recommended practices were implemented, did they make a difference in the legal action taken by the court on behalf of older proposed wards? The practices considered were: (1) inclusion of a specific statement of the medical and/or mental condition of the proposed ward on the petition form; (2) the presence of the ward at the hearing; (3) the presence of counsel retained by the proposed ward and/or the presence of counsel appointed by the court; (4) evaluation by a court visitor of the appropriateness of the proposed guardian; (5) and the assessment by the proposed ward of the need for a guardian. These aspects of the guardianship process were selected because some of them have been identified as problematic and in need of alteration, because use of assessments by court visitors or other neutral parties have been suggested to augment information obtained about prospective wards, and because these data were available in the records studied. These guardianship practices were investigated in relation to the decision by the court regarding appointment of a guardian for older persons. Although some of these safeguards seem rudimentary, they frequently are not implemented.

In the following sections, the aspects of the guardianship process selected for study are described in more detail. It is realized that these practices are not statutory requirements in all jurisdictions in the United States. But they do reflect some of the major concerns of those who would reform the system. Although these practices have been discussed in earlier chapters, the bases for the recommended actions are noted to provide a context for the analysis.

SPECIFIC STATEMENT OF INCAPACITY IN THE PETITION

The petition, which is the document initiating the guardianship process, should clearly state the functional limitations and the physical and mental condition of the proposed ward, indicating why the guardianship is requested. Evidence admitted to support the need for a guardianship often consists of nothing more than a general statement about the ward's physical status. As described earlier, according to scholars and researchers, the amount of evidence provided to prove incapacity often has been scant (Associated Press, 1987; Mitchell, 1978; Peters, Schmidt, & Miller, 1985). For example, Peters and his colleagues observed that in 38 percent of the cases reviewed, the rationale for guardianship was simply that the wards had "mental or physical incapacities." Evidence to link the ward's physical status with functional incapacity often is absent in the court records. Statutory definitions and criteria for incapacity have been described as vague and ambiguous (Venesy, 1990). A stricter standard to prove incapacity has been called for (American Bar Association, 1989).

The physical, mental, and functional limitations noted in the petition are to provide notice to the proposed ward. The statement in the petition sets forth an allegation to be addressed by evidence admitted at the hearing. Although assessments of capacity of proposed wards should not be linked to indices of physical functioning alone (Wang, Burns, & Hommel, 1990), additional measures of functional capacity often are not included in court records. Many petitions fall short of providing information on the "specific nature of the proposed ward's incapacity and . . . examples of recent behavior demonstrating the need for a guardian" (Wang, Burns, & Hommel, 1990:563).

In these analyses, we considered the presence or absence of a specific statement about the condition of the proposed ward in relation to the decision of the court about guardianship. Only petitions including more explicit descriptions of the physical and mental condition of the proposed ward than the statutory language were designated as specific. Although it is not tested in this research, it is likely that specific statements about capacity in the petition would be followed by presentation of more specific evidence of physical, mental, and functional limitations at the hearing.

PRESENCE OF WARD AT THE HEARING

One of the most graphic findings of the study by the Associated Press (1987) was that over 90 percent of the records indicated the proposed ward was absent at the hearing or failed to report whether the respondent attended. At the hearing it is determined if an individual is incompetent or incapacitated and lacks the ability to make decisions about his or her person, property, finances, or all of the these. Witnesses are presented and evidence is submitted about the condition of the proposed ward. Based on this evidence the judge makes a finding about the need for a guardian. A second purpose of the hearing is to review available resources in the community to meet the needs of the proposed ward (Stevenson & Capezuti, 1991).

Increasingly, advocates of change in the guardianship system emphasize the importance of the presence of the ward at the hearing to appoint a guardian (Bulcroft, Kielkopf, & Tripp, 1991; Grossberg, Zimny, & Scallet, 1989). Twenty-five states provide proposed wards the right to attend the hearing but do not mandate their presence. Twenty states and the District of Columbia mandate the attendance of the proposed ward at the hearing (Stiegel, Mason, Morris, Gottlich, & Rave, 1993). The view that the ward should attend the hearing is not shared by those who regard the hearing as informal, nonadversial, and perhaps believe that the hearing should be dispensed with altogether. Without legal representation—an advocate for the interests of the proposed ward—and without the presence of the ward, the evidence likely will remain unchallenged. Twenty-five states provide proposed wards the right to attend the hearing but do not mandate their presence (Stiegel, Mason, Morris, Gottlich, & Rave, 1993).

When finding that only 10 percent of a sample of persons attended their hearings, for example, Stevenson and Capezuti (1991) questioned whether the proposed wards understood the implications of the petition or were unaware of their constitutional rights. In this research the relationship between the presence of the ward at the hearing and the decision of the court was examined.

LEGAL REPRESENTATION

Despite the serious restrictions guardianship may place on the personal freedoms of an individual, the majority of proposed wards are not represented by legal counsel. Stiegel and associates (1993) have included the role of counsel in adult guardianship proceedings as among three issues remaining in guardianship reform. If proposed wards do have representation, it often lacks "active involvement and vigorous advocacy on the part of attorneys representing proposed wards" (Wang, Burns, and Hommel, 1990:564). If there is an attorney, he or she may not be appointed as an advocate but rather as a guardian ad litem to see to the "best interests" of the proposed ward instead of the personal preferences of the ward. Some suggest that vigorous advocacy is needed to protect the rights of the proposed ward and to ensure that his or her wishes are not overlooked. "Without adversary counsel to advise the alleged incompetent of available rights, to prepare the best possible case opposing the petition, and to advocate his or her interests, the prospective ward is destined to lose" (Wang, Burns, & Hommel, 1990:565). There may be confusion for both the court-appointed attorney and the ward regarding whether the attorney serves as an advocate rather than a neutral party who gathers information about the case. Another view is that the appointment of attorneys for all wards is prohibitively expensive. Furthermore, with the appointment of counsel a primarily family issue may become an adversarial situation (Venesy, 1990). Clearly, this latter perspective is not that of those who seek change in the guardianship system.

Conceivably, attorneys appointed by the court might perform in a number of ways. Counsel appointed by the court might serve as a guardian ad litem acting in the ward's best interest as determined by the attorney. In contrast, an attorney may act as a zealous advocate for the ward's spoken preferences. Or, the court may select an attorney who acts in an ambiguous role. Finally, more than one attorney may be appointed; one serves as a guardian ad litem and another acts as an advocate. Role ambiguity of court-appointed counsel remains prevalent in both statutes and practice. "Although the traditional adversarial mode is the dominant method of choice, it is laden with role-confusion for attorneys" (Venesy, 1990:169). The conflicting expectations of guardians ad litem also have been noted (Dubler, 1987). They may be expected to be independent evaluators of the interests of proposed wards, officers of the court, and representatives of the preferences and desires of the aged.

It is unclear in the statutes of the states considered in this research and in their records which type of role a court-appointed attorney may have been expected to carry out. Therefore, we refer to court-appointed counsel as "undefined court-appointed counsel" or "undefined representation."

Presumably if proposed wards obtained their own attorneys rather than using those selected by the court, they might expect and receive vigorous advocacy more frequently, which in turn would be reflected in decisions by the court. In this research we investigated whether outcomes of hearings were different for older persons when they retained their own attorney, had undefined court-appointed counsel, or were not represented.

RECOMMENDATIONS OF THE COURT VISITOR AND THE WARD

In an effort to obtain more information from proposed wards, some states (e.g., California, Colorado) employ neutral persons for precourt interviews and investigations. In Ohio, for example, a qualified and experienced court investigator is interested in the welfare of proposed wards and evaluates their circumstances (Venesy, 1990). Such court investigators or visitors provide proposed wards with information about their legal right to appear at the hearing, to state their objections to the proceedings, to request a different guardian, to obtain legal representation, and to have a trial by jury (Stevenson & Capezuti, 1991). For example, in Colorado the court-appointed visitor presents the court with a functional evaluation of the proposed ward's condition and a recommendation about the need for a guardian (Dice, 1987). In this research, we examined the association, if any, between the recommendations of court visitors regarding the appropriateness of the proposed guardian, limitations on the powers of a guardian, and outcomes of the hearing. Advocates for reform of the guardianship process emphasize the importance of input from the proposed ward. The assessments of proposed wards about their need for a guardian and their recommendations for limitations as revealed in the visitor's report were considered in relation to the decision of the court.

Generally, the literature suggests most guardianship hearings conclude with the appointment of a guardian, a conservator, or both (Venesy, 1990). Most frequently, full powers are granted to guardians, with rare use of partial or limited guardianships (Bell, Schmidt, & Miller, 1981). Peters, Schmidt, and Miller (1985), for example, found all 42 proposed wards they studied were appointed guardians, usually with full powers over both person and property; only one was awarded a limited guardian. In more recent research, Bulcroft, Kielkopf, and Tripp (1991) observed that all of the petitions they reviewed resulted in the appointment of a guardian, although 7 percent of them were limited guardianships. Usually, decisions from the hearings are not examined in relation to characteristics of the guardianship process. In this research we investigated the association between selected guardianship practices and the outcomes of hearings.

PROCEDURES

Data used in this chapter were analyzed from 1,160 court records of guardianship petitions in Iowa, Missouri, and Colorado. The sample and procedures are described in more detail in chapter 2. Characteristics of wards and guardians are presented in chapters 5 and 6.

Measures of practices were drawn from a questionnaire that was completed from examination of court records (chapter 2). The court records questionnaire included items about the presence of a specific statement of the physical or mental condition of the proposed ward in the petition, presence of the ward at the hearing, legal counsel for the ward, and recommendations of the court visitor and of the ward. Questions about the report of the court visitor applied only to records obtained in Colorado.

The presence of a statement in the petition about the specific physical or mental condition of the proposed ward was coded "yes" or "no." To be designated as a specific statement, the physical or mental condition had to be described with more explicitness than merely a repetition of statutory language. For example, a statement that a proposed ward had suffered a stroke with particular consequences would have been coded "yes," indicating the presence of a more specific description than that the proposed ward was "confused" or had a "physical or mental incapacity." Questions about the presence of the ward at the hearing, counsel retained by the ward, or the use of undefined court-appointed counsel also were coded "yes" or "no." These data were coded directly on the questionnaire from the records.

As noted earlier, in Colorado, court visitors complete a standardized questionnaire that becomes a part of the court record. Information on the Colorado visitor's report includes the characteristics of the proposed ward, the ward's understanding of the petition, type of assistance needed as assessed by the visitor, and the physical diagnosis of the ward's condition by a physician. A detailed assessment of functional capacity is not included in the report, but the visitor does make recommendations about limitations on the powers of the guardian.

In this research four indices were used, which were coded directly from the visitor questionnaire. The court visitor's evaluation of the appropriateness of the proposed guardian as "positive," "negative," "neutral," and whether or not the powers of the guardian should be limited ("yes" or "no") were analyzed. Proposed wards were asked by visitors if they needed help in caring for themselves and whether or not there should be limitations on the powers of the guardian; these two questions were answered "yes" or "no." If the prospective wards were incapable of answering, the questions were omitted by the visitor and from the analysis.

RESULTS

Specific Statement of Incapacity in the Petition

Although in recent literature there is the call for provision of specific statements in the petition about the physical, mental, or functional status of wards, only 46 percent of the total sample of petition forms reviewed contained specific statements about the physical or mental condition of the individual considered for guardianship.

Table 11.1
Extent of Powers Granted by Selected Characteristics of the Guardianship Process

Characteristics of the Process		Powers Granted: Full	Powers Granted: Limited or Petition Denied
		Percent	Percent
Inclusion of specific statement of medical and/or mental condition in the petition	Yes	89	11
	No	97	3
Ward present at hearing	Yes	90	10
	No	94	6
Counsel obtained by ward	Yes	68	32
	No	94	6
Counsel appointed by court	Yes	97	3
	No	81	19

Proposed wards for whom a more specific statement about their physical or mental condition was included on the petition form were a little more likely to receive limited guardianships or to have the petition denied than were those for whom no information or a general description was provided (Table 11.1). Few petitions were granted for anything other than full guardianships, but 11 percent of the petitions with specific statements included on the form were limited in some way or denied, compared to 3 percent for which no specific statement was present. Thus, a more specific statement about the condition of a proposed ward was more often associated with a determination for something less than a full guardianship.

Presence of Ward at the Hearing

Those who support guardianship reform usually stress the importance of the presence of wards at their hearings. Of the proposed wards whom we studied, 13 percent attended their hearings. Was their presence at the hearing associated with the action taken by the court? Only slightly more wards who attended their hearings received limited guardianships or had their petitions denied (Table 11.1).

Legal Representation

Historically not only have proposed wards been absent from their hearings, they also have lacked legal representation in their absence. In a

Table 11.2
Extent of Powers Granted by Visitors' and Proposed Wards' Evaluations[a]

		Powers Granted by Court	
		Full	Limited or Petition Denied
		Percent	Percent
Visitors' evaluations:			
Appropriateness of guardian (N = 265)[b]	Yes	83	17
	No	64	36
Limitations on powers of guardian recommended (N = 232)[c]	Yes	70	30
	No	84	16
Proposed wards' self evaluations:			
Help needed with care (N = 274)[d]	Yes	81	19
	No	78	22
Limitation on guardian's power (N = 121)[d]	Yes	71	29
	No	83	17

[a] 394 Colorado cases were analyzed and 370 had some information from a court visitor.
[b] The 17 cases with a neutral recommendation were dropped from the analysis. Other reductions in N are due to missing data.
[c] N is reduced because of missing data.
[d] Data are missing when court visitor failed to ask proposed ward the questions.

national study 44 percent of the wards were not represented by an attorney at their hearings (AP, 1987). Among the cases we reviewed, 4 percent engaged their own attorney, and 68 percent had undefined legal representation appointed by the court. The remainder had no legal counsel.

The presence or absence of counsel retained by the ward and undefined representation appointed by the court were cross-tabulated by the decision of the court (Table 11.1). About one-third of the wards who hired their own counsel received limited guardianships or their petitions were denied, compared to 6 percent of the wards who either had counsel appointed by the court or who had no representation. The number of wards who retained their own attorneys was small ($n = 47$); moreover, they may have been a more able group with fewer needs for assistance.

There was a difference between the outcomes for wards who had undefined court-appointed counsel compared to their peers without representation. Ninety-seven percent of those persons who had an attorney assigned by the court received full guardianships, compared with 81 percent of those individuals with no representation (Table 11.1).

Recommendations of the Court Visitor and the Ward

How were the views of the guardianship held by court visitors and by proposed wards associated with action taken by the court? Visitors evaluated the appropriateness of the proposed guardians by describing them as "positive," "negative," or "neutral." The majority of the visitors (89 percent) were positive about the appropriateness of the prospective guardian. Four percent were more negative, and 6 percent were neutral. Following their contact with the proposed wards, almost one-fifth of the visitors believed there should be limitations placed on the powers of the guardian.

The cross-tabulation in Table 11.2 shows that cases for which the visitors' evaluation of the appropriateness of a guardian was positive or neutral were more likely to be awarded full guardianships (83 percent) than those for which they were negative toward the appointment of the proposed guardian (64 percent). Petitions for which visitors found the proposed guardian inappropriate were more often denied, but the number was small ($n = 3$). Recommendations by visitors for limitations on the powers of the guardian were more often associated with the granting of limited powers or denial of the petition than were recommendations for full powers.

Wards' perceptions of their need for a guardian were included in the report of the court visitors. Of the proposed wards who were studied, 46 percent felt they did not need help in caring for themselves, while 54 percent agreed they needed assistance with certain tasks. Table 11.2 indicates assessments by wards of their needs for a guardian made little difference in the decisions made by the courts. Although the number was small ($n = 5$), proposed wards who believed they did not need a guardian were somewhat more likely to have the petition denied.

Even more of the proposed wards (40 percent) than visitors believed there should be limitations placed on the guardianship. Only wards who recommended the powers of the guardian should be limited had their petitions denied, although the number was small ($n = 5$).

Twenty-nine percent of the proposed wards who believed their guardianships should be limited received guardianships with limited powers, or the petition was dismissed (Table 11.2). Seventeen percent of the proposed wards who recommended full guardianships were granted limited powers. Thus, among both visitors and proposed wards, recommendations for limitation of the guardianship were followed in about 30 percent of the cases by the court granting either limited powers or denial of the petition.

SUMMARY AND DISCUSSION

Previous research has documented the propensity for full powers to be granted in the majority of cases (Venesy, 1990). When recommended practices were implemented, some were associated modestly with decisions for limited guardianship and, in rarer instances, denial of the petition.

Frolik (1981:638) observed that the conduct of the hearing should focus on procedural reform, and noted that the "presence of the alleged incompetent at the hearing could be quite helpful." He suggested the proposed ward might be the best counsel for his or her defense. The alleged incompetent might be able to demonstrate that unusual behavior was not due to incapacity warranting guardianship. Frolik stressed that the presence of the proposed ward would allow the court to judge for itself the level of mental incapacity. Stiegel and associates (1993) identified the right of the respondent to be present at the hearing as one of three issues still remaining in guardianship reform. Courts may rely on a visitor or a guardian ad litem to inform them about the absence of the proposed ward. "Unfortunately, courts have come to rely too heavily upon the observations of the appointee instead of the presence of the respondent at the hearing. If the appointee does not raise the issue of moving the hearing or requiring the respondent's presence, the court will generally enter an order in the respondent's absence" (Stiegel, Mason, Morris, Gottlich, & Rave, 1993). Some courts and judges hold hearings in hospitals, nursing homes, or homes of prospective wards.

In our research, the presence of the ward made little difference in the outcome of the hearing. Of course, it is possible the behavior of the ward during the hearing led to the conclusion that a full guardianship was necessary. This research did not assess whether the proposed ward had an opportunity to participate meaningfully in the hearing. Only the presence or absence of the ward was measured. Because hearings often have been regarded as informal and noncontroversial, wards may not have understood their potentially adversarial role in them, and the role of their counsel. Neutral investigators or court visitors should apprise wards of their option of questioning and opposition. Wards also need to be clearly informed about the nature of the role of court-appointed attorneys and the kind of representation they can expect.

Of the procedural safeguards considered, the findings regarding the influence of the presence of counsel were the most striking. Whereas the need for representation is almost universally endorsed (Frolik, 1981), only 28 states require legal representation (AP, 1987). It is thought the presence of counsel may diminish findings of incompetency (Frolik, 1981). Yet, the majority of state guardianship statutes do not mention the role of an attorney. Some have altered their codes to provide an attorney with some guidance (Stiegel, Mason, Morris, Gottlich, & Rave, 1993).

Our results, however, suggested the influence of counsel was not so straightforward. Undefined court-appointed representation was linked with findings of incompetency and the awarding of full powers. This representation may have consisted of guardians ad litem who did not view themselves in the role of adversarial counsel. State statutes are often silent regarding the duties and roles of guardians ad litem (Frolik, 1981); consequently, the expectations for them are confusing (Peden, 1990). Indeed, the "rolelessness" of attorneys who represent proposed wards has been noted (Wang, Burns, & Hommel, 1990). Although available records did not provide information on the nature of the role assumed by counsel, the data indicated that the likelihood of findings of incompetency was greater when wards had undefined court-appointed attorneys than when they were unrepresented or retained their own counsel.

Because of the role ambiguity of undefined court-appointed counsel, they may not view themselves as advocates for the proposed ward. These findings must be interpreted with this uncertainty in mind. The extent of advocacy engaged in by counsel is not known. This seems to highlight the need to focus on clarification of the role of the court-appointed attorney as an advocate, a suggestion made by those who would reform procedural safeguards for proposed wards (Wang, Burns, & Hommel, 1990).

Despite the function of court visitors as neutral parties, their evaluations were linked with outcomes for wards, although the number who found the guardian inappropriate was very small. Recommendations by visitors for limitations on the guardianship were associated with either the awarding of limited powers or denial of the petition. In this sense they were in a position to suggest implementation of safeguards for the ward and not just to agree to the recommendation of the petitioner.

Advocates of reform recommend obtaining more information from the ward about the circumstances surrounding the petition for guardianship (Wang, Burns, & Hommel, 1990). Preferences of proposed wards secured by visitors may be one of the few pieces of data available directly from wards in the court records, short of the exceedingly rare instance in which the petition is contested. Our research suggested the views of visitors and wards on limited guardianships may have had some influence on the outcome of the hearings. Recommendations of proposed wards and visitors to limit powers of guardians were related to subsequent decisions in almost one-third of the cases. Evidently this information from visitors and proposed wards was influential in precluding the awarding of full powers. These decisions for limited guardianships supported suggestions to obtain more data from wards.

In conclusion, assessments from visitors and wards, and counsel retained by respondents, seemed to be the most influential practices among those studied in diminishing findings of incapacity and in promoting the use of limited guardianships.

Our findings in this research based on unrefined measures of outcomes of hearings, generally indicated that adherence to some of the recommendations for reform did not ensure that decisions for most wards were altered. There are, however, a number of reasons why the findings of this research must be interpreted with caution.

A large proportion of the sample of wards were living in congregate settings which indicates they likely experienced a fairly high level of impairment. Presumably a high frequency of findings of incompetency and subsequent awarding of full guardianships might be expected in such a population. Some of the recommended practices may have the most influence on the needs of a minority of proposed wards and perhaps would differentiate outcomes of only a few.

The outcome measures of petitions for guardianship employed here (full, limited, denial) were very unrefined, and use of them may fail to show accurately some of the positive consequences of due process reforms. For example, the presence of wards at hearings may in time influence the thinking of judges and attorneys about capacity and competency. Because the more able of proposed wards may be observed by the court, they may stimulate the development and eventual use of more community resources. Even though procedural reforms may not be reflected in more denials or limited guardianships, they may shape the treatment of the ward indirectly through instructions to guardians (e.g., investigation of something other than institutional care), more frequent monitoring of guardians, or selection of a guardian different from the person requested in the petition. In these ways procedural reforms may qualitatively change what happens to the ward, although they would not necessarily be reflected in the specific type of guardianship powers used as measures of outcomes in this research. That is, unobserved outcomes of reforms may have occurred that would never have been revealed by the measures used in this study. The major objective is not to avoid guardianship per se but rather to ensure that the determination of guardianship is appropriate, that the process is fair, and that the recommended intervention addresses the needs of the ward.

Each of the reforms considered carry implications for future research. Different roles of court-appointed attorneys should be examined further in relation to findings of incompetency and awarding of full guardianship. Such relationships should be considered in states in which court-appointed attorneys assume the role of advocate and those in which their task may be one of acting in the best interest of the ward. In the present study the differentiation between outcomes associated with undefined court-appointed attorneys and those retained by proposed wards is speculative. The significance of the presence of wards at their hearings and how their presence may influence the judiciary deserve further study.

The unrefined assessments used in this research must be considered exploratory and the findings tentative. Clearly, the subtle consequences of the due process protections were not captured. To amplify what we have learned here with the use of gross measures will require looking beyond the information contained in most court records of guardianships as they are presently constituted.

NOTE

1. This chapter is a revision and extension of Keith, P., and Wacker, R. (1993). "Implementation of Recommended Guardianship Practices and Outcomes of Hearings for Older Persons," *The Gerontologist*, 33: 81–87.

12

A Concluding Glimpse of Wards and Their Guardianships

> The institution of guardianship obviously cannot create love for, or a warm personal interest in, the ward. Nor can it make amenable a person who is not responsive. To one who loves and has a warm personal interest in the ward, it can give authority to make decisions about his care that the relative or friend cannot make in his personal capacity. (Mathiasen, 1963:79)

> Guardians are not encouraged to be imaginative or creative. The view is that a "good" guardian is one who acts conservatively and maintains the status quo. (Frolik, 1981:607)

> Unfortunately, incapacitated older people are often the least attractive, the least responsive, the most demanding and the most difficult individuals to serve. (Mathiasen, 1963:78)

> But with guardianship . . . the fabric of later life, its potential creativity, and personal autonomy at its close hang in the balance. (Hommel & Wood, 1990:12)

Recent innovative legislation on which those who would reform the guardianship system pin their hopes speaks neither of love, warmth, imagination, nor the unattractiveness of age. Rather the hallmark of revised statutes lies in their articulation of procedural safeguards incorporated in the guardianship process. Our interest was to learn whether changes in guardianship legislation were reflected in outcomes for older persons, and whether more innovative statutes would be linked differentially to decisions about proposed wards. In this chapter, we summarize our findings and recommendations and those of others. The chapter is written so that it may be read as a summary that is independent of the remainder of the book.

A major contribution of this research was to link statutory change with decisions of the court and to correlate guardianship practices with outcomes for older wards. These concerns about policies and practice are at the societal or macro-level of analysis. At the individual level, the primary accomplishment of this investigation was the exploration of responses of guardians to their roles. Heretofore, guardians as role occupants, with perhaps considerable troubles of their own, have received little attention.

Some of our findings suggest recommendations that are comparable to those offered by others before us. Recommendations of scholars have been based on a variety of methodologies, including legal commentary, practice, survey research, and anthropological observation. Perhaps more than anything, these findings derived from quite different research procedures have highlighted similar, somewhat intransigent outcomes, even in the face of reform. And new and different analyses once again suggested that statutory reform alone is not sufficient to change behavior substantially. Based on our research and that of others presented in previous chapters, what are we to conclude about changes in legislation and innovative versus more traditional statutes and the guardianship decisions for older persons?

LEGISLATIVE CHANGE AND OUTCOMES FOR WARDS: A SUMMARY OF FINDINGS

Denial of Petitions

Insofar as the search for least restrictive alternatives might be expected to lead to the dismissal or denial of petitions for guardianship, it was an infrequent practice. There was little search for alternatives or subsequent denial of petitions. Although a few more denials were observed following passage of revised legislation, the numbers were very small. Of course, under revised statutes, it may be that more careful scrutiny of petitions and increased counsel with attorneys have resulted in fewer instances in which guardianship clearly was unwarranted, so that some cases never reached adjudication. Even so, denial of guardianship was not a prevalent outcome of hearings conducted after implementation of the revised legislation we studied.

Limited Guardianships

A limited guardianship frequently is recommended in current literature as a least restrictive alternative, although it is more constraining than a substitution for guardianship would be. Even after passage of revised legislation in which limited guardianships were specifically mentioned as options, they were infrequently requested. And the few that were requested were all granted full guardianships. There was an increase in the number of limited guardianships awarded following legislative changes, although none of them had been requested. Even in the post–legislative change period, the number of limited guardians who were appointed was small, about 2 percent ($n = 51$). Yet, this represents a trend not observed before the revised legislation. Almost all of the limited guardianships were awarded in Colorado. In the time period of our analysis the major change in Colorado legislation was the requirement of the visitors' report. And as mentioned in chapter 11, there was some evidence indicating visitors' recommendations for limitations of guardianships were modestly associated with the outcomes for wards. But in Missouri, which had the most innovative legislation of the three states, awarding limited guardianships was infrequent. The data do not show a great deal of difference in the decisions about limited guardianships made prior to or after enactment of legislation in two of the three states.

Limited guardianships may not be requested, in part, because petitioners may think that in a short time the individual will need a plenary guardianship. As noted in chapter 10, court records suggested that some plenary guardianships may be awarded to persons who do not currently need them because it is thought they will require one eventually. Awarding a plenary guardianship at the time of the initial petition precludes a return to court and another hearing, thus avoiding the expense of additional court proceedings. This action, in part, reflects ageism and the thinking that with age will come incapacity of a magnitude to warrant such a drastic measure.

Evidence of Incapacity

Action taken by the court rests on the determination of incapacity of the proposed ward. Presumably, then, the court's decisions will reflect available assessments of the capacity of the proposed ward. A safeguard in some revised legislation addresses the definition of incapacity and attempts to ensure a more careful assessment is made. Were decisions of the court that reflected a fair amount of consistency in the findings between legislative periods also paralleled by a lack of change in the presentation of evidence?

In Missouri, which had more innovative statutes requiring greater explicitness in the evidence of functional capacity, changes in the frequency of presentation of evidence followed statutory revision. The inclusion of medical evidence was similar both before and following passage of legislation, but more substantial changes occurred in the presentation of evidence of functional capacity following enactment of the revised statutes. The absence of functional assessments in the records declined by 25 percent following the adoption of more explicit legislation in Missouri. This change, however, was not accompanied by greater use of limited guardianships. Although most of the petitions for limited guardianships observed in the sample were filed in Missouri, they were awarded full powers. Thus, the greater use of explicit evidence in Missouri was not reflected in selection of a less restrictive alternative as might be represented by a limited guardianship. With its requirements for less explicit descriptions of incapacity, less change in evidence was observed in the Iowa records. The increased information that may have been provided by more explicit indications of capacity was not mirrored in substantially different decisions in the two states. But infrequent use of limited guardianships, of course, may be in part attributable to a tendency for the less serious cases to have been withdrawn or discouraged much earlier in the process and prior to adjudication.

The question, however, remains: Were some guardianships established to address difficulties that could have been resolved in other ways? What we do know is that the majority of the guardians indicated they were not presented with any alternatives to conventional guardianship. The court should present findings that no alternative suitable plan is available to meet the needs of the proposed ward. That is, the court should demonstrate it has considered less restrictive alternatives and that the "powers and duties conferred upon the guardian are appropriate as the least restrictive form of intervention and are consistent with preservation of the proposed ward's liberties" (Wang, Burns, & Hommel, 1990:263).

RECOMMENDATIONS

Assessment and Determination of Capacity

The types of capacity the courts seek to assess are not clear in the statutes. Definitions of capacity in the statutes should delineate at least three areas for assessment: legal (e.g., making a will, entering into a contract); medical (e.g., capacity to consent to medical treatment); and functional (e.g., personal daily decision making such as decisions about living arrangements, managing money). Courts could award limited guardianships by ordering powers for guardians only in the areas of proven incapacity. The ward would retain other areas of decision making. The maximization of the zone of autonomy is attained by employment of the principle of the least restrictive alternative (Carney, 1989).

Standardized assessments could be drafted that measure capacity in each of the three areas. Court visitors, neutral guardians ad litem, or screening committees should conduct the assessment. Nolan (1990) suggests a wide variety of individuals could be involved in the assessment: community health nurses, social workers, occupational and physical therapists, mental health workers, gerontologists, and geriatric assessment units at local hospitals. If the proceeding is truly adversarial, having a person chosen by the petitioner to conduct the assessment may bias the recommendation in favor of proving the need for a guardianship. Nolan further observes that standardized checklists evaluating functional capacity may be more effective if a concise, vivid narrative of the proposed ward is included.

Assessments of capacity should ask what the ward is capable of and what the ward can do. If they are to be accurate, assessments must be conducted more than one time.

If more thorough assessments of function are developed as suggested in chapter 4 and in current literature, there will need to be increased opportunities for training those who use the assessments in drawing up their recommendations and making decisions about the best possible options for proposed wards. This would include training court visitors, guardians ad litem, and other investigators to assess and work with new standards of evidence.

In Colorado, the intention is that the court visitor will provide the court with a functional evaluation of the situation and assess the need for guardianship of the proposed ward (Dice, 1987). In practice, much of the visitor's report is devoted to ensuring that the ward understands the purpose and consequences of the petition and proceedings and their right to an attorney, assessing their feelings about the proposed guardian and the guardianship, evaluating areas in which proposed wards believe they need assistance and would like a guardian to help, and describing limitations on the powers and duties of the proposed guardian recommended by both the visitor and proposed ward. These are important considerations, but little time is reserved for an assessment bearing on the functional capacity of the ward. Indeed, one-third of the visitor reports we studied contained no conclusion about the functional capacity of the proposed ward.

The data reviewed underscore the importance of strengthening the assessments of visitors and other investigators. The recommendations of visitors had a modest influence on the awarding of limited guardianships. Wards for whom visitors recommended limited guardianships were actually awarded them more often than when such a recommendation was not forthcoming. In contrast, wards' requests for limited guardianships were not granted, although in the petitions that were dismissed proposed wards had stated a preference for limited guardianships.

Use of Limited Guardianships

Why are so few limited guardianships requested and awarded? More than 40 states have statutes that specify provisions for limited guardianships (Hommel & Wood, 1990). It may be that limited guardianships are not requested because petitioners do not know the range of powers that can be requested or the advantages of nonplenary guardianships. Frolik (1981:653) suggested that courts and practitioners "feel comfortable" with familiar practices. Use of plenary guardianship avoids the effort involved in awarding powers that address specific needs of proposed wards. Schulte

(1989) noted the reluctance of German courts to use newer and more complicated rules with regard to differentiating the extent of limited capacity. Frolik (1981:653) observed that "plenary guardianship is familiar, uncomplicated, and saves time and effort." Iris (1990a:40) concluded that "much of the bias against limited guardianships arises from misconceptions of their costs and benefits, lack of knowledge about the effect of cognitive incapacity on decision-making ability, and negative attitudes about the aging process and mental disability in general."

Practices have been suggested to facilitate implementation of limited guardianship. Based on research conducted between 1989 and 1992 at the Center for Social Gerontology in Ann Arbor, Michigan, Lisi and Hommel (1992) concluded that limited guardianship was practicable. To encourage the use of limited guardianship orders, they recommended that states develop standardized court forms permitting judges to check off powers assigned to the guardian or conservator.

Nevertheless, as noted earlier, petitioners may request everything all at once to avoid the time and expense of coming back to court. The responsibility lies with the court to investigate and determine if the requested powers match the current needs of the proposed ward, not needs yet to emerge in the future. One way to address emerging needs of wards is to have annual reviews of guardianships conducted by the court, or to have guardians indicate in their annual reports their need for expanded powers. But the House Subcommittee on Health and Long-Term Care observed the courts are so overburdened that monitoring of the progress of guardianship arrangements rarely takes place (House of Representatives, 1987). Schulte (1989) also commented on the slowness of the German courts in reviewing existing guardianships. If reports are going to be unread or receive a cursory review, then they are "nothing but a palliative that squanders the guardian's time and energy" (Frolik, 1990:48). Judges do not have time to review annual reports, but Frolik believes they should demand additional assistance from the legislature. He recommended that court visitors be used to monitor guardian activities after the appointment. However, he observed that visitor programs may be prohibitively expensive.

In a national project, Legal Counsel for the Elderly has monitored guardianships in Atlanta, Houston, and Denver. Volunteers visited persons under guardianship to see if they were receiving appropriate care and whether guardians were fulfilling their responsibilities satisfactorily (Newsnotes, 1990). Findings from the visits by volunteers were provided to the courts. Such efforts to monitor guardians may serve as models for courts elsewhere.

Role Clarity in the Guardianship Process

Coleman and Dooley (1990) note the need for a clear definition of the roles of all participants in the guardianship process. They observe there is a special need for guardians to understand the expectations for them and where to obtain assistance. Our findings strongly support this suggestion.

With the greater use of limited guardianships, there is a need to spell out specifically what is expected of the limited guardian (Rogers, 1984). In describing reform of guardianship laws in Europe, Schulte (1989) urged that the powers of the guardian be clarified and that assistance be given according to the needs of the individual, and not at the discretion of the guardian. Decisions by a limited guardian that will require a hearing in court must be clearly indicated.

The role of the guardian ad litem, which may be confusing for wards, must be clearly specified. The literal meaning of guardian ad litem is an individual who acts as a guardian during litigation (Parry & Hurme, 1991). It refers to a person who in consultation with the ward's attorney, makes legal decisions on behalf of the ward.

Are guardians ad litem to gather information for the court, ensure proposed wards have been notified of their rights, and thereby act as a neutral party in the best interests of the ward? To what extent should their role include advocacy? The position of guardian ad litem has been described as "a profusion of duties, a confusion of roles" (Peden, 1990:19). Some of the confusion may have arisen with the evolution of the role of guardian ad litem. In contrast to the traditional function of a guardian ad litem noted above, an attorney as guardian ad litem may act as both a guardian and counsel during litigation (Parry & Hurme, 1991). Elsewhere, the guardian ad litem may be appointed by the court to report on a controversial matter and act as a monitor rather than a guardian. Parry and Hurme observe that these are three very different functions.

In response to the potential confusion, there have been attempts to make the proceedings in which the guardian ad litem is involved more formal and more adversarial, and thereby clarify expectations of both proposed wards and guardians ad litem (Morrissey, 1982). Ambiguity remains about what constitutes "expert evaluation," as well as the nature of the necessary training for the investigator (Venesy, 1990). Proposed wards may assume that visiting attorneys will provide legal representation for them. The presence or absence of any representation must be made clear to proposed wards. Moreover, attorneys appointed to represent proposed wards should be apprised of their role as an advocate.

Guardians, petitioners, and attorneys who represent wards need to be aware of least restrictive alternatives available in each area of capacity. It is especially important that attorneys appointed to represent proposed wards view their task as being an advocate for their clients as well as being informed about services permitting implementation of least restrictive alternatives. Our findings indicated wards with court-appointed attorneys were more likely to be awarded a plenary guardianship/conservatorship than those without representation. These wards, of course, may have been the most impaired.

No doubt attorneys are familiar with legal mechanisms such as durable power of attorney, trusts, and others. However, they may be less aware of services to address other areas of capacity (medical and functional) and to provide support for wards whose functioning is compromised. AARP, for example, has initiated projects to assist the elderly in paying bills and other daily money management tasks. All participants in the guardianship process would benefit from knowledge of available services. Area Agencies on Aging could be very important in getting information about services to these key persons. Lisi and Hommel (1992) have called attention to the importance of education about aging for the judiciary as well.

Furthermore, if limited guardianships are awarded more frequently or if potential wards are diverted from the guardianship system, there will be a need for additional services. The linchpins of alternatives to guardianships are availability and identification of services. The Michigan Guardianship Diversion Project, working with an Area Agency on Aging, illustrates the necessity of collaborative efforts between state units of government, local probate courts, and networks of human services (Maynard, 1990). An intent of the Michigan project was to assess the need for guardianship and to explore potential alternative actions. Field research establishing whether the outcomes of diversionary programs are superior to those of guardianships is needed (see Wilber, 1991, for an example).

Assistance for Guardians

Guardians need assistance. Concerns about the ward should not stop with the protection of rights of due process. To provide the best care for the ward, assistance must be available to the guardian. Helping the guardian helps the ward.

Guardians are targets of criticism and have considerable power imputed to them, but in this research their personal accounts seldom revealed feelings of efficacy and sometimes even suggested a lack of confidence. The lives of many of the guardians studied were stressful, and their roles were marked by uncertainty and ambiguity. A substantial proportion of guardians who replied to the questionnaire often were not clear about their roles and were sometimes uncertain about the needs of their wards.

Yet, as Rogers (1984) observed, a guardian has a clearly defined role to play and specific responsibilities to discharge. Provision of both a clear definition of the court's expectations and sources of assistance to fulfill the requirements of the role of guardian are a high priority.

In commenting on the situation in Europe and providing a cross-cultural perspective, Schulte (1989) noted that guardians lack experience and skill in working with the aged. There is a clear need for training of guardians.

The formidable myriad of expectations for the "good" guardian as described by the American Bar Association (see chapter 5) suggests a continued need for education and training. Indeed, in an ABA survey almost half of the respondents (48 percent) identified lack of guardian training as a serious problem whereas 28 percent cited it as the most important problem (Hurme, 1991). Schulte (1989:602) advocated mandatory intensive training for guardians, with the intent to impart knowledge about "medical/social/legal aspects of guardianship."

Assessments to determine the most effective means of education and training are needed. The three states we studied, for example, were credited with having instructional brochures for new guardians (Hurme, 1991). Yet, a substantial proportion of guardians that we contacted in the three states experienced strain in part due to insufficient instruction and training.

The guardians we studied were most often in need of information about procedures to accomplish the tasks expected by the courts and family members. Their comments suggested possible directions for additional programming of use to future guardians and to provide greater clarity in their own roles.

Some guardians expressed a need to have persons available with whom they could discuss the problems of their wards. Guardians most often would have liked assistance from social services personnel in arranging services for their wards. Others indicated a preference for obtaining assistance from counselors, attorneys, other guardians, and, to a lesser extent, representatives of the court. In essence, the guardians told us that more explicit guidance to assist them in caring for their wards was needed.

Coleman and Dooley (1990) called for a local standardized guardianship plan that identifies needs of the ward, specifies services, and indicates the mechanisms to obtain appropriate services responsive to the situation of the ward. A clear, detailed individual guardianship plan should provide direction to the guardian and go a long way toward alleviating the ambiguity experienced by several of the guardians studied. Keyser (1987:44) described a model for a plan used by the Volunteer Guardianship Program of Lutheran Ministries of Florida. Included in the plan were "a) a determination of the most appropriate placement; b) necessary services anticipated for at least six months; c) a goal for the ward's functioning level to be evaluated in six months; and d) plans for restoration of competency if possible." Implementation of such a plan requires that guardians are provided with information about available services. Throughout, however, guardians will benefit from the assistance of court staff and social services personnel.

Zimny, Gilchrist, and Diamond (1991) set forth a National Model for Judicial Review of Guardians' Performance, which included the best practices of six states as they go about monitoring the work of guardians. Major aspects of the model were educational materials, general care plans, review of the file, contents of personal reports and accounts, filing and receipt of personal reports and accounts, check and audit of personal reports and accounts, hearing, and feedback to the guardian. Models such as this and instructional materials published by the American Bar Association (Hurme, 1991; Stiegel, 1992) address Mathiasen's request of 30 years ago: "There must be a source of guidance for the guardian, his lawyer and the court in providing care best suited to the needs of the ward" (1963:85).

Choice and Protection

By using only court records, a number of questions about the lives of wards remain untouched. Indeed, information about the preferences of wards, their response to the proposed guardianship, and how they believe they fare once the guardianship is established are poorly represented in the literature. We can conclude little from the fact that few contest the awarding of guardianship. For those who are capable of making some decisions, it is not known which elements of choice remain available to them following the appointment of a guardian.

The appearance of physical frailty should not be a proxy for the engagement of a substitute decision maker. Frolik (1981) indicated that the presence of physical dependency may increase perceptions of the individual as incompetent. Consequently, the choices of the dependent elderly may be under scrutiny.

Because they often cannot bring about their preferences without assistance, their right to choose requires the cooperation of others, both individuals and agencies, thus permitting strangers to scrutinize prospective plans. This involvement of helpers and facilitators may mean that differing standards of judgment and measures of worth will be applied to an elderly individual's choices. Conflicting value systems, which often reflect competing concerns of institutional and individual self-protection and convenience, may be at odds with the elderly person's preferences. Elderly dependent persons are therefore at great risk of losing their right to decide about the course and conduct of their lives (Dubler, 1987:137).

One distinction between minors and adults lies in the range of choices that are usually permitted the latter in American society. The differential legal implications of intervening in the lives of children and the aged have been noted (Hughes, 1989). Adults who are considered competent have the right to agree to or refuse medical treatments and interventions. "By extension, competent adults should also be able to refuse 'caring,' not only care. They should be able to refuse housekeeping assistance, visiting nurse supervision, or other proffered community interventions" (Dubler, 1987:139).

The matter of choice especially may seem to be abridged when behavior is viewed as bizarre or thought to indicate neglect:

The self-neglecting elderly reclusive living in unsanitary and dangerous conditions is often used as an example to illustrate that the adult protection legislation contains value judgements embodied in vague terms and grants wide powers and discretion to professionals to transform a neglected adult's right to receive care and protective services into an obligation to receive the offered assistance regardless of its form or duration. (Hughes, 1989:626)

Without data obtained directly from wards and guardians, our views of the lives of wards following establishment of guardianship primarily come through annual reports contained in the court records. These reports are insufficient to ascertain the range of choice reserved for the ward, the extent the ward is obligated to accept unwarranted assistance, or even that the ward is "receiving the services and treatment he or she requires to enhance his or her development" (Mathiasen, 1963:203). The recommendation is for reform that includes more careful attention to monitoring and assessing the outcomes of the guardianship following its initiation (Schulte, 1989). These assessments should involve the ward insofar as possible. Recently, it has been suggested that issues of choice and protection be considered in voluntary guardianships as well (Weiler, Helms, & Buckwalter, 1993).

While the wards we studied lost degrees of choice, guardians' assumption of decision making was not without stress. Some of the implications of having choice delegated to guardians were reflected in hardships identified by them. For some, the most difficult aspect of guardianship was making the right decisions. Taking into account the best interests of the ward, eliciting the preferences of the ward and incorporating them into decisions, or substituting their judgment for that of the ward were often sources of strain.

We are reminded that "decisions made by the guardian must be as congruent as possible with the values of the dependent adult" (Christie, 1984:204). The guardian is expected to make decisions based on the value system of the ward. Data from the court records and reports in the literature provide few insights into the amount of congruence between the decisions that are made about their affairs, and the actual preferences of wards, if they are capable of providing them, or what they might have been previously when wards had the capacity to express them. Those who advocate reform of the guardianship system likely would project a low level of congruence between the capacities and preferences of at least a minority of wards and the choices made for them by perhaps unwarranted guardians. In fact, the incongruence between values of wards and decisions of their guardians is not known in most instances. And reducing the uncertainty surrounding the match between what is optimal for a ward and action taken by the court is made more difficult by the sparse evidence presented to establish need.

Remaining Questions and Concerns

A number of questions linger. Alexander and Lewin (1972) commented that guardianship provided no observable benefits for wards. How do guardianships benefit wards? What is done for wards that could not have been done before guardians were appointed? What specific activities are done on behalf of the wards? How closely are the needs of wards matched with the powers awarded to the guardians? To what extent do wards and guardians share decision making when the wards are capable of doing so? Increased attention to reports by guardians and other types of monitoring, including greater efforts to assess responses of wards, may answer some of these questions.

As assessments of capacity are improved, it will be possible to document more carefully the specific characteristics of proposed wards who enter the system. The ability to assess the degree of incapacity of proposed wards is critical to a definitive comparison of outcomes of differing state statutes. It is unknown whether proposed wards reviewed under one set of state statutes have a higher degree of incapacity on the average than those entering the system in another state. As it is now, a wide variety of medical evidence is presented, ranging from a single sentence written by a physician to multiple pages of test results and commentary. Standardized assessments will result in more accurate comparisons of court actions across states. Court decisions may appear similar across states, but the level of capacity of wards on which they are based may vary somewhat. In the future, researchers may find that proposed wards in states with more stringent standards of evidence indeed have a lower level of functioning. These wards may have outcomes resembling those in states in which less careful evidence is presented, and in which there is a tendency to grant plenary guardianships with less reason.

There are areas in which further education seems to be called for. Those involved at any point in the guardianship system must become aware of the heterogeneity of the aged with regard to processes of aging and functioning. If key individuals harbor misconceptions about the aged and aging (e.g., belief in reversion to a second childhood, intolerance of idiosyncratic behavior), no amount of legislative change can ensure protection of individual liberties.

Studies of family decision making and of guardianship systems indicate a need for public education about the use of advance directives. Most of the individuals for whom guardianship petitions are filed have not planned for incapacity. Guardianship may be petitioned for in the absence of advance directives. Public education about advance directives may decrease the number of petitions for guardianship.

Some of the lingering questions that may inform future research could be addressed more appropriately with information from wards. Bulcroft (1992) used three theories from social science to raise research questions about the outcomes of guardianship. The theories were stratification, social exchange, and social construction. The hypotheses concerned consequences of guardianship for wards and included role ambiguity, decreased social power, increased use of affective exchanges, and diminished well-being. The hypotheses derived from the three theories suggested that there is little empirical information about the responses of wards to guardianship. Above all, perhaps, little is known about the access of wards to decision making.

Zimny, Gilchrist, Grossberg, and Chung (1991) remind us of the usefulness of longitudinal studies that follow wards. They also observe the importance of being sensitive to the differences between courts within the same state as well as variation in guardianship procedures across states. State statutes can allow considerable leeway in guardianship practices, which are then reflected in intercourt differences. Consequently, Zimny and colleagues highlighted the difficulty of generalizing results both within and between states. Certainly this caution would apply to our research as well. However, as is evident in the review of the literature and in our findings, there are several points of consensus on concerns surrounding the practice of guardianship, common management problems, and the outcomes for both wards and guardians.

CONCLUSION

This book had reviewed some recent thinking about guardianship, presented the substance of proposed reforms, and had suggested needs that continue to be unmet. Writing, advocating, passing, and implementing legislation are costly and time-consuming, and the changes in legislation that we studied did not seem to alter appreciably the prospects of most proposed wards. But the tasks ahead may be much more difficult and complex than the passage of legislation.

Friedman and Savage (1988:273) write: "Stereotypes about old age are pervasive in society, and they leave their mark on the system. Structural reforms may indeed be called for, but a deeper reformation of the process must begin with a change in attitude toward people in the twilight of their lives." And this remaining task cannot be legislated.

Postscript

Mrs.____ is a charming, spry lady of 85. She understands the petition but does not believe that she needs a guardian. She is articulate and cooperative and is well oriented to person, place, and time. But she is unable to recall the name of the President during the Civil War. She cannot subtract serial sevens from 100, and she cannot spell "world" backward.

Appendix: Sample Petition

____________ COURT, ______________ COUNTY OF __________________.
STATE OF COLORADO

Case No. __________________, Division ______

PETITION FOR APPOINTMENT OF GUARDIAN FOR INCAPACITATED PERSON

IN THE MATTER OF

Incapacitated Person.

1. Petitioner, ____,
(name)

(as ____, is interested in the welfare
(nature of interest)
of the above person as is provided by Section 15-14-303 of the Colorado Probate Code) (is the above person).

2. The above person was born on _____________________________________, and resides at
(date)

____________________________________, in the __________________ County of __________________,
(address)

State of __________________.

3. The above person is incapacitated and in need of a guardian as a means of providing continuing care and supervision of the person of the above person.

4. The nature and degree of the above person's incapacity is as follows:

5. The extent to which the guardian should be permitted to give consents or approvals that may be necessary to enable the above person to receive medical or other professional care, counsel, treatment or services is as follows:

Strike parenthetical matter according to fact.

CPC Form 32. Rev. '81. PETITION FOR APPOINTMENT OF GUARDIAN FOR INCAPACITATED PERSON

6. The nature and extent of the care, assistance, protection, or supervision which is necessary or desirable for the above person under all the circumstances is as follows:

7. Venue for this proceeding is proper in this county because the above person (resides in this county) (is present in this county) (is admitted to an institution pursuant to an order of a court of competent jurisdiction sitting in this county).

8. (A) (No) guardian appointed by a Will has accepted such appointment.

9. The welfare and best interests of the above person will be served by the appointment of a guardian for the above person.

10. ____
(name and address of nominee for guardian)

has priority for appointment as guardian for the above person because (state reasons justifying priority)

(10A. It is necessary to appoint a temporary guardian for the above person until a hearing can be held on this Petition because (state reasons))

11. It is (not) necessary to appoint a visitor because (state reasons)

12. The following persons are required by statute to be given notice of the time and place of hearing on this Petition:

Name	Address	Relation to Incapacitated Person

WHEREFORE, Petitioner requests that the Court set a time and place of hearing on this Petition; that notice be given to all persons entitled thereto as provided by law; that the Court determine that the above person is incapacitated or otherwise a person for whom appointment of a guardian is proper; that the Court appoint ______________________________

(name and address of nominee)

____

as the guardian for the above person; (that the Court forthwith appoint a temporary guardian to serve until appointment of a permanent guardian;) (that the Court forthwith appoint a Visitor;) and that Letters of Guardianship be issued to the guardian.

Dated ______________________

Signature of Attorney for Petitioner

Signature of Petitioner

Type or print name, address, telephone number and registration number of Attorney for Petitioner

Type or print name, address and telephone number of Petitioner

CONSENT OF INCAPACITATED PERSON (if applicable)

I, the incapacitated person, consent to the appoint of ______________________________

(name)

as my guardian.

____

Signature of Incapacitated Person

References

Abel, E. (1990). Family care of the frail elderly. In E. Abel & M. Nelson (Eds.), *Circles of care*. Albany: State University of New York Press.

Alexander, G. (1977). Who benefits from conservatorship? *Trial Magazine*, May, 30–32.

Alexander, G. (1979). Premature probate: A different perspective on guardianship for the elderly. *Stanford Law Review*, 31, 1003–1033.

Alexander, G. (1985). Legal perspectives: Issues of competency. In G. Lesnoff-Caravaglia (Ed.), *Values, ethics and aging*. New York: Human Sciences Press.

Alexander, G. (1990). Avoiding guardianship. In E. Dejowski (Ed.), *Protecting judgment-impaired adults: Issues, interventions and policies*. New York: Haworth Press.

Alexander, G., & Lewin, T. (1972). *The aged and the need for surrogate management*. Syracuse, NY: Syracuse University Press.

Allen, R., Ferster, E., & Weihofen, H. (1968). *Mental impairment and legal incompetency*. Englewood Cliffs, NJ: Prentice-Hall.

American Bar Association (ABA). (1986). National conference of the judiciary on guardianship proceedings for the elderly.

American Bar Association. (1989). Guardianship: An agenda for reform. *Mental and Physical Disabilities Law Review*, 13, 274–313.

Anderer, S. (1990). A model for determining competency in guardianship proceedings. *Mental and Physical Disabilities Law Review*, 14, 107–114.

Anderer, S., Coleman, N., Lichtenstein, E., & Parry, J. (Eds.). (1990). Determining competency in guardianship proceedings. Washington, DC: American Bar Association.

Associated Press (AP). (1987). Guardians of the elderly: An ailing system.

Atchley, R. (1991). *Social forces and aging*. Belmont, CA: Wadsworth.

Atkinson, G. (1980). Towards a due process perspective in conservatorship proceedings for the aged. *Journal of Family Law*, 18, 819–845.

Barnes, A. (1988). Florida guardianship and the elderly: The paradoxical right to unwanted assistance. *University of Florida Law Review*, 40, 949–988.

Barnes, A. (1992). Beyond guardianship reform: A reevaluation of autonomy and beneficence for a system of principled decision-making in long-term care. *Emory Law Journal*, 41, 635–760.

Baruch, G., & Barnett, R. (1986). Role quality, multiple role involvement and psychological well-being in midlife women. Working paper no. 149. Wellesley, MA: Wellesley College Center for Research on Women.

Baruch, G., & Barnett, R. (1987). Role quality and psychological well-being. In F. Crosby (Ed.), *Spouse, parent, worker*. New Haven: Yale University Press.

Bell, W., Schmidt, W., & Miller, K. (1981). Public guardianship and the elderly: Findings from a national study. *The Gerontologist*, 21, 194–202.

Berrera, M., & Ainlay, S. (1983). The structure of social support: A conceptual and empirical analysis. *Journal of Community Psychology*, 11, 133–143.

Bhagat, R., Allie, S., & Ford, D. (1991). Organized stress, personal life stress and symptoms of life strains: An inquiry into the moderating roles of styles of coping. *Journal of Social Behavior and Personality*, 6, 163–184.

Blieszner, R., & Hamon, R. (1992). Filial responsibility: Attitudes, motivators, and behaviors. In J. Dwyer & R. Coward (Eds.), *Gender, families, and eldercare*. Newbury Park, CA: Sage.

Borron, J. (1983). The guardianship code revision: An overview. *Journal of Missouri Bar*, Oct./Nov., 453–462.

Braithwaite, V., Gibson, G., & Holman, J. (1985–86). Age stereotyping: Are we oversimplifying the phenomenon? *The International Journal of Aging & Human Development*, 22, 315–325.

Bulcroft, K. (1992). Outcomes of legal guardianship for the elderly ward. Paper presented at meeting of the Gerontological Society of America.

Bulcroft, K., Kielkopf, M., & Tripp, K. (1991). Elderly wards and their legal guardians: Analysis of county probate records in Ohio and Washington. *The Gerontologist*, 31, 156–164.

Carney, T. (1989). The limits and the social legacy of guardianship in Australia. *Federal Law Review*, 18, 231–266.

Carney, T., & Tait, D. (1991). Guardianship dilemmas and care of the aged. *Sydney Law Review*, 13, 61–84.

Christie, J. (1984). Guardianship in Alberta, Canada. In T. Apollini & T. Cooke (Eds.), *A new look at guardianship*. Baltimore: Paul H. Brookes.

Cicirelli, V. (1981). *Helping elderly parents: Role of adult children*. Boston: Auburn House.

Cicirelli, V. (1992). *Family caregiving: Autonomous and paternalistic decision making*. Newbury Park, CA: Sage.

Clipp, E., & George, L. (1990). Caregiver needs and patterns of social support. *Journal of Gerontology*, 45, S102–111.

Cohen, E. (1978). Editorial: Law and aging, lawyers and gerontologists. *The Gerontologist*, 18, 229.

Cohen, E. (1988). The elderly mystique: Constraints on the autonomy of the elderly with disabilities. *The Gerontologist*, 28, 24–31.

Coleman, N., & Dooley, J. (1990). Making the guardianship system work. *Generations*, Supplement, 47–50.

Colorado Revised Statutes §15-14-101 et seq. (1976–1989).

Colorado Revised Statutes §15-14-312 (I) (e) (Supp. 1990).

Comment. (1976). An assessment of the Pennsylvania Estate Guardianship Incompetency Standard. *University of Pennsylvania Law Review*, 124, 1048–1079.

Coulton, C., Dunkle, R., Chow, J., Haug, M., & Vielhaber, D. (1988). Locus of control and decision making for posthospital care. *The Gerontologist*, 29, 627–632.

Coverman, S. (1989). Role overload, role conflict, and stress: Addressing consequences of multiple role demands. *Social Forces*, 67, 965–982.

Coward, R. T., & Dwyer, J. W. (1990). The association of gender, sibling network composition, and patterns of parent care by adult children. *Research on Aging*, 12, 158–181.

Creyke, R. (1989). Guardianship: Protection and autonomy—has the right balance been achieved? In J. M. Eekelaar & D. Pearl (Eds.), *An aging world: Dilemmas and challenges for law and social policy*. Oxford: Clarendon Press.

Dade County Grand Jury. (1982). Final report of the Grand Jury. Miami, FL: Office of the State Attorney.

das Neves, M. (1991). The role of counsel in guardianship proceedings of the elderly. *Georgetown Journal of Legal Ethics*, 4, 855–867.

Dejowski, E. (Ed.). (1990). *Protecting judgment-impaired adults: Issues, interventions and policies*. New York: Haworth Press.

Dice, M. (1987). Colorado guardianship and conservatorship law: A status report. *The Colorado Lawyer*, March, 421–426.

Dickens, B. (1989). Medico-legal issues concerning the elderly—an overview. In J. Eekelaar & D. Pearl (Eds.), *An aging world: Dilemmas and challenges for law and social policy*. Oxford: Clarendon Press.

Doty, P. (1986). Family care of the elderly: The role of public policy. *Milbank Memorial Fund Quarterly*, 64, 34–75.

Dubler, N. (1987). The dependent elderly: Legal rights and responsibilities in agent custody. In S. Spicker, S. Ingman, & I. Lawson (Eds.), *Ethical dimensions of geriatric care: Value conflicts for the 21st century*. Dordrecht, Holland: D. Reidel.

Dudovitz, N. (1985). The least restrictive alternative. *Generations*, Fall, 39–41.

Duke University Center for the Study of Aging and Human Development. (1978). Multidimensional functional assessment questionnaire. Durham, NC: Duke University.

Dwyer, J., & Coward, R. (1992). Gender, family, and long-term care of the elderly. In J. Dwyer & R. Coward (Eds.), *Gender, families, and eldercare*. Newbury Park, CA: Sage.

Eekelaar, J., & Pearl, D. (Eds.). (1989). *An aging world: Dilemmas and challenges for law and social policy*. Oxford: Clarendon Press.

Fillenbaum, G. (1985). Screening the elderly: A brief instrumental activities of daily living measure. *Journal of the American Geriatric Society*, 33, 698–706.

Fillenbaum, G., & Wallman, L. (1984). Change in household composition of the elderly: A preliminary investigation. *Journal of Gerontology*, 39, 342–349.

Frank, J. (1993). Guardianship procedures: A clinical program to assist in the decision-making process. *Thomas M. Cooley Law Review*, 10, 91–114.

Franks, M., & Stephens, M. (1992). Multiple roles of middle-generation caregivers: Contextual effects and psychological mechanisms. *Journal of Gerontology*, 47, S123–129.

Franks, P., Campbell, T., & Shields, C. (1992). Social relationships and health: The relative roles of family functioning and social support. *Social Science and Medicine*, 34, 779–788.

Friedman, L., & Savage, M. (1988). Taking care: The law of conservatorship in California. *Southern California Law Review*, 61, 273–291.

Frolik, L. (1981). Plenary guardianship: An analysis, a critique and proposal for reform. *Arizona Law Review*, 23, 600–660.

Frolik, L. (1990). Elder abuse and guardians of elderly incompetents. In E. Dejowski (Ed.), *Protecting judgment-impaired adults: Issues, interventions and policies*. New York: Haworth Press.

Furrow, B., Johnson, S., Jost, T., & Schwartz, R. (1987). *Health law: Cases, materials and problems*. St. Paul, MN: West Publishing.

Gallo, J., Reichel, W., & Andersen, L. (1988). *Handbook of geriatric assessment*. Rockville, MD: Aspen Publications.

Grace, C., & Wilkinson, P. (1978). *Sociological inquiry and legal phenomena*. New York: St. Martin's Press.

Grossberg, G., Zimny, G., & Scallet, L. (1989). Guardianship of cognitively impaired elderly: Directions for research. In E. Light & B. Lebowitz (Eds.), *Alzheimer's disease treatment and family stress: Directions for research*. Washington, DC: U.S. Government Printing Office.

Groth-Marnat, G. (1990). *Handbook of psychological assessment*. New York: John Wiley and Sons.

Gurland, B. (1980). The assessment of mental health status of older adults. In J. Birren & R. Sloane (Eds.), *Handbook of mental health and aging*. Englewood Cliffs, NJ: Prentice-Hall.

Hafemeister, T., & Sales, B. (1984). Evaluation for guardianships and conservatorships. *Law and Human Behavior*, 8, 335–354.

Hall, M., & Ellman, I. (1990). *Health care law and ethics in a nutshell*. St. Paul, MN: West Publishing.

Handler, J. (1978). *Social movements and the legal system: A theory of law reform and social change*. New York: Academic Press.

Hasselkus, B. (1988). Meaning in family caregiving: Perspectives on caregiver/professional relationships. *The Gerontologist*, 28, 686–691.

Hastings Center. (1987). Guidelines on the termination of life-sustaining treatment on care of the dying: A report of the Hastings Center. Bloomington: Indiana University Press.

Hess, B. (1991). Growing old in America in the 1990s. In B. Hess & E. Markson (Eds.), *Growing old in America*. New Brunswick, NJ: Transaction Publishers.

High, D. (1988). All in the family: Extended autonomy and expectations in surrogate health care decision-making. *The Gerontologist*, 28, 46–51.

Hightower, D., Heckert, A., & Schmidt, W. (1990). Elderly nursing home residents' need for public guardianship services in Tennessee. In E. Dejowski (Ed.), *Protecting judgment-impaired adults: Issues, interventions and policies*. New York: Haworth Press.

Hogget, B. (1989). The elderly mentally-ill and infirm: Procedures for civil commitment and guardianship. In J. Eekelaar & D. Pearl (Eds.), *An aging world: Dilemmas and challenges for law and social policy*. Oxford: Clarendon Press.

Hommel, P., Wang, L., & Bergman, J. (1990). Trends in guardianship reform: Implications for the medical and legal professions. *Law, Medicine and Health Care*, 18, 213–226.

Hommel, P., & Wood, E. (1990). Guardianship—There are alternatives. *Aging*, 360, 6–12.

Horowitz, A. (1985). Sons and daughters as caregivers to older parents: Differences in role performance and consequences. *The Gerontologist*, 25, 612–617.

Horowitz, A., Silverstone, B., & Reinhardt, J. (1991). A conceptual and empirical exploration of personal autonomy issues within family caregiving relationships. *The Gerontologist*, 31, 23–31.

Horstman, P. (1975). Protective services for the elderly: The limits of parens patriae. *Missouri Law Review*, 40, 215–234.

House of Representatives. (1987). *Abuses in the guardianship of the elderly and infirm: A national disgrace*. A briefing by the Chairman of the Subcommittee on Health and Long-term Care of the Select Committee on Aging. House of Representatives 100th Congress First Session. Committee Publication No. 100–641.

Hughes, M. (1989). Personal guardianship and the elderly in the Canadian Common Law Provinces: An overview of the law and charter implications. In J. Eekelaar & D. Pearl (Eds.), *An aging world: Dilemmas and challenges for law and social policy*. Oxford: Clarendon Press.

Hull, L., Holmes, G., & Karst, R. (1990). Managing guardianships of the elderly: Protection and advocacy as public policy. In E. Dejowski (Ed.), *Protecting judgment-impaired adults: Issues, interventions and policies*. New York: Haworth Press.

Hurme, S. (1991). *Steps to enhance guardianship monitoring*. Washington, DC: American Bar Association.

Illinois Revised Statutes §110 1/2 11a-1 et seq. (1988).

In re the Estate of Galvin v. Galvin, 445 NE 2d 1223 (112 Ill.App.3d 677).

In re Estate of Segal, 82 A.2d 309.

In re Guardianship and Conservatorship of Sim, 403 NW 2d 721.

In re Lessard v. Schmidt, 349 F.Supp. 1078.

In re Tyrell, 92 Ohio Law Abs. 253 [28 0.0.2d 337].

Iowa Code §633.635(2)(a)(b) (Supp. 1987); §633.552 et seq. (1983–1989).

Iris, M. (1988). Guardianship and the elderly: A multi-perspective view of the decision-making process. *The Gerontologist*, 28, Supplement, 39–45.

Iris, M. (1990a). Threats to autonomy in guardianship decision-making. *Generations*, Supplement, 39–41.

Iris, M. (1990b). Uses of guardianship as protective intervention for frail, older adults. In E. Dejowski (Ed.), *Protecting judgment-impaired adults: Issues, interventions and policies*. New York: Haworth Press.

Iris, M. (1991). New directions for guardianship research. *The Gerontologist*, 31, 148–149.

Jecker, N. (1990). The role of intimate others in medical decision making. *The Gerontologist*, 30, 65–71.

Jenkins, I. (1980). *Social order and the limits of law*. Princeton, NJ: Princeton University Press.

Johnson, T. (1990). Guardianship in the South: Strategies for preserving the rights of older persons. *Journal of Aging & Social Policy*, 2, 33–50.

Kansas Statutes Annotated §59-3001 et seq. (1988).

Kapp, M. (1987). *Preventing malpractice in long-term care: Strategies for risk management*. New York: Springer Publishing.

Kapp, M. (1990). Evaluating decision-making capacity in the elderly: A review of the literature. In E. Dejowski (Ed.), *Protecting judgment-impaired adults: Issues, interventions and policies*. New York: Haworth Press.

Katz, S., Ford, A., & Moskowitz, R. (1963). Studies of illnesses in the aged: The index of ADL. *Journal of the American Medical Association*, 185, 914–919.

Keith, P. (1989). *The unmarried in later life*. New York: Praeger.

Keith, P., & Schafer, R. (1991). *Relationships and well-being over the life stages*. New York: Praeger.

Keith, P., & Wacker, R. (1992). Guardianship reform: Does revised legislation make a difference in outcomes for proposed wards? *Journal of Aging & Social Policy*, 4, 139–155.

Keith, P., & Wacker, R. (1993). Implementation of recommended guardianship practices and outcomes of hearings for older wards. *The Gerontologist*, 33, 81–87.

Keyser, A. (1987). Legal guardianship for the elderly: A volunteer model. *Journal of Religion and Aging*, 2, 41–46.

Kraus, I., & Popkin , S. (1989). Competence issues in older adults. In T. Hunt & C. Lindley (Eds.), *Testing older adults: A reference guide for geropsychological assessments*. Austin, TX: Pro-ed.

Lehmann, V. (1961). Guardianship and protective services for older people. *Social Casework*, 42, 252–257.

Lewis, S., & Cooper, C. (1987). Stress in dual-earner families. *Women and Work*, 3, 139–168.

Lisi, L., & Hommel, P. (1992). National study of guardianship system and feasibility of implementing expert systems project. Ann Arbor: Center for Social Gerontology, University of Michigan.

Lo, B. (1990). Assessing decision-making capacity. *Law, Medicine, & Health Care*, 18, 193–201.

Maclean, U. (1989). *Dependent territories: The frail elderly and community care*. London: Nuffield Provincial Hospitals Trust.

Mathiasen, G. (Ed.). (1963). *Guardianship and protective services for older people*. Washington, DC: National Council on the Aging Press.

Matthews, S., & Rosner, T. (1988). Shared filial responsibility: The family as the primary caregiver. *Journal of Marriage and the Family*, 50, 185–195.

Maynard, C. (1990). Avoiding guardianship: Linking courts to service agencies. *Aging*, 360, 13.

Menaghan, E. (1983). Marital stress and family transitions: A panel analysis. *Journal of Marriage and the Family*, 45, 371–386.

Merton, R. (1949). *Social theory and social structure*. Glencoe, IL: Free Press.

Miller, B. (1989). Adult children's perceptions of caregiver stress and satisfaction. *Journal of Applied Gerontology*, 8, 275–293.

Minnesota Statutes Annotated §525.539 et seq. (1988).

Missouri Revised Statutes §475.010 et seq. (1982–1989).

Mitchell, A. (1978). Involuntary guardianship for incompetents: A strategy for legal services advocates. *Clearinghouse Review*, 12, 451–468.

Mohoney, F., & Barthel, D. (1965). Functional evaluation: The Barthel index. *Maryland State Medical Journal*, 14, 61–65.

Montgomery, R. (1992). Gender differences in patterns of child-parent caregiving relationships. In J. Dwyer & R. Coward (Eds.), *Gender, families, and elder-care*. Newbury Park, CA: Sage.

Montgomery, R., and Kamo, Y. (1989). Parent care by sons and daughters. In J. Mancini (Ed.), *Aging parents and adult children*. Lexington, MA: Lexington.

Morrissey, M. (1982). Guardians ad litem: An educational program in Virginia. *The Gerontologist*, 22, 301–304.

National Senior Citizens Law Center (1974). Cited in Horstman, 1975.

Nebraska Revised Statutes §30-2617 et seq. (1985).

Newsnotes. (1990). Study finds new ways to recruit older volunteers. *Aging*, 360, 44.

Noelker, L., & Townsend, A. (1987). Perceived caregiving effectiveness: The impact of parental impairment, community resources, and caregiver characteristics. In T. Brubaker (Ed.), *Aging, health, and family: Long-term care*. Newbury Park, CA: Sage.

Nolan, B. (1984). Functional evaluation of the elderly in guardianship proceedings. *Law, Medicine, & Health Care*, 12, 210–217.

Nolan, B. (1990). A judicial menu: Selecting remedies for the incapacitated elder. In E. Dejowski (Ed.), *Protecting judgment-impaired adults: Issues, interventions and policies*. New York: Haworth Press.

Oregon Revised Statutes §126.003 (1988).

Oregon Revised Statutes §126.137(6) (Supp. 1989).

Parry, J., & Hurme, S. (1991). Guardianship monitoring and enforcement nationwide. *Mental and Physical Disability Law Reporter*, 15, 304–309.

Pattison, E. (1973). A theoretical-empirical base for social system therapy. In E. Feulks, R. Wintrob, J. Westermeyer, & A. Favazza (Eds.), *Current perspectives in cultural psychiatry*. New York: Spectrum.

Pearlin, L., Mullan, J., Semple, S., & Skaff, M. (1990). Caregiving and the stress process: An overview of concepts and their measures. *The Gerontologist*, 30, 583–594.

Peden, J. (1990). The guardian ad litem under the guardianship reform act: A profusion of duties, a confusion of roles. *University of Detroit Law Review*, 68, 19–35.

Peters, R., Schmidt, W., & Miller, K. (1985). Guardianship of the elderly in Tallahassee, Florida. *The Gerontologist*, 25, 532–538.

Petrila, J. (1985). Special problems in mental health. In N. Sidley (Ed.), *Law and ethics: A guide for the health professional*. New York: Human Sciences Press.

President's Commission for the Study of Ethical Problems in Medicine and Biomedical and Behavioral Research. (1981). *Making health care decisions: A report on the ethical and legal implications of informal consent in the patient-provider relationship*. Washington, DC: U.S. Government Printing Office.

Ratcliffe, A. (1982). In re Boyer: Guardianship of incapacitated adults in Utah. *Utah Law Review*, 2, 427–443.

Regan, J. (1972). Protective services for the elderly: Civil commitment, guardianship and alternatives. *William and Mary Law Review*, 13, 569–622.

Regan, J. (1978). Intervention through adult protective services programs. *The Gerontologist*, 18, 250–254.

Rogers, P. (1984). Understanding the legal concept of guardianship. In T. Apollini & T. Cooke (Eds.), *A new look at guardianship*. Baltimore, MD: Paul H. Brookes.

Schafer, A. (1988). Civil liberties and the elderly patient. In J. Thornton & E. Winkler (Eds.), *Ethics and aging: The right to live, the right to die*. Vancouver: University of British Columbia Press.

Scharlach, A. (1987). Role strain in mother-daughter relationships in later life. *The Gerontologist*, 27, 627–631.

Scharlach, A., & Boyd, S. (1989). Caregiving and employment: Results of an employee survey. *The Gerontologist*, 29, 382–387.

Schmidt, W. (1990). Quantitative information about the quality of the guardianship system: Toward the next generation of guardianship research. *Probate Law Journal*, 10, 61–80.

Schoenfeld, B., & Tuzil, T. (1979). Conservatorship: A move towards more personalized protective service. *Journal of Gerontological Social Work*, 1, 225–234.

Schulte, B. (1989). Reform of guardianship laws in Europe—A comparative and interdisciplinary approach. In J. Eekelaar & D. Pearl (Eds.), *An aging world: Dilemmas and challenges for law and social policy*. Oxford: Clarendon Press.

Scogin, F., & Perry, J. (1986). Guardianship proceedings with older adults: The role of functional assessment and gerontologists. *Law and Psychology Review*, 10, 123–128.

Seltzer, M. (1976). Suggestions for the examination of time-disordered relationships. In J. Gubrium (Ed.), *Times, roles, and self in old age*. New York: Human Sciences Press.

Shanas, E., Townsend, P., Wedderburn, D., Friis, H., Milhoj, P., & Stehouwer, J. (1968). *Old people in three industrial societies*. New York: Atherton Press.

Sherman, R. (1980). Guardianship: Time for reassessment. *Fordham Law Review*, 49, 350–378.

Sieber, S. (1974). Toward a theory of role accumulation. *American Sociological Review*, 39, 567–578.

South Dakota Code §30-26-1 et seq. (1986).

Spitze, G., & Logan, J. (1989). Gender differences in family support: Is there a payoff? *The Gerontologist*, 29, 108–113.

Stevenson, C., & Capezuti, E. (1991). Guardianship: Protection versus peril. *Geriatric Nursing*, Jan./Feb., 10–13.

Stiegel, L. (1992). *Alternatives to guardianship: Substantive training materials and module for professionals working with the elderly and persons with disabilities. Part I-II.* Washington, DC: American Bar Association, Commission on Legal Problems of the Elderly and Commission on Mental and Physical Disability Law.

Stiegel, L., Mason, D., Morris, D., Gottlich, V., & Rave, M. (1993). Three issues still remaining in guardianship reform. *Clearinghouse Review*, Oct., 577–584.

Stoller, E. (1992). Gender differences in the experiences of caregiving spouses. In J. Dwyer & R. Coward (Eds.), *Gender, families, and eldercare*. Newbury Park, CA: Sage.

Stoller, E., & Pugliesi, K. (1989). Other roles of caregivers: Competing responsibilities or supportive resources. *Journal of Gerontology*, 44, S231–238.

Topolnicki, D. (1989). The gulag of guardianship. *Money Magazine*, March, 140–152.

Turner, J. (1986). *The structure of sociological theory*. Chicago: Dorsey Press.

Venesy, B. (1990). 1990 guardianship law safeguards personal rights yet protects vulnerable elderly. *Akron Law Review*, 24, 161–176.

Vittoria, A. (1992). The elderly guardianship hearing: A socio-legal encounter. *Journal of Aging Studies*, 6, 165–190.

Voydanoff, P. (1988). Work role characteristics, family structure demands, and work/family conflict. *Journal of Marriage and the Family*, 50, 749–761.

Walker, A., Martin, S., & Jones, L. (1992). Benefits and costs of caregiving and care receiving for daughters and mothers. *Journal of Gerontology*, 47, S130–139.

Walker, A., Shin, H., & Bird, J. (1990). Perceptions of relationship change and caregiver satisfaction. *Family Relations*, 39, 147–152.

Wang, L., Burns A., & Hommel, P. (1990). Trends in guardianship reform: Roles and responsibilities of legal advocates. *Clearinghouse Review*, 24, 561–569.

Weiler, K., Helms, L., & Buckwalter, K. (1993). A comparative study: Guardianship petitions for adults and elder adults. *Journal of Gerontological Nursing*, September, 15–25.

Wilber, K. (1990). Material abuse of the elderly: When is guardianship a solution? In E. Dejowski (Ed.), *Protecting judgment-impaired adults: Issues, interventions and policies*. New York: Haworth Press.

Wilber, K. (1991). Alternatives to conservatorship: The role of daily money management services. *The Gerontologist*, 31, 150–155.

Wildner, C. (1971). Chronic conditions and limitations of activity and mobility: United States, July 1965 to June 1967. *Vital and health statistics*, Series 10, No. 61. Washington, DC: U.S. Government Printing Office.

Wisconsin Statutes §880.01 et seq. (1982).

Wood, E., Dooley, J., & Karp, N. (1991). *Court related needs of the elderly and persons with disabilities*. Washington, DC: American Bar Association.

Wood, E., Stiegel, L., Sabatino, C., & Edelstein, S. (1993). Overview of 1992 state law changes in guardianship, durable powers of attorney, health care decisions, and home equity mortgages. *Clearinghouse Review*, 26, 1277–1285.

Zarit, S., Todd, P., & Zarit, J. (1986). Subjective burden of husbands and wives as caregivers: A longitudinal study. *The Gerontologist*, 26, 260–266.

Zenz, G. (1989). The end of guardianship for the elderly? Facts and objectives in current discussions on the proposed reform legislation in the Federal Republic of Germany. In J. Eekelaar & D. Pearl (Eds.), *An aging world: Dilemmas and challenges for law and social policy*. Oxford: Clarendon Press.

Zimny, G., Gilchrist, B., & Diamond, J. (1991). *A national model for judicial review of guardians' performance*. St. Louis, MO: Schools of Law and Medicine, St. Louis University.

Zimny, G., Gilchrist, B., Grossberg, G., & Chung, S. (1991). Annual reports by guardians and conservators to probate courts. *Journal of Elder Abuse and Neglect*, 61–74.

Index

About the Authors

PAT M. KEITH is Professor and Assistant Dean in the Graduate Department of Sociology at Iowa State University. Dr. Keith is coauthor of *Role Relationships and Well-Being over the Life Cycle* (Praeger, 1991) and author of *The Unmarried in Later Life* (Praeger, 1989).

ROBBYN R. WACKER is Associate Professor in the Department of Human Services at the University of Northern Colorado. Dr. Wacker has been author or coauthor of several chapters and refereed journal articles dealing with the elderly.

ISBN 0-275-94424-7
90000>
EAN
9 780275 944247
HARDCOVER BAR CODE